D0212836

DATE DUE

Modern Critical Interpretations

Modern Critical Interpretations

Toni Morrison's
Song of Solomon

Edited and with an introduction by
Harold Bloom
Sterling Professor of the Humanities
Yale University

CHELSEA HOUSE PUBLISHERS
Philadelphia

FRED L. MATHEWS LIBRARY
SOUTHWESTERN MICHIGAN COLLEGE
DOWAGIAC, MI 49047

©1999 by Chelsea House Publishers, a division of
Main Line Book Co.

Introduction ©1999 by Harold Bloom

All rights reserved. No part of this publication may be
reproduced or transmitted in any form or by any means
without the written permission of the publisher.

Printed and bound in the United States of America

10 9 8 7 6 5 4 3 2 1

∞ The paper used in this publication meets the minimum
requirements of the American National Standard for
Permanence of Paper for Printed Library Materials,
Z39.48-1984

Library of Congress Cataloging-in-Publication Data

Toni Morrison's Song of Solomon / edited and with an
introduction by Harold Bloom.
           p.   cm. — (Modern critical interpretations)
        Includes biographical references and index.
        ISBN 0-7910-5193-5 (hardcover)
        1. Morrison, Toni. Song of Solomon.   2. Domestic
fiction, American—History and criticism.   3. Afro-
American families in literature.   4. Afro-Americans in
literature.   Michigan—In literature.   I. Bloom, Harold.
II. Series.
PS3563.08749S638   1999
813'.54—dc21   98–52919
                                              CIP

Contributing Editor: Tenley Williams

Contents

Editor's Note

My Introduction ponders the relationship of *Song of Solomon* to its two unacknowledged precursors, Ralph Ellison and William Faulkner.

I am grateful to Tenley Williams for her skilled assistance in editing this volume.

The critical essays tend to be purely ideological, with only a few exceptions, but then Morrison's critics follow her lead in this political emphasis.

Wilfred D. Samuels reduces Milkman's quest for self to a search for "cultural identity," while Valerie Smith also finds the attainment to be a "communal" self, and not an individualistic one.

Stephanie A. Demetrakopoulos sees Milkman as overcoming the "nihilism and narcissism of Guitar," because he has learned that men and women are interdependent. The moral emphasis appears again in Karla F. C. Holloway's insistence that Milkman finally embodies the ethos of the Black spirituals, and in Harry Reed's view that Milkman represents, at last, the survival power of Black cultural nationalism.

Ralph Story celebrates Morrison's "global understanding" of the Black world, after which Michael Awkward sees *Song of Solomon* as assisting an African-American cultural transformation.

Jan Stryz affirms Morrison's total originality as a Black cosmologist, while Doreatha Drummond Mbalia lauds Morrison as a Marxist, who develops African-American class consciousness. Marianne Hirsch praises Morrison's African-American version of feminism.

Linden Peach agrees with Morrison's insistence that the romance form of *Song of Solomon* is somehow African, while Bertram D. Ashe commends Morrison's construction of a purely African-American standard for female beauty.

Jan Furman expounds Morrison's idea of Black masculinity, after which Gary Storhoff admires Morrison's vision of how "parental enmeshment" can be transcended by culturally informed African-Americans.

Introduction

Toni Morrison's third novel, *Song of Solomon* (1977), seems to me her master-work to date, though *Beloved* (1987) has even more readers. A superb, highly conscious artist from her beginning, Morrison is also a committed social activist. Exemplary as it is, her African-American feminist stance is the prime concern of nearly all her critics, which makes for a certain monotony in their cheerleading. Morrison is scarcely responsible for them, though I detect an intensification of ideological fervor when I pass from rereading *Song of Solomon* to rereading *Beloved* and then go on to *Jazz* and *Paradise*, her most recent novels. A novelist's politics are part of her panoply, her arms and armor. Time stales our coverings; fictions that endure do so despite the passionate commitments of their authors, while claques, however sincere, do not assure literary survival. The very titles of many of the essays in this volume testify to political obsessions: "black cultural nationalism," "myth, ideology, and gender," "race and class consciousness," "competing discourses." Morrison, far cannier than her enthusiasts, at her most persuasive transcends her own indubitable concerns. Her art, grounded in African-American realities and concerns, is nevertheless not primarily naturalistic in its aims and modes.

Morrison has been vehement in asserting that African-American liter-ature is her aesthetic context: she has invoked slave narratives, folklore, spir-ituals, and jazz songs. So advanced a stylist and storyteller is not likely to celebrate Zora Neale Hurston as a forerunner, or to imagine a relation between herself and Richard Wright, or James Baldwin. Her authentic rival is the late Ralph Waldo Ellison, whose *Invisible Man* (1952) remains the most extraordinary achievement in African-American fiction. Morrison subtly wards off *Invisible Man* (1952), from *The Bluest Eye* (1970) on to *Paradise* (1997). Though she has deprecated the "complex series of evasions" of Modernist liter-ature and its criticism, no one is more brilliant at her own complex series of evasions, particularly of Ralph Ellison, unwanted strong precursor. This is not to suggest that Ellison is her prime precursor: William Faulkner shadows

1

Morrison's work always, and inspires even more creative evasions in her best writing.

I am aware that I am at variance with nearly all of Morrison's critics, who take their lead from her *Playing in the Dark: Whiteness and the Literary Imagination*, one of her most adroit evasions of the central Western literary tradition that, in mere fact, has fostered her. But then, as a professional literary critic, I must declare an interest, since my argument for the inescapability of what I have termed "the anxiety of influence" is contested by the culturally correct. There is no anguish of contamination or guilt of inheritance for black women writers in particular, I frequently am admonished. Patriarchal, capitalistic, phallocentric notions must be swept aside: they are racist, sexist, exclusionary, exploitative. If even Shakespeare can become Alternative Shakespeare, then Toni Morrison can spring full-grown from the head of Black Athena.

Every strong writer welcomes the opportunity to be an original, and Morrison's literary achievement more than justifies her sly embrace of African-American cultural narcissism. Her critics seem to me quite another matter, but my Editor's Note is an appropriate context for commenting upon them. Here, in this Introduction, I desire only to discuss, rather briefly, the genesis of *Song of Solomon*'s authentic aesthetic strength from the creative agony with Faulkner and with Ellison. Morrison deftly uses Faulkner while parrying Ellison: out of the strong comes forth sweetness. *Song of Solomon* exuberantly is informed by the creative gusto of Morrison's sense of victory in the contest that is inevitable for the art of literature. Jacob Burckhardt and Friedrich Nietzsche both pioneered in reminding us that the Athenians conceived of literature as an agony. Nietzsche admirably condensed this insight in his grand fragment, "Homer's Contest":

> Every talent must unfold itself in fighting . . . And just as the youths were educated through contests, their educators were also engaged in contests with each other. The great musical masters, Pindar and Simonides, stood side by side, mistrustful and jealous; in the spirit of contest. The sophist, the advanced teacher of antiquity, meets another sophist; even the most universal type of instruction, through the drama, was meted out to the people only in the form of a tremendous wrestling among the great musical and dramatic artists. How wonderful! "Even the artist hates the artist." Whereas modern man fears nothing in an artist more than the emotion of any personal fight, the Greek knows the artist *only as engaged in a personal fight*. Precisely where modern

man senses the weakness of a work of art, the Hellene seeks the
source of its greatest strength.

Probably Morrison would dissent from Nietzsche, but that would be
Morrison the critic, not Morrison the novelist, who is engaged in a
personal fight with *Invisible Man* and with Faulkner's *Light in August*.
Morrison's career is still in progress; it is too soon to prophesy whether she
will yet surpass *The Song of Solomon*. Again, I am aware that admirers of
Beloved, a highly deliberate work of art, believe that Morrison has transcended her earlier work. Since I find *Beloved* ideologically over-deter-
mined, and therefore in places somewhat tendentious, I prefer *Song of
Solomon*. Highly conscious as she is of the American romance tradition,
from Hawthorne and Melville through Faulkner and Ellison, Morrison
wonderfully subverts that tradition in *Song of Solomon*. This subversion is
not primarily ideological, but properly imaginative and revisionary. Great
solitaries—Hester Prynne, Captain Ahab, Joe Christmas, Invisible Man—
are joined by a different kind of solitary, Milkman Dead. Milkman, like his
precursors, quests for the restoration of his true self, lest he remain a
Jonah, but Morrison shapes her protagonist's quest so that it is communi-
tarian despite itself. She does the same in *Beloved*, yet with an inverted
sentimentalism that may be the consequence of too overt a reliance upon
the political myth of a social energy inherent in the souls of Southern
blacks. In *Song of Solomon*, a work of more individual mythopoeia, the
refining of community is aesthetically persuasive.

Ellison's nameless Invisible Man is massively persuasive in his final
judgment that there is *no* community for him, black or white:

> Step outside the narrow borders of what men call reality and you
> step into chaos . . . or imagination. That too I've learned in the
> cellar, and not by deadening my sense of perception; I'm invis-
> ible, not blind.

Morrison's Milkman Dead reaches a conclusion radically revisionary of
Ellison's nameless man:

> How many dead lives and fading memories were buried in and
> beneath the names of the places in this country. Under the
> recorded names were other names, just as "Macon Dead,"
> recorded for all time in some dusty file, hid from view the real
> names of people, places, and things. Names that had meaning

> . . . When you know your name, you should hang to it, for unless it is noted down and remembered, it will die when you do.

The Invisible Man, who will accept no name whatsoever, has stepped into chaos *or* imagination, two words for the same entity, or are they antithesis? Ellison, as an Emersonian, allows for both readings. Morrison, born Chloe Anthony Wofford, has held on to her original middle name as the "real" one. Milkman loses the false name, "Dead," to acquire the ancestral real name, Solomon or Shalimar. Ellison perhaps would have judged that Morrison had kept within narrower borders than she required; I never discussed her work with him, so I do not know, but African-American nationalism, or any sort, was what he had rejected in his poignant and deluded Ras the Exhorter. Milkman's superb poignance is that he is anything but an Exhorter.

Faulkner I find everywhere in Morrison, generally transmuted, yet never finally transcended. In our century, Wallace Stevens wrote the poems of our climate, and Faulkner wrote the best of our novels, particularly in *As I Lay Dying* and *Light in August*. Returning to a fictive South, Milkman also returns to Faulkner, primarily to *The Bear* and its rituals of initiation. I dislike going against Morrison's own passionate critical pronouncements, yet I hardly am attempting "to *place* value only where that influence is located." Joseph Conrad does not crowd out Faulkner, nor does Faulkner render Morrison less gifted, less black, less female, less Marxist. Even the strongest of novelists cannot choose their own precursors. Hemingway wanted to assert *Huckleberry Finn* as his origin, but the ethos and mode of *The Sun Also Rises* are distinctly Conradian. "Africanism is inextricable from the definition of Americanness," Morrison insists. She ought to be right, and as a nation we would be better if she were right. One learns the truth about American Religion, I am convinced, if we trace its origin to the early black Baptists in America, who carried an African *gnosis* with them, in which "the little me within the big me" was the ultimate, unfallen reality. Morrison, like Faulkner, has a great deal to teach us about both "white" American and African-American identity. In a long enough perspective, Faulkner and Morrison may be teaching the same troubled truths.

WILFRED D. SAMUELS

Liminality and the Search for Self
in Song of Solomon

The ultimate quest for self and its realization is found in Morrison's third, award-winning novel, *Song of Solomon* (1977). It tells the story of the quest for cultural identity by its hero, Macon (Milkman) Dead III. Like Pecola's and Sula's, Milkman's story focuses on his turbulent rite of passage into adulthood, into manhood. But more important, like Shadrack's, his journey also reveals the significance of the historical and cultural self. Milkman cannot become complete until he (re)connects the loose historical cords of his memory. He must "re-remember" them.

Consequently, here, too, setting—community and neighborhood, Detroit, Danville, and Shalimar—remains of paramount importance. For it is through the now-familiar kaleidoscopic view of communal black life, which we have come to expect from Morrison, that we find the dramatization of the conflicts her protagonist(s) must experience, confront, overcome, or resolve in the process of becoming. *Song of Solomon* is closer to Ralph Ellison's *Invisible Man*, however, than to her earlier works; it, too, combines the epic quest with the *bildungsroman* motif and the search for the Grail of identity theme.

Like *The Bluest Eye* and *Sula*, as a novel of formation, *Song of Solomon* ultimately aims to achieve a total, authentic personality for its hero. Here, too, secondary characters serve as mentors who aid the protagonist, as

From *Toni Morrison.* © 1990 G. K. Hall & Co.

educators, companions, and lovers. Pilate, Guitar, Hagar, Ruth, and Macon Sr. mediate, interpret, or reflect the alternatives available to Milkman. As in the other texts, however, *Song of Solomon* loudly echoes Morrison's contention that authentic existence emerges from self-affirmation, from making choices that lead to self-ownership, rather than from a life of being-for-others. The ultimate choices are Milkman's to make, much as they are Pecola's, Sula's, and Shadrack's.

Here, again, we find that the central tension of the text emerges from the significant roles the progatonist must assume in charting the direction of a life that must skirt "bad faith and falsehood" and be steeped in the existential responsibility to act, to "express an effort of the will or a freedom of the will." Milkman's ultimate task is to achieve "a strong and centered sense of self, a self that accepts responsibility for his past and reaches out in love for others." As Morrison told Mel Watkins, "If there is any consistent theme in my fiction, I guess that is it—how and why we learn to live this life intensely and well."

Morrison makes this explicit enough through the lessons Milkman learns directly and indirectly from his family, the Deads, whose very name signifies forfeited beings, empty lives: inauthentic existence. Thus, we must begin with an examination of the experience that each member brings to Milkman, the initiate, to assess the lessons he must learn, accept, or reject.

Inauthentic Experience—Ruth Foster Dead

The most significant experience of inauthenticity is offered by Milkman's mother, Ruth Foster Dead, who by herself "ain't nobody." Reared after her mother's death by an affectionate and elitist father, Ruth grows into womanhood without a personal identity, as the extension of her father, the only black doctor in the community. She is known by most as "Dr. Foster's daughter," as the only offspring of the most important black in town. A young lady of manners and culture, Ruth enjoyed an elegant childhood, nurtured by the warmth of her father's love and the sanctuary of his twelve-room citadel. Located on "Not Doctor Street" (named after her father), it offered the trappings of black middle-class life, all hidden behind its heavy doors.

At sixteen, Ruth marries Macon Dead II, a "colored man of property," who by the age of twenty-five would inherit the doctor's place as the most prominent black in the community. He moves into the doctor's mansion: although rather fond of his daughter, the doctor had grown tired of her "steady beam of love" and is relieved when Macon joins them. After two children and fifteen years in a loveless marriage, Ruth gives birth to

Milkman, their only son. Made to face daily a husband whose jealousy and hatred keeps her "awkward with fear," Ruth lives in the memory of the near-incestuous relationship she shared with her now-deceased father. We are told that "she had never dropped those expressions of affection that had been so loveable in childhood. Macon's contempt for Ruth had begun when he found her in bed with her father's dead, bloated body, kissing his fingers.

Ruth verbalizes her awareness of her lack of personal identity when she describes herself to Milkman:

> I was pressed small. I lived in a great big house that pressed me into a small package. I had no friends, only schoolmates who wanted to touch my dress and my white silk stockings. But I didn't think I'd ever need a friend because I had him [her father]. I was small, but he was big. The only person who ever really cared whether I lived or died . . . he cared . . . and there was, and is no one else in the world ever did.

To ensure her father's continued presence, validate her identity, and find meaning while locked in a sterile marriage, Ruth visits her father's grave at night. There she renews that "cared-for-feeling" she had received from him during his lifetime.

The poignancy of Ruth's sitting—empty, alone, and lonely—talking to her father's grave verifies, once again, Morrison's effort to demonstrate the consequences of inauthentic existence characterized by a life that is falsely and selfishly lived for "the Other." Unlike Sula, who guarded her "Me-ness" and unlike Eva, who built her own home (that is, life) according to her own specifications and design, Ruth chooses to accept her father's home, and it "pressed [her] into a small package."

That she is a "small woman" results directly from her personal action, for at no point does she rebel, as does Nel, for example, or her daughter First Corinthians. Other significant influences come into play, however, paramount among which is Ruth's not having had the advantage of a mother to nurture her through significant stages of her girlhood and young womanhood, as did Sula and Nel, whose mothers, despite their life-styles and personalities, were there for their daughters. Ruth's marriage by age sixteen suggests her problem. The fundamental bond between mother and daughter that Morrison in her work insists is necessary is lacking here. She has not had the luxury of blossoming with her mother's milk; her growth is thus artificial, like Pecola's, who is forced to drink white milk from a cup. Although she receives love from her father, Ruth appears psychologically damaged and incomplete. She confuses her father's love, much as Pecola confuses Cholly's, and mistakes it for possession, perhaps out of fear that her father, like her mother, might neglect her or abandon her.

Morrison's naming of her character is thus not coincidental. All three names—Ruth, Foster, and Dead—suggest dependence and absence. Like her biblical counterpart, Ruth is devoted and loyal to the point of forfeiting all rights to her personal life. In her relationship with the doctor, we hear resonances of the Old Testament Ruth who tells her mother-in-law, Naomi, "Entreat me not to leave thee, or to return from following after thee for whither thou goest, I will go; and where thou lodgest, I will lodge; . . . Where thou dies, I will die, and there I will be buried: the Lord do so to me, and more also if but death part thee and me."

Not even in death does Ruth Foster Dead's fear of or loyalty to her father abate. She confesses, "It is important for me to be in his presence, among his things, the things he used, had touched. Later it was just important for me to know that he was in the world." In life, she is "fostered" or nurtured by this relationship, and it robs her of a self that results in meaningful, personal development. In short, it leaves her "dead" though alive.

The water mark she observes on her fine mahogany table, which like the vessel that made the mark is imported and forced into the house, symbolizes her flawed existence, which is also externally anchored: "Ruth looked to the water mark several times during the day. She knew it was there, would always be there, but she needed to confirm its presence . . . she regarded it as mooring, a checkpoint, some stable visual object that assured her that the world was still there; that this was life and not a dream. That she was alive somewhere, inside, which she acknowledged to be true only because a thing she knew intimately was out there, outside herself." Like the table, Ruth's life is blemished and unwhole.

It is also her propensity to fashion an identity outside herself that leads her to validate her essence and being through Milkman, whom she sees as her one aggressive act. He is, after all, the living evidence of the last time her husband made love to her. Here, as with her father, an unwillingness to let go marks the relationship; she nurses her son far beyond infancy for her own satisfaction: "He was too young to be dazzled by her nipples, but he was old enough to be bored by the flat taste of mother's milk." He gains the name "Milkman" at age six when Ruth's ritual is discovered by the town's gossip.

There is little doubt that Ruth's indulgences provide her with the physical contact her husband denies her, but her motives are not merely the fulfillment of sexual needs. This act may even represent efforts to compensate for the aborted relationship Ruth experienced from her mother's death, which would have fractured the nurturing process. Morrison maintains that one person cannot raise a child: "Two people should or either a whole community. And a community is not simply made up of women. It is made up with men in it and the men are as important as the women . . . they are different. They do different things."

Significantly, Ruth's nursing of Milkman also simultaneously meets her maternal need to nurse and nurture. We can, in fact, say that in *Song of Solomon* Morrison looks more expansively at her treatment and characterization of the female character through the complex theme of motherhood, of woman-as-mother, by exploring further the roles of woman-as-(wet)nurse and woman-as-nurturer.

Clearly, the implication here is that woman is more than maker of children, a label that could easily be appended to such Morrison mothers as Pauline, Geraldine, and Hannah, who seem to have no time—no quality time—for their children aside from obligatory care. Ruth is their polar opposite. She lives for her children, especially Milkman, and gains complete personal satisfaction from them, in spite of the fact that Milkman later perceives her as perverted and sullying.

Morrison broadens as well her treatment of the mother/son relationship explored in *Sula*, with some significant differences. Whereas Eva destroys Plum to give him new life, Ruth provides her son with nourishment to sustain his life, making it possible for him to become physically a man while symbolically remaining a child. Aware of this, Milkman objects: "I know I'm the youngest one in this family, but I ain't no baby. You treat me like I was a baby". Morrison explains, Ruth "played house with her son—taking him into the little room and nursing him as though he were a doll, a toy." Ruth did not want her son to mature into adulthood, hence the symbolic overextension of his childhood and the significance of his name, Milkman.

In the end, both Eva and Ruth offer Morrisonian variations of the classical and mythological earth mother, for both are creative, life-giving forces and devouring ones as well. Both women sacrifice themselves for their children; but Eva, unlike Ruth, sacrifices her son as well. Ultimately, Eva's willingness to do so makes her more authentic than Ruth, who remains fostered in a world of Deads. Ruth's failure to explore her own interest leaves her not only in a very circumscribed life, but those she chooses to defer her life for do not reciprocate. In fact, they return her love with distaste. Macon hates her. Milkman, who once defended her against his father, comes to see her as "silly, selfish, queer, and faintly obscene." Her father, we are led to believe, had eventually chosen death over her love.

Rejected by her father, husband, and son, Ruth remains inauthentic, empty, and isolated, because she has no independent self on which to stand. Paradoxically, she does not go insane like Pecola or die like Sula. In fact, we are told that "she was fierce in the presence of death, heroic even, as she was at no other time. Its threat gave her direction, clarity, audacity." What is the source of this undaunting strength? It is certainly not hate, as in Eva's case. No doubt, her sense of motherhood and the complexity of her role in this regard have something to do with this tenacity. Nevertheless, in his quest for authentic existence Milkman concludes that without a personal identity, his mother had very little to give.

Inauthentic Experience—Macon Dead II

As a successful realtor, Macon Sr. has much to offer his son. Unfortunately, what Macon absorbed is mostly material; Macon believes that "Money is freedom . . . the only real freedom there is." Like Ruth's life, Macon's is fundamentally inauthentic; he is monomaniacally driven to acquire material wealth, at all costs, personal and human. Cold, objective, and calculating, he is said to be a "difficult man to approach, a hard man, with a manner so cool it discouraged casual or spontaneous conversation."

Ample evidence is offered to support this description. When Mrs. Baines, a tenant in one of his slums, informs him that she is unable to pay the rent ($4) because she has to feed her children, he replies, "Can they make it in the street, Mrs. Baines? That's where they gonna be if you don't figure out some way to get me my money." When loneliness drives Porter, another tenant, to threaten suicide, Macon surfaces at the site, not to save a life, but to collect his rent. "Put [the gun] down and throw me my goddam money!" he hollers. "Float those dollars down here, nigger, then blow yourself up."

The source of this insensitivity and callousness lies in Macon's past. Like Ruth, Macon blossomed during an early childhood that was quite ideal. He, too, was nurtured by a father who loved him; and he, too, had a mother who died when he was young. The love he received was not fashioned solely in a world of materialism and conspicuous consumption, however, as in the case of Ruth. We are told that Macon worked side by side with his father on their farm at Lincoln's Heaven from the age of four. As the name of the farm suggests, it represented the freedom that his father, a former slave, had hoped to gain and enjoy as a landowner. Moreover, it suggests that theirs was a long-range enter- prise, since it would take sixteen years before a profit would be realized.

The Deads, Macon Sr., his son, Macon II, and his daughter, Pilate, were landowners. In fact, Macon Sr. was killed while protecting his land in a dispute over a question of ownership. One might safely conclude, however, that the material value of the land was unbeknownst to Macon Sr., much less to his son Macon II at the time of his father's brutal murder. In fact, the murder provided the youth with a significant moment of truth. He apparently learned that land had a financial value as well as a spiritual, natural value. This event was also to be the source of Macon's own harshness and brutality in the future.

Despite the absence of economic profits, it is apparent that Macon II had benefited from the profits of "economy," in the Thoreauvian sense, offered by Lincoln's Heaven. He had harvested a higher and more ethereal life from both his salient relationship with his father and from the oneness his father apparently shared with the soil, with an organic and natural world. As the farm's name suggests, theirs was a Walden Pond–like existence, an Edenic world whose fertile soil enhanced bonding between father and son as well as providing the fulfilling experience, that of seeing the products of their joint labor and of being at one with the earth.

The Emersonian and Thoreauvian lessons of nature—physical and spiritual, related to the cultivation of land and, by extension, to the oneness between tiller and soil—were the immediate legacies and profits of the maturing, growing manchild. Macon's reminiscence of his childhood residence reverberates with the sounds and sights of Thoreau's Walden Pond. "It was a little bit of a place. But it looked big to me then . . . About eighty [acres] of it was woods. Must have been a fortune in oak and pine; . . . We had a pond that was four acres. And a stream that's full of fish . . . And we had fruit trees. Apple, cherry." In his recollection one hears strains of Emerson's discourse in the essay "Nature": "Almost I fear to think how glad I [was]. In the woods too a man cast off his years . . . and at what period soever of life is always a child." It is a reminiscence that brings joy to Macon's life; he "paused and let the smile come on." The commodity he recalls is not only the material but the process and result of nature's ministry. It is not merely economic profit but the joy the land and his father's philosophy of the economy of a simple life that bring Macon a brief moment of happiness and wholeness.

Macon was robbed of his material birthright as rightful heir to Lincoln's Heaven, however, when his father was brutally killed, the land illegally taken, and he, along with Pilate, expelled. Aware of no original sin to justify the expulsion, Macon aborts the teachings of his father's examples, replacing them with a life of bitterness, alienation, and quiet desperation, "laying up treasures," as Thoreau writes in *Walden*, "which moth and rust will corrupt and thieves break through and steal." Assessing his struggle in a Marxist dialectic of "haves" versus "have nots," he is driven, like a machine, to own things, as he becomes a member of the bourgeoisie. He marries Ruth strictly for personal advancement rather than love. She is no more than another piece of real estate to which he holds the keys.

His tunnel vision is thus not unlike Pecola's obsession with blue eyes. His reaction to his negative experience is not unlike her response to Yacabowski.

Although he had been shown, through his apprenticeship with his father, a meaningful approach to a more ethereal life, he aborts it for one that, though materialistically fulfilling, requires the prostitution of his spirit. Much as Pecola subordinates her creative anger in place of shame, Macon "subdued his self, his magic, and became an acquirer of things and subordinated everybody to it." A slave driver to himself and others, Macon is not able to overcome his obsession with material treasures, even during old age, and consequently cannot live simply and wisely. He remains locked in an acrid life of unfulfillment that manifests itself in the hatred, criticism, and disapproval of his family, particularly his wife: "His hatred for [Ruth] glittered and sparkled in every word he spoke to her."

Much like Ruth, Macon is driven by emptiness to seek vicarious meaning through Milkman. Hardened by the betrayal of his early childhood experiences, he tells Milkman: "Own things. And let the things you own own other things. Then you'll own yourself and other people too." Ironically, he fails to see that he does not own himself, for he has become enslaved to the things he owns. The slum houses, Packard, and position do not fulfill him: "he felt as though the houses were in league with one another to make him feel like the outsider, propertyless, landless wanderer." Spiritually impoverished and physically alienated from self, family, and community, Macon wanders in the dark one evening to his sister Pilate's house, where, unnoticed, he listens outside her window to her singing: "Near the window, hidden by the dark, he felt the irritability of the day drain from him."

Aware of Macon's sense of nothingness and his inability to love others or himself, Milkman rejects his father. In fact, Milkman does everything he can to be different: "Macon was clean-shaven; Milkman was desperate for a mustache. Macon wore bow ties; Milkman wore four-in-hands. Macon didn't part his hair; Milkman had a part shaved into his. Macon hated tobacco; Milkman tried to put a cigarette in his mouth every fifteen minutes. Macon hoarded his money; Milkman gave his away."

Milkman lacks interest in the choices made available to him by his parent and by his community: "All he knew in the world about the world was what other people had told him. He felt like a garbage pail for the actions and hatred of other people. He himself did nothing."

Aunt Pilate

Pilate, Milkman's aunt, provides him with the ultimate example of authentic existence. From birth, her life has been a continuum of self-actualization. Although her mother died before giving birth to Pilate, the baby "inched its way headfirst out . . . dragging her own cord and her own afterbirth behind her." Signifying a propensity toward self-determination, Pilate is without a navel, a phenomenon that makes her, like Sula, a pariah. More important, it symbolizes her independent and untrammeled spirit; she is not anchored to anyone or anything.

Accepting early her enigmatic characteristics, Pilate makes living itself an art. She becomes both the creator and creation of her art. At twelve she appended her name to her person in a snuffbox that hung from her ear. When the discovery of her smooth stomach thwarts her early efforts to acclimate to the environments in which she found herself, even in her domestic relationships, she "threw away every assumption that she had learned and began at zero. First off, she cut her hair. That was one thing she didn't want to have to think about anymore. Then she tackled the problem of trying to decide how she wanted to live and what was valuable to her. When am I happy and when am I sad and what is the difference. What do I need to know to stay alive? What is true in the world?" Like Eva who designed her own Alhambra to self, Pilate lays the foundation of hers by starting at the bottom, "zero."

Unlike her brother, Macon Sr., and his wife, Ruth, who are driven by external motivations and materialism, Pilate lives a life epitomizing ethereality. Unlike Macon, she remains committed to the higher laws, a spiritual life, that she discovered as a child on Lincoln's Heaven, loving what Thoreau calls "the wild not less than the good." Her life continues the Walden Pond existence she had known at Lincoln's Heaven, physically and spiritually, for she lives in a cabin, a narrow, single-story house on the periphery of town, where she is not a mere traveler in nature but a harvester of its true offerings and strange liberty. Furnitureless and devoid of such modern conveniences as gas, electricity, and running water, Pilate's home provides an avenue through which to live deliberately. It stands in contrast to her brother's citadel, whose emptiness makes it "more prison that palace" and drives him to seek sanctuary outside Pilate's window, where he listens to her improvised song and witnesses her spontaneous life, one firmly grounded in her organic relationship with nature: "No meal was ever planned or balanced or served. Nor was there any gathering at the table. Pilate might bake hot bread and each one of them would eat it with butter whenever she felt like it. Or there might be grapes, left over from the winemaking, or peaches for days on end . . . If another got half a bushel of tomatoes or a dozen ears of corn, they ate them until they were gone too." It is the "economy" of life rather than the economics of life that interests Pilate.

To Milkman, this woman with "berry black lips" "looked like a tall black tree." The sun and odor of pine and fermenting wine permeate the curtainless home of this once "wood-wild girl," who made it a habit to chew on pine needles. Pilate is literally the daughter of Nature: motherless, she was nurtured by the forest during her childhood. Macon tells us that she even smells like a forest. Thus, like Eva, Pilate is a prototype of the "Great Mother," "Mother Earth." As William K. Freiert explains, Pilate's "smooth stomach was a sign that she was not born from human woman— in mystical terms, she is Earth, the Mother of all."

Unlike in *Sula*, however, the concern is not with this archetype's capacity to love or propensity to destroy. Milkman has no need to question Pilate, as Hannah does Eva, about her ability to love. Although she, too, like Macon II, witnessed the senseless killing of her father, and was robbed of her material legacy, Pilate does not relinquish the salient values, relative to caring, that her father sought to teach her by admonishing her not to "leave a body behind." Consequently, her life's agenda is not engulfed, like Macon's, in desperation, bitterness, and hate. She is able to show compassion and love, even for her brother who though once a compassionate sibling now hates her. A spiritual healer, Pilate, we are told, "had a deep concern for and about human relationships."

It is in the significance of these qualities that her name lies. In his blind ritual of naming, Pilate's father thumbed inadvertently through the Bible, choosing "a group of letters that seemed to him strong and handsome" to name his mysterious self-birthing girlchild. He saw in them "a large figure that looked like a tree hanging in some princely but protective way over a row of smaller trees." Although discouraged from naming his child after the killer of Christ, her father was adamant. He explained that he had mediumistically forseen an individual whose sensitivity and strength would lead her to tower above others. Pilate fulfills her father's prophecy: "A tree grounded in her own principles, she thus protectively towers over those about her, not only by her six-foot height but by the ascendancy of her love." Here, again, we see another instance of Morrison's more positive use of biblical referents. As may be further seen in her use of themes, scenes, and names that she takes from biblical mythology, especially in *Song of Solomon*, Morrison's use, as Anne Mickelson notes, is "extensive and varied." It enriches the text rather than suggests, as Edelburg would have us believe, that Morrison wishes to imply that the Bible is "the wrong book for blacks."

Having eked out her own truths about life, Pilate can guide Milkman on his path toward self-realization. By carrying a geography book to denote where she has been and by collecting rocks from each place to denote her determination, her role is specifically that of spiritual guide, the polar opposite of his parents. Barbara Christian correctly notes that central to the novel is the conflict between the values of Pilate and her brother, which Milkman has to resolve for himself. After helping to bring Milkman into the world, she was prepared to direct him away from his fruitless (Dead) existence. She "has as much to do with his future as she had with his past."

Milkman's Quest

By age thirty, Milkman has a need to escape the existential vacuum of his pointless and aimless life, as well as the effort of those around him to work "out some scheme of their own on him . . . Everything they did seemed to be about him, yet nothing he wanted was part of it." As the self he discovered in personal reflection suggested, he "lacked coherence, a coming together of the features into a total self." Milkman resolves to take control of his life by declaring, "I want to live my own life," a pronouncement that, like Nel's self-affirming, "I am me," achieves *nommo*, creating or self-creative.

Yet, it must be noted that his pronouncement does not imply a desire for the experimental life that remained salient to Sula but for a transcendental life, one that surpasses the material world of his parents. Initially, in fact, Milkman identifies material wealth, gold nuggets, as the source of the independence and authenticity he desires. This is not surprising given his father's orientation and the apparent impact he has had on his son. Believing that the "treasure" Pilate keeps hoisted in a green sack in the ceiling of her home is the gold cache she had taken from him, Macon sends Milkman to steal it. Considering his promised share a means of beating "a path away from his parents' past," Milkman agrees, enlisting the assistance of his "main man," Guitar. When the would-be-gold turned out to be a bag of bones, Macon sends Milkman to Danville, Pennsylvania (his father's home), where he believes the gold must still be buried. Failing to find it there, Milkman goes to Shalimar, Virginia (his grandfather's home), in an effort to retrace Pilate's journey and discover the hidden gold.

Paradoxically, although he goes in search of his father's material legacy, Milkman discovers instead his personal treasured legacy: his genealogy, cultural identity, and historical community, embedded in the folklore of his parent's communal past. Ironically, then, in his effort to "beat a path from his parents' past," he literally stumbles right into it. Thus, Milkman, as Susan L. Blake notes, "progresses from his father's values to Pilate's. He sets out seeking gold, his father's concern, but ends up seeking family, Pilate's concern."

His journey to self, in fact, had begun at age twelve—a significant age of initiation—when, despite his father's forbidding, he visited and met his Aunt Pilate. Her role as guide and educator—as *pilot*, as her name suggests— is that of *griot*: She is guardian of cultural and familial lore. This is made evident from the outset, for she provides Milkman with a sense of self in history. Pilate is the first person to tell him about his grandfather and Lincoln's Heaven. Significantly, this begins the process of his reclamation of name, of his identity. Armed with the information Pilate has given him, Milkman is able to get his father to add to the lore about his grandfather, Macon Dead I, who had been given the name "Dead" by a drunken soldier. "[H]e asked him who his father was. Papa said, 'He's dead.' . . . in the space for his name the fool wrote, 'Dead' comma 'Macon.'" Illiterate, the grandfather remained unaware of the fostered identity but agreed to keep it later on when his wife, a free Indian, explained that the new name would wipe out his past of slavery. Ironically, by accepting the surname "Dead," he erased more than the slavery experience—he obliterated his entire legacy, a goldmine that included a past rich in culture, history, and community, that extended beyond slavery to a rich African past. His action thus robbed his progeny of their legacy, relegating them to a life of materialism and inauthentic existence.

Milkman's journey to Danville and Shalimar places him in the presence of his past. It marks the point of his separation from the false community of the Deads and begins the rite of passage that will result in his incorporation into his ancestral community, allowing him to transcend his present fostered existence in a spiritual flight to self. At this point his status as liminal hero is most evident.

According to Arnold Van Gennep, in any given society, an individual's life is characterized by a succession of stages. At each stage, or passage, the individual must undergo a tripartite journey involving a *rite de separate* (separation), a *rite de marge* (transformation), and a *rite d'agregation* (incorporation). The three phases in combination constitute rites of passage. The *rite de marge*, sometimes referred to as the liminal phase (from the Latin *limen*, or margin), represents a period when he is "betwixt and between." No longer assigned to a culturally defined social position or status, the initiand finds himself in limbo.

According to symbolic anthropologist Victor Turner, for the initiand, the liminal state represents, in a sense, a period of "structural impoverishment." He is an individual who is both "no longer classified" and "not yet classified." The final objective is incorporation: the movement of the individual from one well-defined position to another. He is separated for all time from one status and reintegrated into the society in a new status.

Although Milkman's journey indeed imbues him with the characteristics of the hero of tradition, making him akin, for example, to Ulysses, Oedipus, and Daedalus, his journey must also be understood within the context of traditional African culture. Here, ritual incorporation generally occurs after the initiated has been carefully tutored in the art of communal living. In this traditional world, which embraces the living and the "living dead," the significance of the collective society takes precedence over the individual. "Consequently, initiation rites . . . not only introduce the novice to adult life, but more important, they educate him, providing instructions in traditions, institutions, and, above all, in the revered ethical values of the group." Turner correctly notes that the liminal phase is a period not only of structural impoverishment but also symbolic enrichment.

Wearing the trappings of his middle-class identity—a three-piece suit, light blue buttondown shirt, Florsheim shoes, and a watch—Milkman arrives in Danville fifty-eight years after his father left. While there, he is treated benignly by Reverend Cooper and Circe who, as *griots* recite his family history, helping him to unravel his muddled past. Like her mythical name-sake, Circe (who saved Macon's life after his father's death) points Milkman in the direction of Hunter's cave, where, she tells him, he will find his grand-father's remains, for he had not been properly buried. To find the cave, which with the passing of time had become hidden in the woods, Milkman climbs a hill and twenty feet of deep rock, after crossing a creek that runs in front of the cave. With the exception of a collection of boards, leaves, rocks, and a teacup, he finds "nothing at all" in the cave.

Milkman's Danville experience marks the point of his separation from the Deads and begins a rite of passage that will allow him to metaphorically take flight into self. His ascension to the cave as initiand (his cultural womb) is an act that brings him closer to aggregation—to his grandfather and lost community. It necessarily involves the symbolic testing of strength and ritual cleansing (water is the element used here), which he experiences in the climb and by his submersion in the creek, that the liminal hero must encounter. Significantly, this is a process that requires him to shed his artificial past, symbolized by his soiled, torn clothing and his shoe, which he removed, indi-cating his humility as initiand. This ritual cleansing is a form of new birth. Upon reaching the creek's edge, for example, he breathlessly hoists himself from its body, much in the manner that Pilate birthed herself after her mother died during delivery. Most important, this action signifies his completion of the preliminary preparation of his flight to self.

Rebirth is also experienced in Shalimar, when initiatory priests and elders, Luther and Calvin—names one readily associates with reform and rebirth—take him on a hunt. In the woods he overcomes fear by defeating Guitar's challenges to take his life, and he indicates his preparedness for manhood by firing the rifle at the hunted bobcat. In town, the elders end his educational initiation when they ritualistically share the catch with him and give him the bobcat's heart. His middle-class status was of no use to him here:

There was nothing here to help him—not his money, his car, his father's reputation, his suit, or shoes . . . all that he had started out with on his journey was gone: his suitcase with the Scotch, the shirts, and the space for bags of gold; his snap-brim hat, his tie, his shirt, his three-piece suit, his socks, and his shoes. His watch and his two hundred dollars would be of no help out here, where all a man had was what he was born with, or had learned to use.

The striking parallel between Milkman and the recurring image of the peacock in the text clearly indicates this metamorphosis. Royster correctly notes that "the peacock is a symbol of an unregenerated Milkman." When he goes with Guitar to rob Pilate, Milkman sees a white peacock whose inability to fly peaks his interest. Guitar explains that the peacock cannot fly because he has "Too much tail. All that jewelry weighs him down. Like vanity. Can't nobody fly with all that shit." Guitar advises: "Wanna fly, you got to give up the shit that weighs you down." A significant part of the waste that inhabits Milkman's flight to a more "centered sense of self" is his false identity, for in spite of his name, he is not without history and community; in short he is not "Dead." To take flight he must somehow abort this baggage.

Milkman's experiences in the Blue Ridge Mountains and Shalimar allow him to finally divest his fostered self, the life that has become a burden; like the peacock's vanity, it had weighed him down. Like an African initiate who enters the forest at puberty, symbolically dies through the act of circumcision, and returns to his village a man, Milkman enters the woods of his parents' youth and there, stripped of his social trappings, completes his rite of passage. He leaves the forest a new man, one who has been shaped not solely by the environment but also his distinct choices and actions: by his decision to live, to walk the earth as "Self."

In coming to grips with his whole self, Milkman learns that he cannot circumvent his racial and cultural identity. He can now interpret and understand the sacra and lore that he discovered concisely encoded in Shalimar's folklore about Solomon, the flying African. He is in fact the spiritual and biological heir of Solomon, who rebelled against his bondage in slavery with his flight back to Africa and whose history is recorded in Pilate's blues song about "Sugarman," which he heard for the first time when he visited her home at twelve and now hears in Shalimar's children's ring game:

Jake the only son of Solomon
Come booba yalle, come booba tambee
Whirled about and touched the sun
Come konka yalle, come konka tambee

Left that baby in a white man's house
Come booba yalle, come booba tambee
Heddy took him to a red man's house
Come konka yalle, come konka tambee

Black lady fell down on the ground
Come booba yalle, come booba tambee
Threw her body all around
Come konka yalle, come konka tambee

Solomon and Ryna Belali Shalut
Yaruba Medina Muhammet too.
Nestor Kalina Saraka Cake.
Twenty-one children, the last one Jake!

O Solomon don't leave me here
Cotton balls to choke me
O Solomon don't leave me here
Buckra's arms to yoke me

Solomon done fly, Solomon done gone
Solomon cut cross the sky, Solomon gone home.

In unraveling the deeper meaning of the children's game Milkman comes to know his paternal roots. He learns that his paternal grandfather, Jake, was reared by Heddy, an Indian, who rescued him when his father's effort to carry him to Africa failed. His great-grandmother, Ryena, had lost her mind as a result of the desertion. Jake would later marry Singing Bird, the daughter of his surrogate mother, and they bore two children, Pilate and Macon II. As Susan Willis notes, "The end point of Milkman's journey is the starting point of his race's history in this country: slavery. The confrontation with the reality of slavery, coming at the end of Milkman's penetration into historical process, is liberational because slavery is not portrayed as the origin of history and culture."

Milkman finally discovers his inheritance and whole self at the end of his journey when he concludes that the bones in Pilate's "treasure" are Jake's remains. Milkman and Pilate return to Shalimar and give the remains an appropriate burial shortly before Pilate is killed by Guitar. Milkman comes to understand why Pilate's name was appended to her ears. He concludes: "When you know your name, you should hang on to it." Knowing his identity leads to full integration of his self. At the end of the novel he takes flight to signify his ultimate actualization and freedom. He is, without a doubt, the true heir of Solomon.

The Meaning of Flight

Through the tale of Solomon, the flying African, and its central metaphor—flight—Morrison returns to the central issue of existential freedom: the ultimate responsibility of the individual to chart the direction of, to pilot his or her life. Everything about Pilate's life indicates that she has understood and assumed this responsibility. Milkman realizes this at the moment of her death. He concludes: "Without ever leaving the ground, she could fly." But this, too, he concludes, was true of Solomon: "For now he knew what Shalimar knew: If you surrendered to the air, you'd ride it."

Morrison suggests here again, as she has done through Claudia and Freida, as well as Shadrack and Sula, that self-actualization and personal freedom are achieved through individual actions. Without a doubt, the central trope flight "is associated with a spiritual triumph." But as Susan Blake notes, there is a contradiction here. "Although Milkman cannot achieve identity without recognizing community, the identity he achieves is individual." The same would be true of Solomon, whose solo flight—which theoretically reunited him with one community—required that he abort wife and family, at least in Morrison's lore. Blake calls attention to the paradox: "On the one hand, his quest leads Milkman to his kin, close and remote; on the other hand, it sets him apart, like the quest hero of myth and fairy tale . . . On the one hand Solomon is clearly Milkman's hero and model . . . On the other, he dramatically violated the principle of responsibility to other people that Milkman has to learn in order to discover him." As she indicated to Ntozake Shange, however, Morrison is quite aware of this inherent contradiction. If flight is a trope for achieved selfhood in *Song of Solomon*, it is not unproblematic. Flight, Morrison conceded, "also has that other meaning in it; the abandonment of other people." Flight is paradoxically "triumph and risk"—tragedy and triumph. In the end what seems to matter to Morrison is not the violation ("you do leave other people behind") but the willingness to become exceptional, to take the leap. Morrison will save the question of limitation, as we will see, for *Beloved*.

New Depth in Black Male Characters

With her treatment of Milkman as the protagonist, Morrison offers a more in-depth treatment of the black male character than, with the exception of Shadrack, has been heretofore witnessed in her work. Through her characterization of Milkman, we are given a better rounded view of and careful insights into the complexity of the black male, his aspirations, frustrations, and determination. Morrison confessed that her effort here was intentional; she wanted to look at the world from a man's point of view: "I've never considered looking at the world and looking at women through the eyes of men [before]. It fascinated me. It really was, for me, the most incredible thing in the world. I was obsessed by it . . . I mean trying to feel things that are of no interest to me but I think are of interest to men, like winning, like kicking somebody, like running toward a confrontation; that level of excitement when they are in danger." Morrison accomplishes much of this task through the salient friendship and camaraderie that Milkman and Guitar share, but also through the other men. Here, unlike in *Sula*, for example, the men are not superficial or immature; Porter, Macon, Milkman, and Guitar are in fact most complex.

In Porter's story, for example, we see that men, too, can be desperately alone and lonely. That he has a need for more than physical love is suggested in the subtle allusions that make him a Christ figure. He is laden, like Jesus, with a love for humanity, hence the significance of the name "Porter." "I love ya all . . . I'd die for ya, kill for ya. I'm saying I love ya . . . Oh God have mercy," he tells a crowd that mocks him much as Christ was mocked while on the cross. He acknowledges the congruence of their experiences when he states: "You [Jesus] know all about it. Ain't it heavy?" The implications are related not solely to the difficulty involved in loving one's fellowman but also to doing so unselfishly, without the expectation of reciprocity. This quality is lacking in black male/female relationships, Morrison seems to have concluded in her previous assessments. Porter's unselfish love is responsible, in the end, for Corinthian's resurrection from the "Dead," from the meaningless world of materialism of her father's home.

Morrison's treatment and characterization of Macon Sr. is equally significant. Although we may not approve of his actions, we are given ample information to understand the source of his behavior. This does not lead to justification but to empathy. We feel the depth of Macon's loneliness and emptiness, for example, in the poignant image of this ostensibly powerful man hiding in the dark outside Pilate's house. For a brief moment we are drawn into the chaos within him. More important, Macon does not abandon his family, as Boy-Boy does. Although we may conclude that he perceives them as his possession, we must acknowledge that the territorial instinct is also present. He seems willing to guard and protect that which is his, in spite of his inability to openly show affection.

The intricacy of Morrison's black male characters is seen, however, in the special friendship that develops between Guitar and Milkman. It is akin to that which developed between Nel and Sula, in that there seems to be reciprocity until, through misunderstanding, one experiences betrayal. These men also differ from Nel and Sula in that they are independent of each other, each complete within himself. Nevertheless, like Pilate, to whom he introduces Milkman, Guitar serves as mentor; he is a friend "wise and kind and fearless." Above all, Guitar seems to be a surrogate father, replacing Macon, whom Guitar does not resemble in any way. Milkman considers Guitar "the only sane and constant person" in his life. He finds sanctuary in Guitar's home as well as a willing listener and an understanding friend in his more experienced comrade. Guitar shows sensitivity to Milkman's confusion when he tells him, "Looks like everybody's going in the wrong direction but you, don't it?," at the point that Milkman was thinking about his inability to conform. He encourages Milkman to assume the responsibility for his own life. "You got a life? Live it!" he tells him.

In spite of his admirable qualities, however, Guitar is potentially dangerous, as his membership in the Seven Days, a vigilante group, suggests. He lacks not only Pilate's shamanistic powers but, more important, her spirit of forgiveness and love for humanity. Like Macon II, he harbors and is enslaved by a deep hatred of whites as a result of his father's brutal death at the hands of whites. The degree to which this hatred becomes a destructive force for Guitar is manifested when he joins the Seven Days. Insecure and paranoid, he is unable to trust anyone, even his devoted friend. When Macon evicts Guitar for back rent, he holds Milkman responsible and considers it a breach of their friendship. Desperate for money, he agrees to accompany Milkman on his search for the lost gold, but believing that Milkman is "not being serious," he is not trusting. He tells Milkman, "I'm nervous. Real Nervous." Convinced that he has been betrayed by Milkman, whom he believes does not intend to uphold the agreement to share the buried gold, Guitar stalks him to kill him. Paradoxically, he reveals his intention to kill Milkman. When Milkman asks why he has chosen to tell him, Guitar responds, "You're my friend. It's the least I could do for a friend."

Guitar seems honest in his response: He is torn between commitment to his friendship and his membership in the Seven Days, his only apparent source of a sense of place. Ironically, in counseling Milkman, Guitar has told him that everyone has desired his life. Now, it becomes obvious that *everyone* is indeed all inclusive, for it includes his best friend. In the end, Milkman makes the ultimate sacrifice and gives his life to his friend: "You want my life?" he asks Guitar, "You need it? Here." Consequently, even here there is a paradox, for in the final moment between the two, Milkman experiences triumph when he learns the ultimate sacrifice: "Not love, but a willingness to love," by unselfishly giving oneself to mankind, by meeting the challenge of his friend-become-nemesis, Guitar.

Male/Female Relationships

Through Milkman's relationship with Hagar, his cousin, Morrison continues to illustrate the detrimental effects of male/female relationships that result when in romantic love one willingly forfeits self for the love of "the Other." Ironically, Hagar's demise does not result from the incestuousness of the relationship or her abandonment by Milkman after he grows tired of her dependence. Initially, Milkman was the aggressor and Hagar the reluctant prize. By the third year of their relationship, however, she has made Milkman's life more important than her own. She tells Ruth that Milkman is "my home in this world." She commits, in the world of Morrison's fiction, a cardinal sin. Although the relationship lasts an unusually long time, by the twelfth year, Milkman has grown bored with her accessibility: "Her eccentricities were no longer provocative and the stupefying ease with which he had gotten and stayed between her legs had changed from the great good fortune he'd considered it, to annoyance at her refusal to make him hustle for it, work for it, do something difficult for it. He didn't even have to pay for it. It was so free, so abundant, it had lost its fervor. There was no excitement, no galloping blood in his neck or his heart at the thought of her."

Morrison next uses one of the most powerful "masculine" tropes of her canon to convey the negative place Hagar, having become a "permanent fixture in his life," came to occupy in Milkman's world: "She was the third beer. Not the first one, which the throat receives with almost tearful gratitude; nor the second, that confirms and extends the pleasure of the first. But the third, the one you drink because it's there, because it can't hurt, and because what difference does it make." Like Sula, who had confused love with possession, Hagar wants to own Milkman, even if she has to kill him. Psychologically distraught, she is unable to wield a fatal blow symbolic of castration (she uses such public symbols as a knife and ice pick) when, after stalking him for months, she finally catches him. Undoubtedly, she would have killed a part of herself had she succeeded.

In words that seem to capture the crux of Morrison's argument, throughout her collected works, relative to "doormat women" Guitar tells Hagar:

> You think because he doesn't love you that you are worthless. You
> think because he doesn't want you anymore that he is right—that
> his judgment and opinion of you are correct. If he throws you

out, then you are garbage. You think he belongs to you because you want to belong to him. Hagar, don't. It's a bad word, 'belong.' Especially when you put it with someone you love. Love shouldn't be like that . . . You can't own a human being. You can't lose what you don't own.

Finally, Guitar reminds Hagar that if her life "means so little to [her] that [she] can just give it away, hand it to [Milkman], then why should it mean any more to him? He can't value you more than you value yourself." Hagar's death is inevitable; she dies at the moment Milkman stands at the threshold of his manhood.

Communities of Women

This novel, like the others, has several communities of women. Significantly, though composed of threes as before, the clusters are no longer generic, as they are in *The Bluest Eye*. They are eclectic, and the women tend to be more eccentric. For example, Ruth and her daughters First Corinthians and Magdalene called Lena, are quite like the women of Helene Wright's house in that they conform to social conventions. That they spend their time making artificial flowers clearly suggests the stagnant quality of their false, hollow, virginal lives, which, paradoxically, also have some stability. These women are not abandoned to care for themselves by the likes of a Boy-Boy or Jude Green. Corinthians' educational pursuits and her brief employment as a maid indicate her desire for personal freedom. When Corinthians falls in love with Porter, however, she deviates completely from the mold and role of caretaker and centerpiece for her father's status.

Confessing that she had initiated the task of artificial flower making in the family because it kept her "quiet," Lena finally gets the strength to confront Milkman, whom she felt had exploited his role as male heir. She tells him, "Our girlhood was spent like a found nickel on you." Like her plant on which he urinated, she withers and dies in the gloomy world of the doctor's house. Unlike Corinthians who abandons everything, Lena finds escape in alcohol. Unfortunately, Lena, like the mother she felt a need to protect always, never gets around to acting, to doing "something terrible," although she seems to resolve to do so when she warns Milkman: "I don't make roses anymore, and you have pissed your last in this house."

A similar complexity can be found among the other significant cluster of women: Pilate, her daughter, Reba, and her granddaughter, Hagar, who to some degree are reminiscent of the women in Eva Peace's house. Their wine making and improvised music illustrate their generally creative and fulfilling lives. Yet, we know from a close examination of their characters that this remains true of Pilate alone. Although they are not degraded in their home like Lena and Corinthians, Hagar and Reba do not seem to benefit directly from Pilate's example of self-actualization.

They remain confused about love, for example, associating it with possession and gift giving. They never arrive at Pilate's level of independence or her realization that true love is unselfish, caring, and above all free. Reba, who gives "away everything she had," is turned "on for everything in pants," so much such that she is taken advantage of by men. Hagar is the weakest of the two, however, because she is not "strong enough, like Pilate, nor simple enough, like Reba, to make up her life as they had."

Like Eva, Pilate and Reba are deeply engrossed in their role as mothers. This is particularly true of their instinct to secure and protect their offspring. When one of Reba's lovers hits her, Pilate comes armed to her defense. She tells him, "Women are foolish . . . and mamas are the most foolish of all . . . Mamas get hurt and nervous when somebody don't like they children."

Unlike Eva, whose behavior suggests that motherhood and love involve the realization of the appropriate time to let go of one's siblings, Pilate and Reba remain devoted mothers, catering to the every desire of their daughters. We get the impression that Pilate wishes to compensate for the years when, abandoned by husband and friends who feared the implications of the absence of her navel, she wandered aimlessly about and Reba did not have a stable home. Hagar, however, is the very reason for settling down. Pilate decides that Hagar "needed family, people, a life very different from what she and Reba could offer." They spend their lives giving Hagar everything that she wants, as Reba tells her: "We get you anything you want, baby. Anything." Their propensity to overindulge Hagar begins when she is two and ends with her death. To some degree, then, they are responsible for Hagar's inability to accept Milkman's rejection. She was not accustomed to being told no. As if to justify their behavior, Pilate declares at Hagar's funeral: "And she was *loved!*"

We may conclude in the end that such untrammeled maternal love is as destructive as Macon's blind materialism. Ironically, one may also conclude that the significant difference between Pilate and her daughter and granddaughter lies in the tangible relationships they have established with men. Though the community of women is important, so is the absence of men in their lives. Morrison reminds us that Pilate spent twelve important years of her life in a meaningful relationship with her brother and father, which made her fierce and loving: "Her daughter had less, that daughter's daughter had none. So her relationship to men was curious and destructive, possessive . . .

the stuff that Pilate has is not transmitted by DNA; you need other people."
There must be a shared responsibility, Morrison maintains, for the child to
begin to approach wholeness.

Myth and Mysticism in *Song of Solomon*

Structurally and thematically, *Song of Solomon* draws heavily not only from
the world of folklore but also from the worlds of mysticism and magic. Far
more than in *The Bluest Eye* and *Sula*, Morrison muddles the division
between the real and the fantastic, among folklore, myth, and history. The
mythic structure of *Song of Solomon*, as Chiara Spallino notes, is that of the
hero's quest myth. It fits well, as noted above, into a pattern of the heroic
myth. In fact, it is possible to agree with Leslie Harris that the myth structure is responsible for the cohesiveness of the novel; it prevents it from
being meandering and confused. Significantly, however, as Spallino points
out, "Morrison's characters . . . are portrayed as mirroring their communities and culture, and it is the strength of the continuity of the Black
heritage as a whole which is at stake and being tested here."

Consequently, Milkman's quest, as noted earlier, must also be
assessed within the context of an African communal rite of passage.
Although allusions to classic myths are visible from the very beginning, as
in the Icarusian flight of the insurance agent Robert Smith, Morrison is
obviously borrowing from the black "folk stuff" that she knows intimately,
including the tale of the flying African. As she reports, "I've heard all my
life that Black people could fly, just as I heard the tooth fairy story, and I
accepted it. Then I used to read about it in the slave narratives."

Then there is otherworldly Pilate, whose distinct characteristic is the
absence of her navel. This, more than the fact that she was apprenticed to
a root worker, is believed to endow her with magical powers. As shaman,
she is able to assist Ruth in getting Macon to make love to her. Pilate put
a small doll on Macon's chair in his office; "A male doll with a small
painted chicken bone stuck between its leg and a round red circle painted
on its belly." Thus, much like Isis, the wife of Osiris, who is often associated with the dead, Ruth (who is married to a Dead) is able to conceive
magically after sleeping with the dead/Dead.

Equally significant is the presence of the mythological shaman/witch
Circe in the form of her Morrisonian counterpart. Much in the manner
that Circe provides the information that guides Odysseus through the
River of Ocean, offering him advice on how to deal with the ghost of Tire-
seas, Morrison's Circe, with her toothless mouth but mellifluent voice,

directs Milkman on his Odyssean path to self, "Go north until you come to a stile. It's falling down, but you'll see it's a stile. Right in there the woods are open. Walk a little way in and you'll come to a creek. Cross it. There'll be some more woods, but ahead you'll see a short range of hills. The cave is right on the face of those hills. You can't miss it." Circe also becomes "healer and deliverer" who guides Milkman to the site of his ancestral past by telling him about his grandmother, Sing. She above all sets him on the correct path to his desired treasure.

It is Pilate, however, who maintains direct contact with her mythic past. She communicates with her dead father, and although unaware of it, she keeps his remains hanging from the ceiling in her home. Morrison thus successfully weaves into her tale here again African cosmological views of the reciprocity that exists between the world of the living and the living dead. Simultaneously, she includes folk notions of propitiation, of appeasement, evident in the fact that Macon Dead, Sr. had not been appropriately buried. Circe tells Milkman, "The dead don't like it if they're not buried. They don't like it at all." His ghost returns as an apparition, though not as a poltergeist, until he has been appropriately buried.

Moreover, Pilate is a paradigmatic folk heroine, the trickster as hero. We see her protean quality when she changes both voice and size in going to rescue Milkman from jail. While in the jail, she appears shorter and whines as she speaks. On her way home, however, "Pilate was tall again. The top of her head, wrapped in a silk rag, almost touched the roof of the car . . . and her own voice was back." Milkman's father tells him that, like a snake, Pilate has the power to step out of her skin, and neighbors maintain that she "can set a bush afire from fifty yards, and turn a man into a ripe rutabaga—all on account of the fact that she had no navel."

What seems to remain most important, however, is Pilate's role as *griot:* she knows and guards the family history; her blues song about Sugarman is not a lamentation but a celebration of Solomon, the ancestor who escaped slavery by taking flight. She alone can carry her identity firmly sealed in her person because she alone knows who the family really is, and she alone can pass it on to Milkman to allow him to become fully realized. It is only by tracing his ancestry through the myth to the flying African that he, too, can take flight at the end in a symbolic death that leads to rebirth and transcendence. Interestingly enough, when they meet for the first time, Pilate offers Milkman an egg, a symbol and foreshadowing of the rebirth he will eventually realize. The incorporation of myth and mysticism into the text is inevitable, because they are legacies of the Afro-American experience that is Milkman's.

Through the major characters of *Song of Solomon*, Morrison reveals that the struggle for self is indeed complex. The quest for authentic self inevitably involves the quest for truth, love, survival, and even power and forgiveness. For most of the characters, the search for external fulfillment proves unrewarding. Macon is materially rich, but he remains empty. Yet, whether externally or internally, the characters are marked with a sense of incompleteness that drives them toward some form of wholeness. Morrison also suggests through her characters that to achieve some equilibrium, love is paramount—love of oneself and of one's fellowman.

In the end, Milkman is a riddle solver, as Dorothy Lee points out: he brings "his treasure . . . the gift of [self-] knowledge . . . to his people." Only when self-knowledge and self-love are in place can one experience true transcendence, can one ride the air, "fly" like Pilate and Milkman, can one sing her/his "song of songs"—her/his song of Solomon.

VALERIE SMITH

Song of Solomon: *Continuities of Community*

In her first three novels, *The Bluest Eye* (1970), *Sula* (1973), and *Song of Solomon* (1977), Toni Morrison explores the interplay between self-knowledge and social role. Her characters, like Ralph Ellison's Invisible Man, inhabit a world where inhospitable social assumptions obtain. But Morrison does not provide her people with the option of living underground, in isolation, beyond community. Those whom social relations exclude (like Pecola Breedlove of *The Bluest Eye* or *Sula*) lack self-knowledge and are destroyed by themselves or by others. My analysis here centers on *Song of Solomon*, the only one of Morrison's novels in which her protagonist completes successfully his/her search for psychological autonomy. Yet, no discussion of the search for identity in *Song of Solomon* would be complete without some mention of Morrison's two earlier novels. The structure and thematic concerns of these two works establish a framework in terms of which we may understand the meaning and status of Milkman's discovery.

I

The black characters in Morrison's early novels are especially vulnerable to the defeats that accompany isolation; in *The Bluest Eye* and in *Sula*, she examines the complex economic, historical, cultural and geographic

---

From *Toni Morrison: Critical Perspectives Past and Present.* © 1993 Henry Louis Gates, Jr. and K. A. Appiah.

factors that problematize their relations within the black community and the world beyond. Pecola Breedlove, on whom *The Bluest Eye* centers, typifies Morrison's outsiders. Her story illustrates the destructive potential of a culture that recognizes only one standard of physical beauty and equates that standard with virtue. Ostensibly, Pecola is driven mad by her inability to possess blue eyes. But her insanity really results from the fact that she serves as the communal scapegoat, bearing not only her own self-loathing, but that of her neighbors and family as well. Soaphead Church's failure to provide her with blue eyes is thus simply the proverbial back-breaking straw.

The Bluest Eye does not address the hard questions directly. The book does not undertake to explain, for example, why black Americans aspire to an unattainable standard of beauty; why they displace their self-hatred onto a communal scapegoat; how Pecola's fate might have been averted. The metaphors of Claudia MacTeer that frame and image Pecola's story, and the very structure of the novel itself, suggest that such considerations are irre-solvable. "This soil is bad for certain kinds of flowers," Claudia remarks. "Certain seeds it will not nurture, certain fruit it will not bear." Claudia accepts as given the fact that certain "soils" will reject both marigolds and plain black girls. To her, the reasons for this incompatibility are structural, too intricately woven to distinguish. She therefore believes that any attempt to explain Pecola's deterioration will be fruitless and concludes that *"There is really nothing more to say—except why. But since why is difficult to handle, one must take refuge in* how."

I would argue that not only Claudia, but the novel itself, avoids "why," taking refuge instead in "how." Claudia, the narrator of the primer, and the ostensibly omniscient narrator all tell stories—tell "how" fast and furiously. These stories, in general, demonstrate what it means to find inaccessible the possessions and attributes that one's culture values. Their thematic similarity reveals the representative nature of Pecola's story: self-loathing leads inevitably to some form of destruction. Perhaps more importantly, the remarkable number of stories symbolizes the complex sources and effects of this cycle of self-loathing. The form is therefore a figure for the cultural condition the novel addresses.

The structure of *The Bluest Eye* underscores the proliferation of stories and of narrative voices within the novel. The body of the text is divided into four chapters which are, in turn, subdivided. Each begins with an episode, usually involving Pecola, told from the point of view of Claudia the child but shaped by her adult reflections and rhetoric. Claudia's stories then yield place to one or two stories told by an apparently objective, omniscient narrator. This narrator usually recalls information to which Claudia would not have had access: he/she tells stories from Pecola's life that involve other characters and weaves flashbacks from the lives of these other characters (Polly or Cholly Breedlove, Geraldine, or Soaphead Church, for example) into Pecola's story. In addition, in each chapter several garbled lines from the primer separate Claudia's voice from that of the omniscient narrator.

The chapters counterpoint three moments in time: a past before the narrative present (the flashbacks), the eternal present of the primer, and the narrative present of Pecola's story as told by Claudia. The different narratives in each chapter provide variations on a specific theme. This technique demonstrates here and throughout Morrison's fiction the interconnectedness of past and present. The form implies that the meaning of Pecola's story may only be understood in relation to events that predated her birth.

The cacophony of voices in *The Bluest Eye* demonstrates that Pecola is inextricably linked to the linguistic community that forms the novel. Yet she is clearly denied a place in the world the text purports to represent; her involuntary isolation from others leads to her psychological disintegration. *Sula* as well features a scapegoat-protagonist, although Sula clearly cultivates those qualities that distinguish her from her neighbors. Here, too, Morrison's plot relies on a multiplicity of narratives to implicate Sula in the very community from which she is alienated. Although Sula, unlike Pecola, chooses her isolation, it is precisely that distance that destroys her.

Sula centers on a character who believes that she can create for herself an identity that exists beyond community and social expectations. "An artist with no art form," Sula uses life as her medium, "exploring her own thoughts and emotions, giving them full reign, feeling no obligation to please anybody unless their pleasure pleased her." She thus defies social restraints with a vengeance. She disavows gratuitous social flattery, refusing to compliment either the food placed before her or her old friends gone to seed, and using her conversation to experiment with her neighbors' responses. As the narrator remarks: "In the midst of pleasant conversation with someone, she might say, 'Why do you chew with your mouth open?' not because the answer interested her but because she wanted to see the person's face change rapidly." Worst of all in her neighbors' judgment, she discards men, black and white, as rapidly as she sleeps with them, even the husband of her best friend, Nel.

There are moments when the text seems to validate Sula's way of life; the narrator suggests, for example, that Sula's independence has bestowed upon her a kind of immortality:

> Among the weighty evidence piling up was the fact that Sula did
> not look her age. She was near thirty and, unlike them, had lost
> no teeth, suffered no bruises, developed no ring of fat at the waist

or pocket at the back of her neck. It was rumored that she had
had no childhood diseases, was never known to have chicken pox,
croup or even a runny nose. She had played rough as a child—
where were the scars?

But by interweaving Sula's story with Shadrack's and Nel's, Morrison demonstrates structurally the collective nature of human identity.

Sula's story stands in analogous relation to Shadrack's, symbolic
evidence that her situation, like Pecola's, is hardly unique. The communal
response to Sula is identically Shadrack's response to the unexpected.
Shadrack, the insane World War I veteran whose story opens the novel,
exemplifies in the extreme this need to explain or find a place for the inexplicable. By creating National Suicide Day, he finds a way of controlling his
fear: "If one day a year were devoted to [death], everybody could get it out
of the way and the rest of the year would be safe and free."

The people of the Bottom of Medallion, Ohio, ridicule Shadrack's
holiday, but their survival, like his, depends upon finding ways of controlling
their terrors. Superstitions, which recur in the narrative and in their collective discourse, help them explain disturbing disruptions. When Hannah,
Sula's mother, dies suddenly, Eva, Sula's grandmother, reflects that she would
have been prepared for the tragedy if she had read properly the omens she
had received. Likewise, the denizens of the Bottom remark that they should
have anticipated Sula's deleterious effect on their community, because her
return was accompanied by a plague of robins. Like Eva, the townspeople
find a sign or reason for their trouble after the fact. Their retrospective justi-
fications are finally no different from Shadrack's.

And just as they must find a way of controlling the unexpected evils that
beset them, so do they find a place for Sula. Since they do not understand
her, they call her evil and hold her responsible for the injuries and deaths that
befall their community. As the narrator notes, the townspeople actually
become more generous when they shun Sula because they assign to her their
own baser impulses. For all her efforts to transcend the community, then,
Sula remains an integral part of it.

Morrison also undercuts Sula's aspirations to originality by characterizing her as only half a person. As several critics have argued, Sula and Nel
complement each other psychologically, and neither is fully herself after
geography, and Sula's relation to Jude, separate them.

Sula and Nel are products of two different styles of childrearing: their
friendship grows out of their fascination with their dissimilarities. Sula's
family is the source of her independence of mind and sexual nonchalance.
Her mother is known especially for her sexual generosity; her grandmother,

Eva, for selling her leg to support her children. Eva's home provides a figure for her family, replete with an ever-changing cast of boarders, gentleman callers, and foundlings:

> Sula Peace lived in a house of many rooms that had been built over a period of five years to the specifications of its owner, who kept on adding things: more stairways—more rooms, doors, and stoops. There were rooms that had three doors, others that opened out on the porch only and were inaccessible from any other part of the house; others that you could get to only by going through somebody's bedroom.

Nel, on the other hand, is raised in a well-ordered but repressive household, and is thus prepared to choose a life of limited options such as the one she shares with Jude. Haunted by the image of her own mother, a prostitute, Nel's mother tries to launder the "funk" out of her daughter's life. During their childhood and adolescence, Nel provides Sula with restraints, and Sula offers Nel license. More importantly, they offer each other a kind of security that neither finds in her own family. Together they begin to discover the meaning of death and sexuality. As the narrator remarks:

> Because each had discovered years before that they were neither white nor male, and that all freedom and triumph were forbidden to them, they had set about creating something else to be. Their meeting was fortunate, for it let them use each other to grow on. Daughters of distant mothers and incomprehensible fathers (Sula's because he was dead; Nel's because he wasn't), they found in each other's eyes the intimacy they were looking for.

Their relationship is permanently destroyed when Sula sleeps with Jude, although Sula reflects that she never intended to cause Nel pain. Without Nel, "the closest thing to both an other and a self," Sula is cut off from the only relation that endowed her life with meaning, and she drifts to her death. Nel, too, is rendered incomplete when her friendship with Sula ends. She may think that her inescapable grief is the result of having lost her husband, but as she realizes at the end of the novel, what she had missed for so many years was not Jude, but Sula.

The descendant of a line of relatively autonomous women, Sula attempts to go them one better and create herself outside of the collective assumptions of women's behavior. Morrison denies the feasibility of such a choice most obviously by killing off her protagonist. But the narrative structures she employs in *Sula* further undercut Sula's aspirations. By characterizing her as both a scapegoat and the second self of her more conventional best friend, Morrison denies Sula the originality she seeks.

II

Song of Solomon centers on Milkman Dead's unwitting search for identity. Milkman appears to be doomed to a life of alienation from himself and others because, like his parents, he adheres to excessively rigid, materialistic, Western values and an attendant linear conception of time. During a trip to his ancestral home, however, Milkman discovers his own capacity for emotional expansiveness and learns to perceive the passage of time as a cyclical process. When he incorporates both his familial and personal history into his sense of the present, he repairs his feelings of fragmentation and comprehends for the first time the coherence of his own life.

Milkman's father, Macon Dead, Jr., is a quintessential self-made man. Orphaned and disinherited in his adolescence, he wheeled and dealt his way into his position as the richest black man in town. Milkman can therefore brag about his father's houses, cars, assets and speculations, to the delight of the Reverend Mr. Cooper and his Danville companions. The avid materialism and rugged individualism that made Macon financially successful have exacted their price from him in other ways, however. Macon has come to believe that money, property and keys are what is real in the world; his financial success has thus cost him his capacity for communication and emotion. As he advises his son:

> "Come to my office; work a couple of hours there and learn what's real. Let me tell you right now that one important thing you'll ever need to know: Own things. And let the things you own own other things. Then you'll own yourself and other people too."

The Macon Deads exemplify the patriarchal, nuclear family that has been traditionally a stable and critical feature not only of American society, but of Western civilization in general. The primary institution for the reproduction and maintenance of children, ideally it provides the individual with the means for understanding his/her place in the world. The degeneration of the Dead family, and the destructiveness of Macon's rugged individualism, symbolize the invalidity of American, indeed Western values. Morrison's depiction of this family demonstrates the incompatibility of received assumptions and the texture and demands of life in black American communities.

Macon, Jr. believes that a successful businessman cannot afford to be compassionate. Reflecting that his first two keys to rental units would never have multiplied had he accomodated delinquent accounts, he sees his tenants only as so much property. Moreover, he objectifies his family. He brutalizes his wife Ruth both subtly and overtly because he suspects her of incestuous relations with her father and son. Despite his concern for Milkman, he only speaks to him "if his words [hold] some command or criticism." And by refusing to acknowledge Pilate as his sister, Macon denies her humanity as well. His resentment is based in part on the belief that she stole the gold that the two of them should have shared. More significantly, though, he eschews her company because he considers her deportment to be socially unacceptable. He fears that the white bankers will cease to trust him if they associate him with a woman bootlegger.

Weak and pathetic as she is, Ruth finds a subtle method of objectifying the members of her family as well. She retaliates against her husband's cruelty by manipulating him. Since she cannot attract his attention in any other way, she demeans herself until, out of disgust, he lashes out at her. Similarly, she remarks that her son has never been "a person to her." Before he was born, Milkman was "a wished-for bond between herself and Macon, something to hold them together and reinstate their sex lives." After she realizes that her husband will never again gratify her sexually, she uses Milkman to fulfill her yearnings by breastfeeding him until he is old enough to talk, stand up and wear knickers.

Pilate Dead, Macon's younger sister, provides a marked contrast to her brother and his family. Like Macon, Pilate presides over a household which is predominantly female. But while Macon's love of property and money determines the nature of his relationships, Pilate's sheer disregard for status, occupation, hygiene and manners enables her to affirm spiritual values such as compassion, respect, loyalty and generosity.

If the Macon Deads seem barren and lifeless, Pilate's family bursts with energy and sensuality. Pilate, Reba, and Hagar engage ceaselessly in collective activity, erupting spontaneously into harmonious song. On his way to his own emotionally empty house one evening, Macon, Jr. peeks through the window of his sister's home in search of spiritual nourishment. He hears the three women sing one song, Pilate stirring the contents of a pot, Reba paring her toenails and Hagar braiding her hair. Macon is comforted both by the soothing and unending motion of each character in the vignette and by the harmony and tranquility of the music they make together.

As Pilate introduces vitality into her brother's life, so does she introduce a magical presence into the otherwise spiritually lifeless world of Part I of the novel. The circumstances of her birth make her a character of larger-than-life dimensions—one who has transcended the limitations of her historical moment and milieu. Pilate delivered herself at birth and was born without a navel. Her smooth stomach isolates her from society, since those who know of her condition shun her. Moreover, her physical condition symbolizes her thorough independence of others; even as a fetus she did not need to rely on another person for sustenance. Her isolation and self-sufficiency enable her to "throw away every assumption she had learned and [begin] at zero." She is therefore neither trapped nor destroyed by decaying values as her brother's family is. Like Macon she is self-made, but her self-creation departs from, instead of coinciding with, the American myth. Pilate decides for herself what is important to her, and instead of appropriating collective assumptions, she remakes herself accordingly. After cutting her hair:

> [Pilate] tackled the problem of trying to decide how she wanted to live and what was valuable to her. When am I happy and when am I sad and what is the difference? What do I need to stay alive? What is true in the world?

Quintessential self-made man that he is, Macon predicates his behavior on a linear conception of time. To his mind, future successes determine identity and justify one's actions in the past and present. Macon's futuristic, linear vision of time and of identity is evidenced by his failure to consider his past as part of himself. He denies the importance of his relationship with his sister and of their shared past. Moreover, as he remarks, while telling Milkman about his days in Lincoln's Heaven, he does not even allow himself to think about his past:

> He had not said any of this for years. Had not even reminisced much about it recently . . . For years he hadn't had that kind of time, or interest.

Macon's linear vision of time is also partly responsible for his sense of family and of morality. Because he believes that the coherence and significance of his identity lie in his future, he cares only about his relationship to his son. To his patriarchal mind, it is in that connection that the most important genealogical transfer occurs. But Macon has no time whatsoever for any connection that would cause him to exercise his capacity for horizontal or (what would be to him) peripheral vision.

Macon's ability to see the world only in linear, exclusive terms, explains his lack of sympathy in yet other ways. He believes that the ends justify any means; as a result, he excuses his own corruption by considering only the financial profits it brings him. He feels no need to offer Mrs. Bains (one of his tenants) charity because charity will not increase his wealth. And he encourages Milkman and Guitar to steal what he thinks is Pilate's gold, despite the kindness she has shown them all.

In contrast to Macon's, Pilate's vision of time—indeed, of the world—is cyclical and expansive. Instead of repressing the past, she carries it with her in the form of her songs, her stories and her bag of bones. She believes that one's sense of identity is rooted in the capacity to look back to the past and synthesize it with the present; it is not enough simply to put it behind one and look forward. As she tells Macon:

> "You can't take a life and walk off and leave it. Life is life. Precious. And the dead you kill is yours. They stay with you anyway, in your mind. So it's a better thing, a more better thing to have the bones right there with you wherever you go. That way it frees up your mind."

Before Milkman leaves Michigan, he perceives the world in much the same way that his father does. His steadiness of vision and lack of compassion allow him to abuse remorselessly and unself-consciously the people around him. For instance, his letter to Hagar reveals his inability to understand her feelings and psychology despite their years of intimacy. Instead, he writes little more than a business letter suggesting that he leave her for her own best interest. Moreover, his sister Lena tells him that he has "urinated" on the women in his family. That is, he has demanded their service and shown them no consideration. He has presumed to know what is best for them without knowing them at all.

Milkman's search for gold indicates further the similarity between his father's vision of the world and his own. He thinks that leaving his hometown, his past and his responsibilities will guarantee him a sense of his own identity. As he becomes increasingly implicated in the scheme to retrieve Pilate's gold, Milkman acquires a clearer but equally false sense of what freedom means. He believes that gold will provide him with a "clean-lined definite self," the first sense of identity he has ever known.

Milkman's assumption that the key to his liberation may be found in Danville and Shalimar is correct, although it is not gold that will free him. In his ancestors' world, communal and mythical values will prevail over individualism and materialism; when he adopts their assumptions in place of his own, he arrives at a more complete understanding of what his experience means. When Milkman arrives in the South he wears a "beige three-piece suit, button down light-blue shirt and black string tie, [and] beautiful

Florsheim shoes." He ruins and loses various articles of clothing and jewelry as he looks first for gold and then for the story of his people. Indeed, just before his epiphanic moment in the forest, he has changed from his cosmopolitan attire to overalls and brogans. Similarly, the people he meets in Shalimar force him to throw off his pretenses before they offer him the help and information he needs. Only when he ceases to flaunt his wealth and refer to their women casually do they admit him into their community. Until he sheds the leaden trappings of materialism, Milkman is like the peacock he and Guitar see: too weighted down by his vanity to fly.

While in Michigan, Milkman believes that when he finally achieves his freedom, he will no longer need to submit to the claims of others. In the woods, away from the destructive effects of "civilization," he realizes that human connection—horizontal vision—is an inescapable part of life:

> It sounded old. Deserve. Old and tired and beaten to death. Deserve. Now it seemed to him that he was always saying or thinking that he didn't deserve some bad luck, or some bad treatment from others. He'd told Guitar that he didn't "deserve" his family's dependence, hatred, or whatever. That he didn't "deserve" to hear all the misery and mutual accusations his parents unloaded on him. Nor did he "deserve" Hagar's vengeance. But why shouldn't his parents tell him their personal problems? If not him, then who?

While previously he had dehumanized his friends and relations, he now empathizes with his parents and feels shame for having robbed Pilate:

> . . . the skin of shame that he had rinsed away in the bathwater after having stolen from Pilate returned. But now it was as thick and tight as a caul. How could he have broken into that house— the only one he knew that achieved comfort without one article of comfort in it. No soft worn-down chair, not a cushion or pillow . . . But peace was there, energy, singing, and now his own remembrances.

In keeping with this new awareness of others and of his personal past, Milkman, insensitive to Hagar and unwilling to accept responsibility for her in life, understands her posthumously and assumes the burden of her death. He acknowledges the inappropriateness of his letter to her and realizes that he has used her. Moreover, he knows without being told that she has died and he is to blame. As Pilate carried with her the bones of the man she believes she has murdered, so too does Milkman resolve to carry with him the box of Hagar's hair: a symbol of his newly acquired cyclical vision of a past he no longer needs to escape.

Macon, Sr., Milkman's grandfather, was an American Adam, a farmer who loved the land and worked it profitably. Moving north cost Macon, Jr. some of the talent he had inherited from his father; still able to manipulate cold cash, he lost his father's connection to the soil. In the south, Milkman, too, seems disconnected from nature. Graceful in the "civilized" world, he is clumsy and obtuse when he enters the wilderness. However, he becomes increasingly attuned to nature's rhythms as he grows in self-awareness. During the bobcat hunt he senses through the contact between his fingertips and the ground beneath him that someone is about to make an attempt on his life. And as he returns to the town, Milkman feels as if he is part of the "rock and soil" and discovers that he no longer limps.

Finally, however, Milkman's discovery of his identity lies not so much in his connection with the earth, or in his ability to understand his own past; these accomplishments only attend his greater achievement—learning to complete, to understand and to sing his family song. Milkman comes to know fully who he is when he can supply the lyrics to the song Pilate has only partially known. Throughout his life, Milkman has had an inexplicable fascination with flight. Robert Smith's abortive attempt to fly from the hospital roof precipitated his birth. Riding backward makes him uncomfortable because it reminds him of "flying blind, and not knowing where he [is] going." And as he approaches Circe's house, he recalls his recurring childhood fantasy of being able to take flight. When Milkman knows the entire song, however, and can sing it to Pilate as she has sung it to others, he can assume his destiny. Flight is no longer a fantasy that haunts him, appearing unsummoned in his consciousness. He now understands it as a significant action from his ancestral past. Indeed, the ultimate sign of his achievement of identity is his ability to take flight in the way his grandfather did. In the process of assuming himself, Milkman discovers that his dreams have become attainable.

Milkman acquires a sense of identity when he immerses himself in his extended past. He comes full round from the individualism his father represents and advocates. Assuming identity is thus a communal gesture in this novel, as, indeed, Morrison suggests in her two earlier novels. Knowing oneself derives from learning to reach back into history and horizontally in sympathetic relationship to others. Milkman burst the bonds of the Western, individualistic conception of self, accepting in its place the richness and complexity of a collective sense of identity.

STEPHANIE A. DEMETRAKOPOULOS

The Interdependence of Men's and Women's Individuation

While *Sula* is the most moving of Morrison's works for me, I have found myself coming back over and over to *Song of Solomon*: first, for the fierce wisdom of Pilate, which I wrote on in *Listening to Our Bodies*; then for the wisdom and clarity and originality of Morrison's analysis of masculine archetypes and how they underlie men's individuation; and finally, for lessons about women's life stages, since the novel gives a cross section of women on the boundary line of passages into various new life stages.

Like her other novels, Morrison's *Song of Solomon* crosses seveal generations; the major action of the novel takes place when all the women have grown middle-aged or old. Although this novel develops in depth Morrison's vision of masculine archetypes, the portraits of the women are as strong and compelling as her more centrally feminine previous novels; as Gloria Snodgrass Malone says, "men [are] more prominent in this novel, but women bear the brunt of suffering." The female figures are for me more memorable than the males. And although the novel's protagonist is male, he is finally redeemed by the strength and spirituality of several women in his family and the witch figure Circe, whom he meets on his journey South. Milkman is thirty-one when this happens. The older women in his family are his mother, Ruth, sixty-two, and his aunt, Pilate, sixty-eight; these women comprise the portraits of women in the last stage of life, well past middle age. His sisters, Corinthians and Lena, are forty-two and forty-three respectively, thus

From *New Dimensions of Spirituality: A Biracial and Bicultural Reading of the Novels of Toni Morrison.* © 1987 Karla F. C. Holloway and Stephanie A. Demetrakopoulos. Reproduced with permission of Greenwood Publishing Group, Inc., Westport, CT.

moving into middle-age during the last section of the novel, as does Reba, Pilate's daughter, although her age is never actually given. Hagar, Milkman's cousin and lover, dies at thirty-six, apparently unable and unwilling to move towards middle-age. But before examining the women's life stages in depth, we need to set the stage with Morrison's development of masculine archetypes.

The Archetype of the Masculine: Flying and Dominion

Morrison herself says of the men in *Song of Solomon:* "Men are more prominent. They interested me in a way I hadn't thought about before, almost as a species." *Species* is an apt term for the polarized masculine in this novel. Morrison's masculine archetypes are often pathological ones because they are so one-sided, so out of balance. They are not linked to or grounded in nature or the feminine. They are also alienated, isolated from and rejected by masculine white culture. So they exist in a sort of vacuum. Yet theirs are universal masculine values, I believe, not characteristic only of Black males, although these values gain their particular style from Black culture. But I would say that most men in the world have never really known a woman. Certainly men never know a woman in the way that women know each other; women unconsciously don personas around most men to protect themselves from the contempt and loathing that men so often feel towards women's values and deepest selves. Thus men generally live unknowingly cut off from half of humanity.

Appropriately then, the major symbol of the book is flying, men out of touch with the ground. Milkman's mother Ruth begins labor as she stands and watches Robert Smith leap off a hospital to fly across Lake Superior; the sister of Milkman's father, Pilate, sings Smith off. At age four, Milkman loses interest in life when he finds he cannot fly; as an adult he is euphoric during the plane ride down South where he finds his roots. The image of the Black man flying back to Africa that Morrison builds on is integral to Black culture. This portion of Robert Hayden's poem "O Daedalus, Fly Away Home" reflects the songs and images with which he and Morrison must have grown up:

> Night is an African juju man
> Weaving a wish and a weariness together to make two wings.
> *O fly away home fly away*
> Do you remember Africa?
> *O cleave the air fly away home*
> My gran, he flew back to Africa,
> Just spread his arms and flew away home.

Pilate sings her own form of this litany to Robert Smith:

> O Sugarman done fly away
> Sugarman done gone
> Sugarman cut across the sky
> Sugarman gone home.

Milkman finds that his first American ancestor, Solomon, flew home to Africa, and the local children have a song on the subject that ends this way:

> Solomon done fly, Solomon done gone
> Solomon cut across the sky, Solomon gone home.

Morrison herself has spoken eloquently on this theme:

> Flying is the central metaphor in "Song"—the literal taking off and flying into the air, which is everybody's dream. My children [both boys] used to talk about it all the time—they were amazed when they found they couldn't fly. They took it for granted that all they had to do was jump up and flap their arms. I use it not only in the African sense of whirling dervishes and getting out of one's skin, but also in the majestic sense of a man who goes too far, whose adventures take him far away . . . black men travel, they split, they get on trains, they walk, they move. I used to hear those old men talk about traveling—which is not getting from here to there, it's the process—they even named themselves after trains. It's a part of black life, a positive, majestic thing, but there is a price to pay—the price is the children. The fathers may soar, they may triumph, they may leave, but the children know who they are; they remember, half in glory and half in accusation. That is one of the points of "Song": all the men have left someone, and it is the children who remember it, sing about it, mythologize it, make it a part of their family history.

I quote this passage at such length because it is important to see that Morrison looks at this archetype from women's and children's points of view. She doesn't redefine this archetype of masculine flying, but she surely does broaden and complicate the myth by looking at it from an outsider's vantage point rather than Robert Hayden's lyrical, masculine point of view. Morrison has said she finds this flying "one of the most attractive features about the black male life. . . . It's part of that whole business of breaking ground, doing the other thing. . . . It's very beautiful, it's very interesting, and in that way, you know, they lived in the country, they lived here, they went all over it." Yet she insists upon the cost of this freedom. We remember Eva and Nel in *Sula*, both trying to raise children after their husbands abandon them. Milkman hears the wailing winds of Ryna's Gulch, named after his great-great-grandmother, who was deserted with twenty-one children when her husband, Solomon, flew away. As Milkman's Southern informant, Susan Byrd, says, although the myth is that Ryna could not love again because she was a one-man woman, the truth is probably that she went mad trying to take care of the children by herself. And Milkman's grandfather Jake was deserted as a baby by the mad Ryna and raised by an Indian woman.

The children of flying men suffer discontinuity of every kind. They lose their names, a sense of their fathers, a sane and stable mother, and even their racial roots in this case of the boy raised by the Indian. This desertion of family is not as specific to Black culture as Morrison implies. There is data that suggests that as many families were broken up before the advent and acceptability of divorce in America, but that they were broken up by the desertion of fathers. Sometimes the mother simply broke under the weight of trying to support her family alone. The protagonist of *Anne of Green Gables* is orphaned because of these same circumstances. One of the ways *Song of Solomon* looks at this problem in a fresh way is in the point Morrison makes of the ramifications of masculine flying for women and children.

But the loss to men's own soul development is perhaps an even more devastating result. Virginia Woolf says there is a space the size of a shilling in the back of each gender's head that must be described by the opposited gender because it cannot be seen except by the other; in the case of men, more than such a small aspect of their selves needs naming. I believe men in general need to read women's works for precisely this reason. It is especially hard for American men to see their loss of soul, to recognize it, in a culture that celebrates masculine isolation as heroic—Huck Finn and John Wayne both ending their stories by disappearing into distances. Cutthroat ambition is another symptom of being cut off, and this again is often admired in our culture. Interaction with others solely in terms of politics is another way men can become cut off; in their response to white culture, Black revolutionaries can fall prey to this. For example, the Days, a group of seven black men who avenge Black people killed by white people, must remain absolutely "loose" and unconnected to family or friends. Smith, a "Day" who begins the novel with his leap to death, became convinced that he could fly, really fly. Henry Porter, another one of the Days, climbs to his roof top and threatens to leap, demanding sex, a woman; he avows his general and abiding love for everyone and especially for all women—a high flying, abstract love. To hate or love universally is easy; actual persons give us trouble. Remaining forever ready to fly as one of the Days, Guitar's universal hatred of all whites takes over his one loving friendship, and he tries to kill Milkman, his oldest and best friend. Having spent his life "loose" as a free-flying assassin getting even with white culture, Henry Porter gets a double dose of the worst of white values when he ends up with the light-skinned and immature Corinthians, a forty-two-year-old aristocratic virgin afraid of her parents. But Porter wants her and they do end up together, perhaps maturing with each other at long last.

I think here again of James Hillman's precept that people can only go as far with themselves as they have gone with another: these unattached men seem eternally adolescent, emblems of the *puer eternal*. This is especially tragic in Guitar's case who is deeply intelligent and passionate, even compassionate when he sees how Hagar is suffering—he alone understands why. Guitar is one of Morrison's most appealing male characters, and I feel a real loss when he continues his vendetta to the end of the novel. As always with all her male characters, Morrison shows us why Guitar feels as he does, how a white man killed his father and then paid off Guitar's mother with money and sweets for the children. He is named Guitar because he wanted one and could never afford one; this is the art form his creative urge would have taken. Like Cholly (*The Bluest Eye*) and Sula, he is the *artiste*, specifically the musician *manqué*. His creativity and brilliance turns to a smoldering, lifelong revenge. He is, of course, also cut off from his emotions because of his bereft childhood. One adult after another abandoned Guitar as a child and he now does not trust anyone.

Certain Black writers complain about how their culture has been studied to death. Besides the absurd amount of studies, I would complain further about the naming of phenomena discovered in these studies. Anthropologists such as Carol B. Stack and Nancy Tanner study what they call "matrifocality" in Black American culture and give the stamp of approval to what Morrison's works and my own observations show to be destructive patterns. Stack studies the moves and shifts in childcare, children being shifted from mother to grandmother to aunt and uses these examples to demonstrate the "domestic authority of women." I would name this phenomenon rather the crushing responsibility of women and a serial inability of female caretakers in a distressed culture to cope. Simply because the children survive does not mean this is a healthy pattern. I know two men very well, one Black and one Greek, who were given by their impoverished biological mothers to aunts and uncles at the ages of six and ten respectively. Both men are professionals, good fathers and husbands, but both are insecure, often pained, isolated persons who live encased away from strong emotions. Yes, these men survived, but at what price? I know also that one of the mothers suffered a lot for having to give up her son because she could not support him. Stack and Tanner fall prey, it seems to me, to a wistful desire to find female strength in what is really exploitation by society of the mother-child bond; this bond and the maternal drive for her child's survival do assure that the mother will find a way to feed her child even if it means breaking that bond. Tossing children around hither and yon results in angry, hurt, cut-off adults. Tanner admits that among Black Americans, "arrest rates are high and school-performance rates are low" but attributes these facts purely to lack of opportunities for Blacks in the society at large. She goes on to claim that these data have nothing to do with Black family structure and that in this structure the "mother-child units . . . function effectively on their own." Yet, do they if there is such a lack of continuity? These anthropologists' essays suggest that the way Black American mothers are forced to function due to poverty is healthy for the individuation of their children. While certainly economics underlie Black arrest rates, this pressure on the mother-child unit also contributes to Black adult malaise, pain, and anger.

There is also an unthinking acceptance of victims' assessments of their plights and values. We now know that many incest victims try to understand their experience as "normal," some even writing books now about how good it was for them. But even the most cursory examination of these persons and their lives reveals how these experiences have twisted them and warped their lives. We do not take the victims at their word. Yet Stack appears to support the values of Black women who encourage their sons to father illegitimate children; she congratulates these women for the pride they take in the twenty-two-year-old son with three children, and a nineteen-year-old son with one child; this woman made boasting of these children her first priority to visitors. Yet her sons lived with her and apparently had no responsibilities towards their children. As Morrison points out, Black children too often live cut off from their fathers. I do *not* think the live-in, constantly changing boyfriends, uncles, or brothers are adequate substitutes as Stack does.

This pattern of migratory men underlies many of the problems in Morrison's characters, especially Guitar. Guitar cannot take his great energy and passion into mature love relationships; instead he turns them to hate. Like Sula, he is an artist without a constructive form, a medium. He stays ready to fly and can kill with equanimity, much more easily than he can love, because of his very lack of connections. His soul and intelligence finally shrink to only a cunning compulsion to stalk and murder.

Their insistence on the right to instant flight as their masculine prerogative also hurts the men in another way. Many writers have discussed the idea that the masculine sense of time is more linear, the feminine more cyclical. This is probably why men sense death itself as inexorable, devouring. I think men especially need women to keep in touch with, for grounding in, cyclical time. Women's bodies and their children mark time out in cycles and stages. Attempting to track time in the narrowness of his all-male world, Henry Porter wallpapers his room with calendars. He measures time by the killings he has done for the Days: he has many kinds of calendars, yet ironically

> most of them were from the North Carolina Mutual Life Insur-
> ance Company. They literally covered the walls, each one turned
> to December. It was as though he'd kept every calendar since 1939.
> Some of them were large cards displaying all twelve months and
> on those she noticed circles drawn around them.

Thus the flying with no real point of return costs the men maturation, individuation, connections—in short, their souls.

The flying counterpoints the other archetype of masculinity, the image of power through dominion by ownership. The men try to ground themselves in things; instead of turning to relationships, their life instincts root into *materia*. Milkman understands his father's drive to own things when he goes to his father's southern home town and finds out about the town's image of his grandfather Jake beside whom Macon worked so proudly. The town's men idealize Jake's farm as a prelapsarian Garden of Eden, shaped out of the virgin American territory by a godlike Black man. This masculine conquest over virginal territory is also imaged in Jake's marriage; Jake ploughed and planted a natural American woman, the Indian woman Sing. When the white men kill Jake for his property, all the Black men in the area give up trying for dominion through property-owning. When Milkman tells them how well Macon has done, their hopes reawaken, and they eagerly conjecture that Jake's son somehow has an innate ability for exercising dominion through property like white men can. They want to believe again in masculine *perfectio*, the possibility of "complete power, total freedom, and perfect justice."

So while most of the other Black men in this novel remain airy, committed to flight, Macon, Milkman's well-to-do father, is just as bad off, but in a different way. The men in flight enact only one side of the masculine principle—airiness; he, of the masculine elements of fire and sulphur. Macon is described as existing like a volcano, ready to erupt, his anger and bitterness drying up even the watery feminine, the relatedness, in the women around him; his daughters are "boiled dry from years of yearning," and his wife's feminine nature is also completely dried up. His son is corroded with self-doubt because of Macon's vicious (sulphur-like) criticism. He rules his family through fear. He is borne down by his property, his *materia;* as Guitar points out, the male peacock cannot fly because of its tail. Morrison uses the peacock imagery several times to develop the masculine narcissism of Macon. And Macon's keys to all the houses he owns lock him out of the Black world and into isolation. Early in the novel, we see him evicting Guitar as a little boy with the woman who was trying to care for the child. Furthermore, Macon emulates and reflects his unconscious acceptance of white values when he marries "up" in color to a light-skinned doctor's daughter. At least the flying Black men know their brothers.

Macon's desire for property as dominion is almost impossible for a Black man to accomplish anyway; the male prophets of this novel deliver a doom liturgy to the small boys Guitar and Milkman on the series of things that Black men will never have:

> And you not going to have a governor's mansion, or eight thou-
> sand acres of timber to sell. And you not going to have no ship
> under your command to sail on, no train to run, and you can join
> the 332nd if you want and shoot down a thousand German
> planes all by yourself and land in Hitler's backyard and whip him
> with your own hands, but you never going to have four stars on
> your shirt front, or even three.

Railroad Tommy goes on to tell them what they will have: a broken heart "and folly. A whole lot of folly. You can count on that." Flying away from the whole problem is an easier answer. The Black man will not get what he earns, and even when he does manage to tear something out of the American earth itself (like Jake's farm), that will be taken away. The unconnected flying and the folly are, in other words, twisted and inverse masculine ambition, all that's left to the disenfranchised Black male. Flying is dynamic, frontier breaking, if it is grounded in some kind of psychic anchoring in the real world, as Milkman finally learns from Pilate, his picaresque and strong aunt. But it becomes folly when it is indulged in simply for itself, as an escape mechanism. Flight and dominion are polarized forces in these men's world, rather than complementary forces, like adventure and home, work and family.

Milkman's natural masculine tendency is towards the pattern of flying; even as a small boy he dreams of it. But he is entrapped, entangled in his father's values of dominion. Not even allowed to go off to college, he is kept at home to learn his father's business. Consider the etymology of business— "busy-ness"—the frenetic extroversion of the American male taking the economic world as his hunting ground. The predator/prey metaphor under-lies the evicting of the orphans. Macon takes over his father-in-law's house, launches his career of ego-inflation through acquisition, and loses his soul through and in *materia*. His money hoarding symbolizes the anal retentive spirits, the unawakened hearts of such men; they mistake movement of money through hands as psychic movement or growth. As depth psychologists say of money:

> *Money is the most powerful, practical and experienced form of transformation.* In the most starkly real way, one can turn money into anything in the world. Nothing else achieves this range of transformational possibility in actuality or in fantasy. In this direct sense, money symbolizes everything. Byron went correctly to the heart of the matter when he observed that "every guinea is a philosopher's stone." The life and soul of money must lie in this transformational potentiality. This is the deepest reason for the psyche to be drawn into a fascination with money. As with the search for alchemical gold, or the search for true love, one experiences something of the possibility of transformation in oneself when in the grips of the transformational power of money.

Saving money without purpose then, just to own it, is an economic manifestation of psychic blockage, failure to change or grow. And we grow or we rot. So Milkman becomes lost in his father's world and finally lost to his friend Guitar, whose avenging at least originated from true passion, not emulation of the father role like Milkman's prestige and power and moneyed position.

Milkman and Guitar become the polar faces of dominion and flying. Guitar is pure mobility; Milkman, pure stasis in things. Yet the two archetypes of flight and desire for property (*materia*) merge in Milkman's flight south to seek gold. This archetype of the hero leaving home to seek his fortune seems innate to the first stage of life of men; the establishment of the self within the social sphere requires this strong and autonomous ego development. Erik Erikson even sees relationships as impeding the young male's entry into the world where he finds his individuation through achievement, a form, surely, of dominion.

But Morrison gives her hero a different task in his quest for maturation, for self. For Milkman to become a whole person, he must undergo an ego death that makes both flying and owning, fear and ambition, no longer the prevailing forces in his life. The patterns of Morrison's novels reinforce certain gerontological theory that women and men undergo different life stages and development. For Nel in *Sula* to be reborn, she must let go of her fantasy that losing Jude was central to her life pattern; she must embrace all the sides of her feminine soul, including the Sula side, to really consolidate her ego strength. It is as if the *birth* of the feminine ego begins the mid-life, or second stage of life, for a woman. But Milkman needs to undergo the *death* of the masculine ego to become a complete person at only age thirty-one. As Jean Shinoda Bolen warns in her *The Tao of Psychology*, "When fear or ambition are decisive, the heart is not even consulted. And eventually, as Don Juan warns, such a path will make you curse your life." Milkman can connect authentically and deeply with women and his own anima only through and after this ego death.

Milkman's first and most important epiphany of himself and his place in the world comes as he lies alone on the ground, one-to-one with the skin of the earth, during a night hunt with the Southern Black men. As he pants, exhausted, "The thoughts came, unobstructed by other people, by things, even by the sight of himself. There was nothing here to help him—not his money, his car, his father's reputation, his suit, or his shoes." He rejects ambition, property, and dominion criteria of manhood. Guitar sneaks up at this point and attacks him with a wire around the neck; unafraid, he fills with "sadness to be dying, leaving this world at the fingertips of his friend." In this powerful and lyrical sequence, Milkman sloughs off the fear and ambition that have made him so ego driven. Fittingly, Guitar tries to cut off his head as Milkman lets go of his overblown ego, a kind of head or mind castration, a relinquishing of power, that releases him to growth. He escapes from Guitar and the whole rest of the novel portrays his new found self. For Milkman this death of his ego is the beginning of his real life.

The pathology of Guitar is what sets off and counterpoints Milkman's final individuation. Memories of gifts of candy at his father's death mean that Guitar cannot bear candy, but Milkman's final baptism into an abiding connection with his anima is with a woman named "Sweet," who bathes him and swims with him, a double baptism into humanity, community. Milkman also resists, and argues cogently against, the murder of anonymous white victims by the "Days." It is Milkman's final negation of all that Guitar comes to stand for that makes their final duel almost like matter and antimatter colliding; but it really is not important from Milkman's point of view who lives because he has discovered and established his own soul and self as distinct from his previous egoizing and painfully separate, isolated nonexistence: the ending of the novel frustrates if the reader is only interested in the narrative questions of who is going to live, what is going to happen. Morrison does not give, permit the reader that psychological ease and climax. We are left with Milkman's state of mind, his intra-psychic integration. That is what matters and Jacob lived to see the dawn after wrestling with his shadow/angel. I believe they both live, but I must warn the reader that I like happy endings. (Guitar does throw the gun down.)

Both the initial causes and the final results of Milkman's relinquishing his ego for his true humanity lie in the world of women. Unfortunately the women who have most sacrificed their very beings to Milkman's original egocentricity are never able to benefit from his new sense of the value of the feminine. Helene Moglen has written of the full humanity Rochester achieves at the end of *Jane Eyre* when he leaves his privileged upper-class male, yet driven, life-style and enters the women's world of family, love, home, and children that Jane / Brontë gift him with. Access to this world is what Mr. Ramsey, bereft as he now is of his wife, seeks from Lily at the end of *To the Lighthouse*. The happy ending of *Pride and Prejudice* also features Darcy connecting with his own sister anew as Elizabeth constructs a family life for him. Like these foremother writers, Morrison obviously likes her male protagonist; even his nickname, Milkman, foreshadows the fullness of self he will find through the feminine principle and women themselves. I think that women writers often see family life as a great achievement and grace their favorite male protagonists with it, not castrate them with it—as certain critics, for example, accuse Charlotte Brontë of doing through Rochester's blindness and his marriage to Jane. In his realization of his love for Pilate and Ruth, Milkman begins his first steps towards true adulthood. Sweet is like Dante's Beatrice, the living, present guide. As Pilate dies, he imbibes, achieves her ferocity and leaps like a Samurai warrior, with faith in his own instincts, to his final bout with Guitar.

Milkman's Femine Ground of Being
Lena and Corinthians: Middle-aged sisters in a brother-centered home

Morrison's development of Milkman's two older sisters is masterful. For the first three-quarters of *Song of Solomon*, they are interchangeable as Tweedledum and Tweedledee. Light-skinned like their mother, they serve as twin status symbols for Macon to dress up and parade in the family car around other Black people, almost all of a lower economic class than Macon. When not on parade in the public, they sit in their rooms and make roses out of red velvet. They are a true, bitter, virulent portrait of what happens to sisters who are made subservient body-servants to a selfish, adored brother simply because he is male. I have often seen this family pattern among Greek families; and Greek women with brothers are the angriest of those culturally disenfranchised women. Morrison's Lena says what I think many of these Greek women would articulate if they were not so strongly repressed and cut off from the sources and roots of their own bitterness.

Not until she is forty-three years old does the oldest sister Lena tell Milkman how subordinate they have been to him:

> Our girlhood was spent like a found nickel on you. When you slept, we were quiet; when you were hungry, we cooked; when you wanted to play, we entertained you; and when you got grown enough to know the difference between a woman and a two-toned Ford everything in this house stopped for you. You have yet to wash your underwear, spread a bed, wipe a ring from the tub, or move a fleck of your dirt from one place to another. And to this day, you have never asked one of us if we were tired, or sad, or wanted a cup of coffee. . . . Where do you get the *right* to decide our lives? . . . From that hog's gut that hangs down between your legs? . . . You are a sad, pitiful, stupid, selfish, hateful man. I hope you little hog's gut stands you in good stead, and that you take good care of it, because you don't have anything else. . . . I don't make roses anymore, and you have pissed your last in this house.

Lena's diatribe is triggered by the death of a tree she planted that he had urinated on. She seems to have identified her own being with that tree and when it dies, her passive nurturing side dies too; in its place comes her ego, unsoftened by any feminine values that had been appreciated and so rooted in or linked with the masculine world. She has contained and anesthetized her anger with alcohol. The same repressed female, dedicated to servitude, is the protagonist of Margaret Laurence's *A Jest of God* and of Mary Gordon's *Final Payments*. My experience in teaching *Song of Solomon* is that many female students become fiercely joyful when Lena finally rejects Milkman's living off her; few women grow up without experiencing a certain amount of servitude to some man just because (as Lena says) of his "hog's gut."

The other sister, Corinthians, has been touched through her connection with Henry Porter. Corinthians received an education and European travel, but there is no man that her parents deem worthy as a marriage partner for her. She is also rejected by ambitious young Black men who want a strong, upwardly mobile spouse, not a pampered flower. She becomes a maid to a spiritually vacuous, repulsive old white woman. Corinthians also discovers her own ego at age forty-two.

Corinthians sets out on a heroic quest of her own that is perhaps more risky than Milkman's; certainly Porter as her future holds even less promise than the pot of gold that Milkman pursues. She also will have no one to fall back on; her parents' love is clearly contingent on her never stepping out of line. She is a perfect example of the educated, Ivy League daughter who is to use her class and learning only as a persona, as a decoration for her family. Further proof of her status as family property is Milkman's attempt to stop her from relating with the "unworthy" Porter. He tries to round her back up and into the family's treasury of prestigious objects. When we consider that Milkman is younger and has no sense of her as a person, let alone as a sister, his cheek and arrogance, his sense of the whole world existing as a prop for his aggrandizement, becomes absolutely infuriating. Again, I have seen Greek male cousins and brothers casually and cruelly change irrevocably the lives of Greek women, forcing marriages or stopping them—and since marriage is the main institution for female individuation in that culture, both in Greece and here in the States, this influence (often capricious) is devastating. The contempt for women as persons with rights is so deep and radically a priori that it is terrifying to observe. Corinthians' dilemma is not unlike that of some of these Greek women I have seen. She is expected to live her life in abeyance until the acceptable man (to her family) comes along. Hers is an easy life, but one that yields emptiness. We can only congratulate her for making this leap that for her must be into a kind of abyss. She can no longer live out her parents' fantasies, and she settles for the very untender, harsh, probably psychotic Henry Porter rather than for living as a vestal virgin, a role Lena seems headed for.

Lena is a craggy, ferocious spinster, like many of the older single women of Mary Wilkins Freeman's *The Revolt of Mother*. She is not sad to be unencumbered with a man; she is in the beginning stages of the Spinsterian Selfhood that Mary Daly defines this way:

> A woman whose occupation is to spin participates in the whirling movement of creation. She who has chosen her Self, who defines her Self, by choice, neither in relation to her children nor to men, who is Self-identified is a Spinster, a whirling dervish, spinning in a new time/space.

Psychologist Nor Hall would see her as a woman early given over solely to the duties of the Mother and now at middle age embracing also the pole of the Amazon or Artemis. As Lena deflates Milkman's phallocentric and unconscious existence, she becomes stronger and more autonomous: "Her eyes doubled in size behind the lenses and were very pale and cold." Until middle age these sisters have been trapped in a Persephone-Demeter, Hestian mode, all feminine roles that depend on others for their identity. The sisters both break into new modes at middle age when their egos suddenly solidify and become fiercely separate.

They are like the sisters of Margaret Laurence's Manawaka world, Stacey/Aphrodite and Rachel/Artemis, who also suddenly individuate towards opposite poles as they approach middle age. Like Rachel, Lena is a caretaker of her mother; these women appear doomed to live out only this role and relationship. Like Stacey, Corinthians chooses to define herself in terms of a man, but both characters have less than satisfying relationships with their men. All four of these women are portraits of what gerontological data calls the increased extroversion of women in the second half of life. As middle age nears, these women's drowsing ego-selves suddenly flare, come alive, individuate into the world. But these two sisters' egos will always be grounded in a childhood filled with cruel images of relatedness; their beginnings were framed by a bitter reality of entrapping relationships. They have been allowed no privacy, independence, autonomy. In a way Lena and Corinthians are retarded, but in another and more deep way, they are bitterly aware of the stinging salt of existence, of the misery human life can hold. Their egos will never drowse in the unconscious selfishness that so sustained the younger Milkman's ego.

Hagar

While Lena and Corinthians have had to deal with the bitterest faces of the masculine—a cruel father, an indifferent brother, and a literal killer-lover (for Corinthians)—their cousin Hagar has had an insulated and pampered childhood. The sisters have grown strong enough (although warped) in coping with the harsh reality of their home life.

As Guitar so astutely notes, Hagar's feminine typology needed a traditional community of women to help her reach adulthood. Hagar does not want to be unattached and floating like Reba and Pilate; Morrison says that at age twenty-three she dreams of a Prince Charming who will change her life. She has grown up completely surrounded by a chaotically feminine yet providing world. She has never had to strive for anything. Like Sula she has never had to carry any responsibility; she apparently does not work although she does help with the wine making sometimes. She is able to spend her life drifting because Pilate and Reba see themselves as the providers for her. They obviously love her to distraction as seen in her funeral when they sing her back to themselves, internalize her as their baby, their "sugar lumpkin." But for all the poignancy of this matriarchy's tender love for its own, still Hagar is dead. Ironically, their totally uncontingent and supportive love may have taken from her the development of strength she needed to survive Milkman's abandoning her. Also missing in her life are male relatives to help build her animus, her sense of the way to deal with men; when Pilate tries to make her see Milkman as a cousin/brother, Hagar immediately seduces him. She sees him as one more gift from her mothers for her self-indulgence. As he gains maturity, she projects the total numinosity of the masculine onto Milkman, making him carry the divine animus, her soul. Without him she feels she will lose her grounding in the feminine world, in the world itself even. She is like Sula vis-à-vis Ajax.

For Hagar, time is only cyclical, tied to feminine rhythms; she cannot comprehend the irrevocable passage of linear time. She is ruled by the moon, her hair standing up like a thundercloud on the thirtieth day of each menstrual cycle when she attempts to kill Milkman. Hagar is at age thirty-six still a girl; she has not tracked the irrevocable linear passage of time and cannot believe that she has given nineteen years of her life to Milkman and that he can write her off. She thinks that she can metamorphose back into a perfect young girl like Cinderella through a mad shopping trip in which she pathetically dons all the Madison Avenue clichés. She tries for rebirth by simply changing her exterior, her persona. When Guitar finds her on her last murder attempt, she sits holding her breasts like rejected fruit, sensing herself as the barren yet vegetative feminine.

Because Hagar has been so pampered, she does not really know how to assert herself except by murdering the demonic and rejecting masculine or by repackaging her body. She has been terribly "over-mothered," calling both Reba and Pilate "Mother"; and Pilate beats her, a thirty-six-year-old woman, when she tries to kill Milkman. Everyone in the community sees her as the two women's daughter. She is trapped in a Persephone/Kore role that has reduced her to a Baby Bear or Goldilocks slot within her family. She has absolutely no resilience. She and Sula are the tail ends, the remnants of a purely matriarchal line that has no connections to the masculine world. Hagar looks like Pilate and reflects Pilate's creative energy in the wild growth of her hair; but she does not have Pilate's strength for going it alone. Hagar's hair is a metaphor for the wild and chaotic feminine in her that has no form, no institution like that of a traditional marriage or a role in her community (like teacher, nurse, doctor) into which it can flow. She dies close to the advent of middle-age, dolled up like a young girl. This is no particular person's fault by any means; in fact, Hagar's mothers have had only good will towards her. But by totally protecting Hagar as a symbol of the future of their line, as their baby, Pilate and Reba may have unwittingly participated in her destruction. Three other elements are at least as present in her demise: her own temperament, Milkman's cynical indifference towards her, and the commercial values of American culture. Yet I think the aspect most missing in her is the strength that comes to women from the ardor of either raising children or working to support oneself. Sula dies the same way as Hagar, and when an author tells us the same pattern twice, we should believe she means it.

In these women of the younger generation—Lena, Corinthians, and Hagar—Morrison uses life-stage boundaries to delineate character change and growth. The women explode out of the niches others have made for them, individuating in bent and killing ways, but nevertheless insisting on change. Their explosions further Milkman's individuation; he has, as his father's delegate, tried to force Corinthians to give up Henry Porter—but she escapes. Then Lena tells him of his selfishness. Hagar kills herself and Pilate gives Milkman Hagar's hair, saying that he must carry his guilt.

Part of Milkman's ego death is a self-crucifixion when he realizes how selfishly he has treated Pilate and Ruth when only these two old women have really cared for him. As Pilate dies in his arms in the conclusion, she instructs him about *caritas*, love of all humans, his oneness with the cosmos. Milkman realizes her lesson on grounded-in-relatedness flying; he knows now how to construct a true self and a good life too. He leaps to wrestle his own shadow, the nihilism and narcissism of Guitar. He has already won.

KARLA F. C. HOLLOWAY

The Lyrics of Salvation

Last summer, my children intensely devoted themselves to flight. My daughter's attack was methodical. She planned the mechanics of her flight first on paper, with da Vinci–like designs. Then, scisssors, scraps, and collected pigeon feathers in tow, she'd lug her imagination to the backyard and attempt to implement her plan. My son was more direct. He'd scale the nearest tree and, wings of plastic garbage bags extended, magnificently thrust himself into the air. As he and the wings crumpled to the ground, he'd extract himself from the pile of grass clippings he had chosen as his landing site and return to the tree.

I watched their adventures from the kitchen window. I was, at the time, involved in reading Black spirituals for references to flight. I had what I had felt was the magnificent idea that such symbolic networks as were developed in *Song of Solomon* were directly related to those spirituals. I thought that the source for the networks of the text was hidden somewhere within those early Black songs. But as I watched my children play at what I was researching, I realized that the network is far more extensive than just those musical folk traditions.

I had felt, for quite some time, the elusiveness of *Song of Solomon*. For a long time I was unable to write this chapter because I could not grasp some single solid sense of this novel and have been therefore uncomfortable with

From *New Dimensions of Spirituality: A Biracial and Bicultural Reading of the Novels of Toni Morrison.* © 1987 Karla F. C. Holloway and Stephanie A. Demetrakopoulos. Reproduced with permission of Greenwood Publishing Group, Inc., Westport, CT.

what I felt as a shifting presence. But watching my children at play and remembering the scene that initiated the research clarified the novel's situation. The extensiveness of this network of flight and song is the theme, and its multifaceted and shifting presence *is* its identity.

Early last spring, before the summer of my children's obsession, my uncle had died. It was an especially sad occasion. My aunt had died only a few years earlier; they had been a young and wonderful family, and two sons were left parentless.

At the funeral service, the minister prayed an extemporaneous prayer designed to give us strength and hope and some guidance. The cadence of his voice rose and fell, counterpointing the few audible sobs in the gathering, and the room was heavy with the sorrow of that moment. As if to relieve some of this pressure, someone in the back hummed. Then someone else sang, others softly relinquished tears or sighs into this music, and the minister's voice became the rhythmic punctuation to that song. Soon, instead of his prayers, it was the words to that song he called out to us and we responded: "Soon one morning when this life is over, I'll fly away. . . ." And we flew. Our spirits were literally lifted out of that sorrowful place and sent to rest in the strong places that we needed to sustain us. It was an overwhelmingly emotional event. Later, as I remembered the day, I remembered most of all that sensation of being elevated from my sorrow. Either that song or that collocation of music and event and emotion sustained and rescued us.

Demetrakopoulos discusses the haunting Hayden poem that carries the myth of Morrison's *Song of Solomon*. Its rhythm is the rhythm of many of these spirituals I read and remembered, and its message is repeated again and again in the music of Black folk. The "two wings" reference in Hayden's poem is possibly his poetic restructuring of the spiritual "Lawd I want two wings to veil my face, Lawd I want two wings to fly away. . . ." In another Black spiritual, the goal is expressed as "I'm gonna fly from mansion to mansion when I'm gone."

Flight is a recurrent image in these Black songs, and Morrison has structured the importance of this racial sense of flight and dominion into the bedrock of her text. This symbolic opportunity for oppressed slaves to free themselves spiritually from the shackles of slavery, as expressed in Black spirituals, is the source of the myth of Morrison's text. Solomon is a member of the tribe of "flying Africans"—those Blacks who liberated themselves from slavery—who "flew" away from oppression. How else could their escape have been mythologized and used as inspiration for those who would follow? We can call this flight "escape"; however, the rich and complex spirituality of these African peoples also paralleled what they understood as a miraculous liberation with a similarly miraculous event—the power of flight as transformation and transcendence. Christianity may have offered a religious ground for the displaced African to replant the symbols of his spirituality—but the growth from that soil was distinctly Black and African. In *Souls of Black Folks*, DuBois's description of a southern revival is dominated by imagery that suggests flight:

> The black and massive form of the preacher swayed and quivered as the words crowded to his lips and flew at us in singular eloquence. The people moaned and fluttered and then the gaunt-cheeked brown woman beside me suddenly leaped straight into the air and shrieked like a lost soul. . . .

The physical power of both flight and song is woven together at every crucial juncture in this novel. Milkman's birth is accompanied by the song of his ancestor Solomon. Hagar, Reba, and Pilate sing it to him and Guitar when the boys visit their home. At the end of the novel, Milkman says that the children's "sweet voices reminded him of the gap in his own childhood," and this memory is painful because he realizes how close (yet blind) he had been, since birth, to understanding the heritage of his line.

That summer Saturday, as I watched my children's developing design on flight, I realized that the background of their play was the background of this novel. Pilate's song that accompanied the spiritual liberation (through physical suicide) of Robert Smith interrupted the tension of the moment of Smith's death in the same way that "Soon One Morning" elevated our spirits during my uncle's funeral.

The extensively networked metaphors of song and flight connect this novel first to universal childhood memories, then to specific racial mythologizing and finally reemerges with a universal and mystical epiphany that compels our spirits towards dominion over earthly mansions. I know now that my discomfort with *Song of Solomon* has been with its completeness and its scope and depth. I had been looking at it as a part of the line from her earlier novels. But it is not a part of the network of *The Bluest Eye* or *Sula* or *Tar Baby*. These novels have themes that link them. The girlhood trauma of *The Bluest Eye* is background to the young womanhood of *Sula*. Jadine (*Tar Baby*) is no surprise for readers of Morrison's earlier novels about girls, women, and Blackness.

Looking for these threads in *Song of Solomon* was a frustrating task. Pilate and Circe seem spiritually related to each other, and although Eva in *Sula* is one of their lineage, she is not mystical in an ancient, primal sense, as they are. Nel, Sula, Jadine, and even Pecola are modern women and girls too; and therefore, in a book that pulls us backwards in time, as *Song of Solomon* does, these modern females are out of place—almost creatures not-yet-imagined.

In many ways, *Song of Solomon* is a beginning book. It places value, establishes identity, and unequivocably shows us point-of-origin. If later we suffer as Pecola suffers, or lose touch as Nel and Sula and Jadine did, then *Song of Solomon* is there to tell us why and remind us of where we were before the destructiveness of Western civilization corrupted and displaced our African selves. This book is a whole and it fills in all gaps and all questions and compels our attention to its quintessential song of the African individuation patterns that underlie Black Americans' quests for survival.

Countee Cullen's poem "Heritage" invokes a similar sense in its rhythmic pulse that discomfits the poet and reminds him of his African heritage—an African remembrance that taunts him and destroys his equilibrium. In a similar way, the myth of *Song of Solomon* is unrelenting. Until we call it our own, until Milkman makes the necessary journey back to his past, we will be discomfited by the myth, uneasy with its song. From its first gripping funeral imagery of those red velvet rose petals scattered across the frozen snow, we know something will be buried in this book—and something born.

> The singing woman . . . walked through the crowd toward the rose-petal lady. . . . she whispered . . . "A little bird'll be here with the morning." . . . The women were looking deep into each other's eyes when a loud roar went up from the crowd. . . . Immediately the singing woman began again:
>
> > O Sugarman done fly
> >
> > Sugarman done gone . . .
>
> Mr. Smith had seen the rose petals, heard the music, and leaped on into the air.

Demetrakopoulos's approach to this novel is much more deeply embedded in archetypes than mine. The calls of the goddess figures, for example, are for me less tangible than the call of the clan. There are, nevertheless, archetypal children's needs, and these show in Black children's special need for memory. There is, for me, cultural wisdom imparted through song—a wisdom that affirms our pasts and promises us a future. I think this essay and Demetrakopoulos's clarify the distinction, the difference between a Black woman's and a white woman's writing. What speaks to us, compels us, gives voice to our thoughts is the principle that orders our reality. For me, and I suspect for Black women, that principle is memory—direct or indirect. For Demetrakopoulos, and I suspect for white women, memory is far more objective—(and probably more easily recovered). The language and the music of *Song of Solomon* form my memory and become the kinds of archetypes that I believe are culturally connected. Morrison describes this memory as a "spoken library" of Black culture. In a speech in 1977, Morrison expresses a sentiment that she later gives to a character (Son in *Tar Baby*). "I have to tell you," she said, "Nothing I ever read or was taught helped prepare me to be a Black person . . . a woman in 1977."

> The spoken library was . . . children's stories my family told, spirituals, the ghost stories, the blues, and folk tales and myths, and the everyday . . . instruction and advice of my own people . . . . I wanted to write out of the matrix of memory, of recollection, and to approximate the sensual and visceral responses I had to the world I lived in . . . to recreate the civilization of Black people . . . the manners, judgments, values, morals. . . .

Morrison effectively transfers to me, as a Black reader, her sense of the images and cosmology of Black language. Whether song or story, the universe of this novel comes through the metaphors of its language—its synthesis or rendering of families and events, its myth making or spiritualism—all of this is at the center of this novel for me.

While the figures and appearances of men and women suggest for Demetrakopoulos a way of living in and understanding the world, the language and song of those characters suggest for me their places in my world.

Earlier in this book, I spoke of the memories of women in my family that came rushing back to me as I read Morrison. Instead of being models and examples of life-styles and values, Morrison's characters are my grandfathers and cousins, aunts and grandmothers. They are the children I played with, fought with, and went to school with. As I read, they surrounded me with their memories—the touches, the smells, the sensations of love and fear I'd felt as a mere child were with me once again.

So the distinction between our reactions I think is basically that I have felt this book like my life, and Demetrakopoulos has felt the life in this book.

In this chapter, I will explore the myths that link childhood, race, and adulthood. It is important that this is a novel about children, young women and old, young men and old. It is also important that there are no "real" white characters in this novel. It is a Black event. Morrison shows us the wholeness of a Black cycle. She affirms that although white people figured in the gyrations of a Black universe, they have been catalysts only for Black mythologizing. Morrison gives us the entire race in *Song of Solomon*—the men and the women and the children—and unfolds us into their myth of flight and its musical configurations.

Childhood

It is appropriate that this novel opens with a scene that places children squarely in the midst of a life/death situation. Macon Dead's daughters adorn this death scene as they scatter rose petals as the accompaniment to Robert Smith's suicidal leap from the top of the hospital. There are a number of ironies in the scene. The white people who observe the incident turn to the children to direct a rescue. "Tell him to tell the guard to get over here quick" a white nurse tells the child Guitar. But she misspells the name of the admissions office, and Guitar notes her incompetence. The betrayal of white and adult imperfection will figure later in Guitar's adulthood. Young Corinthians and Magdalena are responsible for the decorations—the funeral flowers that are scattered over the snow later remind Corinthians of death. Both girls will grow to resent their decorative and ineffectual posture in their family. That they decorate a death-scene in their childhood is prophecy of their adult situations.

In this novel, children are responsible for sustaining the remnants of the myth of Milkman's ancestor Solomon. Their rendition of the song "Sugarman done gone" makes it "child's play" and yet, it is much more than this. Milkman comes to realize that his play, because it was different from other children's, has kept him from learning the song that is his heritage. It is not until he is fully grown that he realizes that the song is about his ancestor and that he is intimately involved. Morrison spends a considerable part of the novel detailing the childhood experiences of Magdalena, Milkman, and Corinthians so that we can understand that being kept "awkward with fear" as children inhibits growth and endangers adulthood. Ruth's father insures her separation from her Black self in his perverted rearing of her. Dr. Foster is uncomfortable as Ruth grows into womanhood and he seeks to marry her quickly because he is not only unsure of the quality of her devotion—but the extent of his dependence on it.

> Fond as he was of his only child, useful as she was in his house since his wife had died, lately he had begun to chafe under her devotion. Her steady beam of love was unsettling. . . . Perhaps it was the loud silence of his dead wife, perhaps it was Ruth's disturbing resemblance to her mother.

Foster rears Ruth away from her heritage—establishing her as the "doctor's daughter" and therefore less Black than the townfolk he services. He values her lighter skin precisely because of his desire for demarcation between his daughter and other Black people. As adults, Ruth and Macon Jr.

perpetuate this distancing. The "Dead" children are almost maliciously kept away from other children and dressed to emphasize their difference from them. Macon seems to take macabre pleasure in this separation and uses his children as decoration for the lifestyle he has assumed.

> There were other children there. Barefoot, naked to the waist, dirty. But we stood apart, near the car, in white stockings, ribbons and gloves. And when he talked to the men, he kept glancing at us, us and the car. . . . You see, he took us there so they could see us, envy him. . . . First he displayed us, then he splayed us. All our lives were like that: he would parade us like virgins through Babylon, then humiliate us like whores in Babylon.

It is the removal of the children from their Black selfhood in this novel that dictates the events of the journey Milkman takes to discover his past. Guitar, Milkman's friend, tells the tragic tale of his own father's death at the sawmill. It makes Guitar physically ill to remember. It's an event that has followed him all his life in a bittersweet twist of memory: "I can't eat sweets. . . . It makes me think of dead people. And white people . . . My father got sliced up in a sawmill and his boss came by and gave us kids some candy. Divinity. His wife make it special for us."

In some sense, he blames the brutal insensitivity of the white boss for the lingering of that memory. His ability to cast blame enables his membership in the Seven Days, the organization that seeks retribution against whites for the deaths of any Blacks. Because white characters in this novel are less than "real people" and "flat" in a literary perspective, the kind of vengeance Guitar wreaks happens without serious (or effective) questioning of his right to effect this violence. It is a lifting of the standards of morality and justice that allows the mystical story of Solomon and the surreal atmosphere of many of the events in this novel to take place. Ironically, Guitar's activity is not the only actual connection this book has to Black history. The death of Emmett Till and the murder of four children in Birmingham on that tragic Sunday in 1963, are among the events that the Seven Days revenge. But this reality is peripheral—it touches the tale of *Song of Solomon* only indirectly as if to warn us away from questioning the legitimacy of Morrison's myth.

This suspension of reality is accomplished by a collection of events in the children's lives that make us want some other reality for them. Guitar is tragically deprived of his father. Ruth is tragically attached to, then deprived of, her father. We are afraid that her sexuality will play itself out as incest. The ambivalent scene that accompanies her father's deathbed is never really settled for the reader. We have both Macon's and Ruth's views of this incident, and neither one of them is trustworthy because their child-hoods were also bereft. Macon and Pilate had lost the security of their father's parenting, and Macon, spiritually emptied by this loss, is emotionally unable to sustain a relationship with his sister, Pilate. Their angry separation reinforced the gulf of their parents' absence—evidence that Pilate literally carried with her. Her father's bones hang from the ceiling of her house and she has no navel—no physical evidence of her connection to her mother. Both Macon and Pilate suffer from their disconnection from each other as well as the loss of their parents. Their fierce and often dangerous love of their own children is evidence of the qualitative weight of their loss. Pilate surrounded her daughter and granddaughter so thoroughly with her own warmth that the womblike home that kept these women made life outside of it dangerous and threatening. Both Pilate and Macon must go backwards in time and mythology to a community that remembers them as a part of it. Milkman accomplishes this journey for them, and Hagar becomes their ritu-alistic sacrifice emblematic of the link between their present and their past. She reincarnates the myth of Ryna, her great-grandmother who died after her husband Solomon "flew" back to Africa:

> It like to killed [her] . . . she's supposed to have screamed out loud for days. . . . You don't hear about women like that anymore—the kind of woman who couldn't live without a particular man. And when the man left, they lost their minds or died or something.

But we have just learned about a woman like that—and Hagar has been like her great-great-grandmother, who "couldn't live without a particular man." Morrison intentionally juxtaposes the event of Hagar's death with the event of Milkman's awakening understanding. We learn that Hagar is like the woman before her—that her psyche is linked, albeit tragically, to her past. Hagar may not "survive," but she reverts to "type," and returns to the myth.

For Milkman, "It was becoming a habit—this concentration on things behind him. Almost as if there were no future to be had." As he became an adult, it was obsession.

> Milkman closed his eyes and then opened them. The street was even more crowded with people, all going the direction he was coming from. . . . He turned around to see where everybody was going, but there was nothing to see except backs and hats pressing forward into the night. . . . Not a soul.

Although Milkman is the focus of the return—because he retraces Pilate's journey—Corinthians, Lena, Guitar, and Hagar travel too. Milkman's may be the only obvious journey, but these others travel within their spirits, and Morrison reminds us that their sojourns are covered with as much travail.

The childrens' stories that are played out in this novel are tragic tales. They involve loss, betrayal, conflict in roles and values and lack of nurturance—for whatever reasons. Whites do figure in all of this tragedy, as the murderers of parents, as the source of the conflicting values within the family, as the reason the family will never have a life-style that might allow it some stability. But more important than this white complicity in the stories of these children are the indications of how this interference and betrayal and loss have separated them from what superficially seems desirable—participation in a white world and how the children have been left in serious need of a Black myth if they are to survive.

It is not as important that Guitar murders white people as it is that he can murder without regret. It is less important that Corinthians works for a white woman who demeans her than it is that she loves darkly. It is less important that Milkman's grandfather was murdered by whites than it is that Milkman solves the secret of the song and gains his soul through the experience. Pilate's "soul-felt" cry at her granddaughter's funeral—"and she was loved"—underscores the essence of Hagar's too quickly spent life. As we turn to the tales of the women and the men in this novel, it is important to understand that they were made necessary because of the quality of life that was lost or denied or too quickly spent as children and that Morrison sees their survival critically connected to their return to the sustaining and dependable mythology of their pasts.

The music of this novel is the umbilicus between these children and the men and women they become. Macon, in the earliest pages of the novel, finds himself "surrendering to the sound" of the woman who had been "his first caring for." It is through song that the children receive the archetypal imagery of their race, and it matters not whether a loving mother or a rejecting mother sings these songs, so long as the children hear them. The songless childhood of the "white" household of Milkman held no singers. Even he, in his effort to erase his past and forge ahead into the sterility of a "white-like" existence, cannot deny his need for this link. As Pilate sings, Macon feels "himself softening under the weight of the memory and the music" as if ready to return to the nurturance that once marked their relationship. Morrison establishes quite early that his music coming from these women and children is the lifeline of survival for those lost souls.

Adult Reclamation

The children who come to be adults are Milkman, Lena, Corinthians, and Guitar. They work through their own mythologies and emerge into some activity that makes them acknowledge their Blackness. And there are also the adults of this novel, past and present, who are either the fertile loam that lines their way back to the past, or the dangerous dryness that "sifts down like ashes" around them. Ruth's father, Ruth, and Macon, Jr., are the dangerous adults. Their control must be destroyed before any progress can be made by their children.

As much control as Dr. Foster has had in the life of his daughter Ruth, she surrendered it all under the taint of his memory. Macon's story is vivid with images of sexual defilement—and it is because he believes he saw Ruth naked in bed with her father's bloated and diseased body that he refused to touch her and renew their sexual intimacy. Ruth's story is full of over-whelming bereavement over the death of this man and her loss of sexual fulfillment from her husband. She holds her husband responsible for her father's death. Her rendition is that although her father was not a good man, and although she was "pressed small" by living in that house surrounded by its bigness and the bigness of his ideas, she had only knelt by her father's bedside at his death and kissed his fingers—the only part of his body that wasn't deformed by the disease. Dr. Foster insured in his stingy and malicious living, and in the ugliness of his dying that his daughter and her husband would never be free of his perverted values and able to separate themselves from the ugliness of his memory.

Her daughters, Magdalena and First Corinthians, labor under this memory as well. They are brought up as she was. Ruth's only memories of other children were not as playmates, but as children who wanted to "touch her dresses and white silk stockings." Her daughters become women who are as much objects as was their mother. We know they are eternally infantile—their "work" of crafting the velvet pieces into roses for a department store occupies them through their childhood and into their adulthood. They were raised to be childlike brides of "correct men"—but none of these men wanted women like them.

> It had been assumed that she and Magdalene called Lena would marry well—but hopes for Corinthians were especially high since she'd gone to college. Her education had taught her to be an enlightened mother and wife, able to contribute to civilization—or in her case, the civilizing—of her community. . . . High toned and high yellow. . . . Corinthians was a little too elegant.

Magdalene called Lena seemed resigned to her life but when Corinthians woke up one day to find herself a forty-two-year-old maker of rose petals . . . she made up her mind to get out of the house.

Corinthians's escape from her father's house took her back to a traditional Black woman's role—maid to a white woman. It was as if this step backwards, away from the pseudo-life-style designed by her parents, gave her entry into a self-designed reality, and made the potential of her coming to touch herself as a woman a possibility. The work as a maid is not as important as it was that this work allowed her to meet and love Henry Porter. Again, the white connection serves as a sort of catalyst. A college-educated woman having to assume the position of a maid (and lie to her parents that she is an amanuensis) illustrates the psychological and social abuse suffered and endured by Black women who work in these roles, subjugating their pride for some personal goal. Corinthians's goal of escape is the important point, as well as the fact that her escape was found in the antithesis of the "correct" man. Even her brother was appalled when he discovered she was involved with Porter, whom he knows to be a member of the Seven Days. But we get a sense that his outrage is not so much an effort to protect his sister as it is an effort to preserve his reputation in the town. Corinthians, perhaps not so much in love as she was "in escape," would fight to save her relationship with Porter to "escape the velvet." She remembers the suicide leap on the day her brother was born and how she and her sister were collecting the rose petals they had made from the snow.

It was all mixed together—the red velvet, the screams, and the man crashing down on the pavement. . . . They spoke to her of death. First the death of the man in the blue wings. Now her own. For if Porter did not turn his head and lean toward the door to open it for her, Corinthians believed she would surely die.

Corinthians knew that her involvement with this man would be "the only thing that could protect her from a smothering death of dry roses."

It was Corinthians's strike for freedom that gave Lena the courage to confront Milkman with the staleness of his life and his selfishness. Her accusation that "our girlhood was spent like a found nickel on you" is a message that liberates her. She lets loose her hatefulness of Milkman, appropriately focusing her anger on his maleness ("the hog's gut that hangs down between your legs"), the accident of gender that gave him the social sanction to narrow the realm of his sisters' experiences while enlarging the potential of his own world. But Lena warns him that he will "need more than that." She doesn't tell him for what—but she is the impetus that sends him on a journey where maleness is no safe guide.

Pilate, Reba, and Hagar are the other half of the women in this novel. They are qualitatively different from the ineffectual doctor's daughters. These are women of substance and sustenance. It is as if their removal from males has forced the awakening of the potential within feminine bonding and assured them their health. Insulated in Pilate's fertile home, their strength is intact. Outside of this home, however, the fragility of their exclusive unit is exposed to a world that needs the strength of a family and community, complete and healthy, to survive.

Morrison assures Pilate's survival by making her womanhood an intense acknowledgment of its own completeness. Whenever Pilate is present, we are overwhelmed with the strength that her stature commands. Milkman sees this once, when Pilate grows to a regal stature, reminiscent of an African queen ("the top of her head wrapped in a silk rag"). This vision awes him and commands his respect for the woman who was responsible for his birth.

It is not as if Pilate lives in any luxury. The contradictions in her image ("silk rag") are a clear acknowledgment of the contradictions of her lifestyle. She is alone but yearns for a community; she is whole but bereft of her legacy; she is poor but emotionally she is rich. Macon Jr. senses her ability to nurture through these contradictions and knows the power, both mythic and real, that she sustains. He hides under the window of her home and "surrenders to the sound" of the music of these women. Softening under the "weight of memory and music" Macon vaguely recalls his link to this unit. Pilate frames the picture of the singing women and sways "like a willow," tall, serene, strong and gentle, over this scene.

There is important imagery in Pilate's home. It is natural and fertile. Children are offered eggs to eat—symbols of the feminine dominion in the household. The home has a fruity odor, more imagery of the womb, and the women fiercely protect their solidarity. Until Milkman enters this home, breaking their unit with his threatening (rather than complementing) maleness, these women gain strength from each other. Although Hagar's loving her cousin destroys her, their peacefulness—until his intrusion threatens all of them—is almost serene and certainly powerful. These are women who have survived because their womanhood has not been violated. Only Milkman was able to destroy their unit—and I believe his access to their circle was gained because of his feminine *potentia* (having been breastfed so long by his mother—linked to her womanhood long enough to recognize it) and because Hagar was a woman needy of a particular man.

When Milkman destroys this mystical unit of three, he owes the three something. Although his motives are impure and selfish, what he learns finally from his sister's accusations and from Hagar's violent love is how to return life to those who gave it to him, who shared theirs with him, who sacrificed theirs for his. The magical and rhythmic vibrations of song teach him the way. His 'flight' is surrender to this mysticism, and he earns his place alongside Pilate's newly released soul. It was she who enabled his life, and it is she whose soul is reborn with his understanding.

Circe, the sorceress who dominates the childhood memories of Macon and Pilate, assures that Milkman's regeneration will happen. She is the incarnate Pilate. Had Pilate remained South, the real potential for Circe's truly mystical stature would have been hers. When Milkman reaches Circe's home, he is overwhelmed by an odor that is eventually reminiscent of the fruity ripe smell of Pilate ("like ginger root—pleasant, clean seductive"). Circe's witchlike appeal forces Milkman's surrender to her, and he is "helpless to pull away." Again, the presence of some white folks' evil is behind the appearance of this woman. Circe has vowed to remain in the house, watching the white vision of the world rot, and relishing in its dissolution. But again, this is less important than is Circe's function to renew the spirit of the myth that will save Milkman's soul and enable him to return to Pilate what he has stolen from her. Circe appears to retell the story Milkman will need to complete his journey. Her appearance is fraught with the symbolic natural imagery that surrounds Pilate; her memory is of "her Macon and her sweet little Pilate," and she is the woman who had saved these children years ago so that they could return to discover their pasts—these are the keys to his life with which Circe hastens Milkman on his way. Once she has accomplished this, she fades back into the fabric of this story and we wonder whether or not his encounter with her was real. "They think you're dead," Milkman tells her. But she lives long enough to tell him the story he needs for survival. Once again she is "healer deliverer" and had he known, Milkman could have added his own name to the list of those for whom Circe had ensured survival.

The men in this novel are connected through Milkman's journey. Suckled so long by his mother, he has so much womanness in him that he alone gains the power to return to the feminine myth of the song, learn his heritage, and share this sustaining myth in an intimate reconnection of the men and women who have been "dead."

Guitar functions in this return. Denied nurturing by women or men (his father has been murdered, and we are never given a sense of his mother's being able to compensate for this loss), Guitar's adulthood is achieved by denying life to others. Unknowingly, he pushes Milkman back to a confrontation with his past. It is Guitar who frightens Milkman into the discovery that his relationship with this primal ground is the critical discovery of his sojourn. Milkman believes at first that he "had come here to find traces of Pilate's journey, to find relatives she might have visited, to find anything he could that would lead him to the gold." But he learns instead the language of the woods and realizes his connection to this language "when a tiger and a man could share the same tree, and each understood the other." He turns in time to listen to the feminine earth and save himself from Guitar's attack. Once "grounded," he is safe.

Guitar initiates the visit to Pilate's house that later prompts Milkman's questions to his father and allows Macon, Sr., to remember his father's strength and love and how he had "worked right along beside him." Although Macon, Jr., loves to "excess" the things his father loved, although he had "distorted life, bent it, for the sake of gain," Milkman learns from his father that this "was a measure of his [Macon's] loss at his father's death." Macon's ways are rejected by his son, although Milkman shares his greed. So the journey South is a quest for both of them. The father learns through the child. The child learns by acknowledging his own guilt and complicity:

> Hating his parents, his sisters seemed silly now. . . . His mind turned to Hagar and how he had treated her. Why did he never sit down and talk to her? He had used her—her love, her craziness. . . . Suddenly he was tired, although the morning was still new.

This father and son, Macon and Milkman, form an allegiance like Pilate's and Reba's and Hagar's, but unlike the culturally and spiritually nurturing connections of the women, their goals are to disconnect themselves from their clan rather than to connect. Their search for white values pulls them away from each other. In consequence, they have heard all their lives, although without recognition, the music that is the key to their pasts—Macon, Jr., under the window of Pilate's house, Milkman in Pilate's home and at his birth. But Macon denied its healing power, and Milkman almost misses its solace and its potential to be "helpful and defining."

But as well as being a novel that documents loss, *Song of Solomon* is a novel in which something is born. When Milkman realized that the children in Shalimar were "singing a song about his people . . . [and that] somewhere in the pile was a gift for him. . . . He was as eager and happy as he had ever been in his life." As Milkman receives this gift, Pilate is relieved of her burden.

The weight of her father's bones, which Pilate had carried with her through her childhood and adult life, should, by rights, be buried. Pilate's destiny was flight. She had gifted her children and her family with the music of their pasts. She had carried their truths along with her burden. As she relieves herself of that last burden, Guitar is the accompaniment and Milkman learns to sing. Milkman's is the song of his renewed spirit: "Sugargirl don't leave me here . . . and . . . he could not stop the worn old words from coming, louder and louder. . . ." Two birds swoop down to the dead Pilate and the reborn Milkman. "Lord I want two wings." Milkman, in a final epiphany, literalizes Pilate's flight and his own salvation. He surrenders to the air, and he rides it. That little bird, Milkman, born the day after Robert Smith's tragic flight, had fought for reclamation of the power of flight all his life. It had been denied by his father's betrayal of his filial link to Pilate, obfuscated by his mother's impotence, and threatened by his own avarice. Only through his liberation into myth does Milkman re-member his birthright.

Childhood is a time of intimacy with things spiritual. As we become adult, we can claim the strength of song to carry us back to our spirits and renew them with the power and strength of ancestry. *Song of Solomon* begs our attention to this potential. When Pilate sings, her face is "all mask; all emotion and passion . . . left her features and entered her voice." When that Black spiritual calls for "two wings to veil my face," it is both an affirmation and a promise of the strength of the African spirit in Black folk that assures us endurance, staying power, and spiritual dominion.

Last summer, when my son pulled himself back into that tree and when my daughter furiously erased her design and modified her drawings, they were assuring themselves a future where flight was always in *potentia*. It did not need to have been actualized during that summer. This spring, Ben has rediscovered that tree, and Ayana whirls in the March winds as if she had wings. Childhood is a promise of return to the soul, a moment of memory for our spirits, and the challenge to hold fast to these powers as we grow into adulthood.

HARRY REED

Toni Morrison, Song of Solomon and Black Cultural Nationalism

Black nationalism's origins probably date to the 1780s with the founding of the Free African Society of Philadelphia. Immediately the organization spawned auxiliaries in several other northern cities. Chiefly, the organizations desired to serve a multitude of functions for the growing northern free black community. They served to centralize discussions of black religious freedom; they sought to organize black self-help efforts; and they also provided the first organized political defense of the community. While these activities did shape the black political awakening, they did not constitute modern black nationalism. They lacked a developed ideology for creating a separate political entity. Most early black political activists worked for equality and acceptance within the American political framework. Modern black nationalism is a concept incorporating attitudes and actions which seek to control, direct, and shape political destiny. The hoped-for results of black nationalism have focused on two ideas. One, to build a political entity, a modern Black Nation State. Or, to achieve the acceptance that the group (Black Americans) constitutes a nation.

Cultural nationalism, one of a variety of nationalist expressions, contends that black people possess a culture, style of life, world view, and aesthetic values distinctly different from white Americans. Since the 1950s we have witnessed the growth of two black cultural nationalist positions.

From *The Centennial Review* 32, no. 1 (Winter 1988). © 1988 *Centennial Review*.

Militant cultural nationalists such as Ameer Baraka assert the superiority of black cultural nationalist products (music, dance, literature) on moral and aesthetic grounds. They claim that black artistic impulses have neither been sullied by nor saddled with the guilt of capitalist oppression. They further assert that the entire world recognizes jazz, a black American original, as the only legitimate American contribution to world culture. Conservative cultural nationalists maintain that Afro-Americans are one of many subcultures that make up American society. They refrain from making value judgments about any subcultural element. Ralph Ellison is usually cited as representative of the second form of black cultural nationalism. For the creative artist, BCN outlines several missions to the black community. Artists should not only present alternative archetypes to help shape black personality but also develop distinctive cultural forms for the community.

In the voluminous literature critiquing Toni Morrison's work, one analytical perspective is conspicuous by its absence: no critic has viewed Morrison's novels through the prism of black cultural nationalism. Morrison's stories, however, are ripe with a cultural nationalist thrust. Perhaps several reasons account for this oversight. One, black women usually are not cited as representative black cultural nationalists. Two, even as black male critics and writers engaged in a sometimes raging dispute, their definition of black cultural nationalism was extremely limited. Not only were the definitions limited to two expressions, conservative and militant cultural nationalism, but also their conception of BCN was equally restrictive. Most male nationalists viewed BCN in the limited terms of an end in itself or as a hand maiden to politics. No political activist critic viewed BCN as the most important foundation for black survival. Toni Morrison and other black female writers perceive of cultural survival as more important than—or at least equally important with—political progress. Generally these writers who have taken a holistic approach to BCN have been drowned out by their more political opponents. Three, in the politically moribund 1980s, black cultural nationalism seems passé. The current quietude makes it imperative that we understand that black women writers have always been contributing but unacknowledged black cultural nationalists. Finally, the pervasive subject of Toni Morrison's work—the lives of black women—has not aligned her work with cultural nationalism. Black women's lives are continually undervalued in American culture; any balanced representation of those lives in fiction had to await both the civil rights and the women's liberation movements. Ironically, the black female writers' focus on the lives of black women offers a more penetrating look at all black life and simultaneously a more deeply satisfying and more deeply disturbing interpretation of black culture.

Toni Morrison's *Song of Solomon*, her third novel, is a major contribution to nationalist thought. Like that of other black female writers, Morrison's work poses a threat to the present limited perceptions of black cultural nationalism. She suggests a need to expand BCN to permit a focus on regenerating the community from within. Her work, then, is a tour-de-force; a simultaneous affirmation and criticism of black cultural nationalism. In this novel we see the black female writer working on the broadest possible imaginative nationalist canvas. Her study encompasses a multidimensional quest: the search for roots, family and identity; the acquisition of autonomy and commitment; the pursuit of humanity, clarity and growth; and the ability to define and make choices. Deeply imbedded in Morrison's work are some of their viable and distinctive elements of black culture. A Pan-African motif envelops the entire novel. Essential to the story's development are the emphases on oral recall, the premium blacks place on the spoken language, and Afro-American musical motifs: rhythm, the Blues and the call-and-response pattern.

A deep reverence for black females and black female networks pervades Morrison's novel. She avoids romanticizing or idealizing women's hard circumstances, but every woman, except possibly Hagar, has small moments of triumph. And Morrison loves them and their moments of feistiness and overcoming odds. Granny who looked "as though she might move the earth if she wanted to" ultimately bests the white nurse. Certainly Granny had to show deference to the white authority figure but she emerges as more aware: she knows what's going on and she knows the people. Granny's final comment, after the nurse has departed, reaffirms her dignity and makes clear that she, Granny, possesses a humanity absent in the white nurse.

Moreover one can view three of Morrison's women—Pilate, Circe, and Ruth—as nationalist archetypes. Despite their surroundings, both Pilate and Circe survive partly by utilizing the past. Pilate's unconscious Africanism is demonstrated through her identity with nature, the aura of magic, and a sense of deep wisdom. Circe's uses of the past manifest the survival power of black women in the institution of slavery. Her superiority helped her survive when lesser pressures drove her mistress to suicide. Circe was a colored woman; her mistress, a white lady. Both women illustrate a nationalist precept: the unity of the black historical experience. Their personae incorporate bits of Ancient Africa, New World Slavery, Southern Reconstruction and the present. Morrison's reverence for her three women and their representation of nationalist ideas is somewhat difficult to grasp because it represents a departure from cultural nationalist norms. Like Pilate and Circe, Ruth does not experience a revolutionary change. Her awakenings come come in fits and starts: a quiet rage against her son, a *rapproachment* with

Pilate, and demands on her husband to provide Hagar's funeral expenses. What Morrison depicts is a slow, long period of change and adjustment. Like other black female writers she depicts an image of cultural survival that eschews the quick-fix resolution. Instead these writers focus on the transformation within the individual and with the race. Morrison's female networks do not always solve existing problems but that must not invalidate our appreciation of her reverence for black females.

II

While Milkman is central to the resolution of the dense thematic thrust of *Song of Solomon*, his quest is buttressed by his female relationships. The fluid constellations of black women loving him, supporting him, guiding him and even rejecting him confirm the nurturing aspects of black life. Milkman is generally unconcerned about his effect on the females in his life. He neither knows about nor cares about the sacrifices they make to keep him whole and healthy. He accepts without question his mother's protection, but he cannot reciprocate when she needs support.

> Milkman leaned against a tree and waited at the entrance. Now he knew, if he'd had any doubts, that all his father had told him was true. She was a silly, selfish queen, faintly obscene woman. Again he felt abused. Why couldn't anybody in his whole family just be normal?

As Morrison shows, Milkman neither realized nor cared that he was the most recent in a long line of men who had oppressed her.

Ruth's father, Dr. Foster, had never approved of his future son-in-law, Macon Dead. Later he refused to give Macon a loan to complete a business deal. Macon, in turn, never forgave his wife for siding with her father. He also resented his wife's seeming distaste for sex, but the final straw in his rejection of her was the scene he witnessed between her and her dead father. Later Macon relates that story from his male perspective to his son. Even Ruth's handyman perceives of her as weird and then circulates stories about her.

Through all of the refracted male views of Ruth, none of the viewers pauses long enough to listen to her. Even her son—reflecting on his own sense of betrayal—does not understand her explanation. What she describes is her oppression by the black males in her life, not the oppression of an undefined white power structure. People she expected to love her, to accept her and to nurture her had not, as she explains to her son.

. . . Because the fact is that I am a small woman. I don't mean little, I mean small, and I'm small because I was pressed small. I lived in a great big house that pressed me into a small package. I had no friends, only schoolmates who wanted to touch my dresses and my white silk stockings. But I didn't think I'd ever need a friend because I had him. I was small, but he was big. The only person who ever really cared whether I lived or died. Lots of people were interested in whether I lived or died but he cared. He was not a good man, Macon. Certainly he was an arrogant man, and often a foolish and destructive one. But he cared whether and he cared how I lived, and there was, and is, no one else in the world who ever did. And for that I would do anything. It was important for me to be in his presence, among his things he used, had touched. Later it was just important to know he was in the world. When he left it I kept on reigniting that strange cared-for feeling that I got from him. I am not a strange woman. I am not a strange woman. I am a small one.

Poignant as it is, Ruth's story evokes Milkman's interest only when she mentions his Aunt Pilate. His attention then is only momentary: he is more concerned about asking "Were you in the bed with your father when he was dead? Naked?" "No," she answers, "but I did kneel there in my slip at his bedside and kiss his beautiful fingers. They were the only part of him that wasn't. . . ." Milkman cuts her off and hurls the accusation "You nursed me." When Ruth answers in the affirmative Milkman then asserts "Until I was . . . old, too old." His indictment is answered with chilling force from Ruth:

And I also prayed for you. Every single night and every single day. On my knees. Now you tell me. What harm did I do you on my knees?

For the moment the question is lost on Milkman. Like the other men in her life, Ruth's son is convinced that she is indeed a strange woman.

Had Morrison left Ruth at this point it would have been just another example of the madonna/bitch theme that the work of so many male nationalist writers perpetuates. The Madonna/bitch theme illustrates the ambiguity that black males feel for mothers and wives, but especially mothers. Conflicts inherent in the theme are exacerbated when the black male attempts to gain autonomy *vis-à-vis* the white power structure. A standard resolution of this tension is the black male's condemning of the love and protection of the black female, possibly because she has diverted his attention from confronting whitey and denigrated his manliness by suggesting what he sees as cowardly alternatives.

Morrison offers a different and more compelling resolution of the mother-son conflict. First, any attempt to reach an immediate mediation dissolves. Milkman has had his biases corroborated and so fails to comfort his mother. Second, telling the story triggers the remembrance of Pilate's support. And it is this other black female who helps Ruth begin to shape her life and to shed her smallness. Thus Morrison opens new views of black life by incorporating the black woman's quest for selfhood, autonomy, and growth. Ruth begins to assert herself, not in a domineering way but with newly discovered ego-strength. Significantly her new assertiveness is not structured to educate black males about their shortcomings, or to castrate them for them. Instead she works on behalf of other black women.

Equally important, she begins to identify once more with Pilate, her sister-in-law. Initially they are drawn together because of Ruth's son, Macon, (she refused to call him Milkman) and Pilate's granddaughter, Hagar. Several years older than Milkman, Hagar refused to accept his ending of their relationship. She had indeed made several inept attempts to kill him. Ruth warns Hagar to leave her son alone. Unseen by Ruth or Hagar, Pilate listens to each say why she is important to Milkman. Pilate puts both of their relationships to him in the proper perspective by noting, "He wouldn't give a pile of swan shit for either one of you."

III

When Pilate takes center stage, Morrison's concept of black life, black survival, coalesces. Pilate condemns neither of the women. She instead commands their attention by reciting her experiences. She is the embodiment of black folk wisdom, which gives Pilate an equilibrium that neither Ruth nor Hagar possesses. Pilate has survived the suspicions of numerous lovers who always became alarmed when they learned she has no navel. The lack of an essential anatomical feature gave Pilate notoriety if not status in the community. In the eyes of many she was, like Ruth, strange. But she possessed the basic quality of the old black world. "Old timey" was the way that some young people perceived Pilate. Even though the older generation was generally embarrassed by her presence, Morrison makes it clear that everyone depended on that wisdom even as they rejected it. Pilate scorned property, money, book learning and slavish dependence on males. Her wisdom is the wisdom of the ages, and Morrison implies that we are all the poorer for our inability to understand, to accept, and to utilize the old ways.

Pilate's old way makes it possible for her to accept if not flourish in her isolation. More importantly her old black way allows her to nurture two women one of whom, Ruth, was ready to murder her granddaughter. Morrison has no problem envisioning a black society whose generative force is the black woman. She, however, does not envision a matriarchy. Pilate acts to give black women strength and black men freedom. Her love frees. She chastises Ruth and Hagar for trying to possess Milkman. " . . . talkin' 'bout a man like he was a house or needed one. He ain't a house, he's a man, and whatever he need, don't none of you got it." Morrison values love and freedom for blacks individually and collectively. The house motif incorporates Morrison's definition of intraracial sexual oppression. Women concern themselves with rooms, with houses: how to acquire them, how to clean them, how to live in them. Men, on the other hand, build houses and leave them. Pilate transcends that gender-related oppression and is therefore eccentric but free. She can not only support and live happily within a woman-centered environment but she can also accept the love of men without being devastated by its absence.

Pilate's freedom (and Morrison's nationalism) converges in the activity surrounding Hagar's funeral. Pilate seems scarcely aware of the usual arrangements for burial; Ruth, rather, had to get the money and organize the ceremony. Pilate—deeply rooted in the world of the black folk—knows and must act on her sense that death is personal. She fashions her release in a powerfully evocative ritual.

> Two days later, halfway through the service, it seemed as though Ruth was going to be the lone member of the bereaved family there. A female quartet from Linden Baptist Church had already sung "Abide with Me," the wife of the mortician had read the condolence cards and the minister had launched into his "Naked came ye into this life and naked shall ye depart" sermon, which he always believed suitable for the death of a young woman; and the winos in the vestibule who came to pay their respects to "Pilate's girl" but who dared not enter had begun to sob, when the door swung open and Pilate burst in, shouting "Mercy!" as though it were a command.

She rivets the congregation; only two men try to stop her progress to the front of the church. Over and over she shouts "Mercy!" changing her intonation to reflect a variety of moods.

> It was not enough. The word needed a bottom, a frame. She straightened up, held her head high, and transformed the plea

into a note. In a clear bluebell voice she sang it out—the one
word held so long it became a sentence—and before the last
syllable had died in the corners of the rooms, she was answered
in a sweet soprano: "I hear you."

The people turned around. Reba had entered and was singing
too. Pilate neither acknowledged her entrance nor missed a beat.
She simply repeated the word "Mercy," and Reba replied. The
daughter standing at the back of the chapel, the mother up front,
they sang.

In the nighttime
Mercy.
In the darkness
Mercy.
In the morning
Mercy.
At my bedside
Mercy.
On my knees now
Mercy, Mercy, Mercy, Mercy.

They stopped at the same time in a high silence.

The congregation had witnessed an ancient rite, older than slavery, older
than the middle passage, back through time to the African homeland. While
the ritual was timeless, it was slipping away in the memory of most of their
listeners.

Through Reba and Pilate we have witnessed one of the most
powerful celebrations of a black musical heritage in Afro-American letters. In
form and content the ritual was African although neither mother nor
daughter was aware of it. African and Afro-American music are marked by
the call-response pattern, and the African content is also striking. Through
her actions, Pilate rejected the empty Christian sermonizing. Her references
were to activities Hagar shared with the living: the music, the morning and
the evening. Pilate's words reflect the basic unity of African life where physical death is both an end and a beginning. Pilate and Reba released their grief
but also sent Hagar off to the ancestors. Finally Pilate interjects a sense of
revitalization with her last words "And she was loved."

IV

At precisely the time of Hagar's funeral, Milkman is working his way toward solving the riddle of his family background. Significantly he has had to retrace the steps to the south and follow the oral accounts back to slavery. On his second visit to Susan Byrd, the granddaughter of the woman who took in his grandfather, Milkman inquires:

> What was Jake's last name?
> Can you tell me?
> I don't think he had one he was
> one of those flying African
> children.

Bit by bit, Susan Byrd tells of Jake's father Solomon, an African who, tired of slavery, took off and flew home to Africa. He had tried to take Jake, his youngest, with him, but flying close to some trees he had brushed one and the baby fell to earth. Weeks earlier before his sojourn through the south, Milkman would not have believed such a story. Down home has had a maturing effect on Milkman. Even when he least understood the direction or speed of change, it had prepared him to accept flying African ancestors. Clearly Morrison validates flying Africans through the device of oral recall.

Milkman travels a highway preserved, in part, in the stories of his father and Pilate. All along the way the stories are reinforced by other people he meets. People remember. Recall is not always complete or accurate but tantalizing details are always apparent. A name, an incident, a song fragment are compelling incentives to Milkman. Not once does anyone produce written proof of anything. When writing/record keeping does intrude, blacks are victimized by it. A drunken Yankee soldier's misrecorded information caused Milkman's grandfather Jake to become Macon Dead. Morrison projects an interrelatedness in Afro-American culture by the ease with which Milkman, from his literate background, adapts to the oral oriented culture. His adaptation was not without problems, but it was basically painless.

He was initiated into a sometimes brutal but often exhilarating and deeply satisfying cultural milieu. These new black people are different yet familiar. They accept their cultural distinctiveness, generally without apology. Milkman learns by experiencing the land, the people and their ways.

Simultaneous with the focus on oral recall and the interrelatedness of black culture, Morrison also employs other Afro-American cultural elements. The premium blacks place on the spoken language and its rhythm is celebrated throughout her work. Movement is everywhere and especially in black speech. Using a narrative voice, in the opening section, that sounds like a black grandmother in the 1940's, Morrison depicts the verbal byplay between Mr. Smith and the onlookers. In the crowd a cat-eyed boy, a gold-toothed man, and a sinning woman with a funny knit hat also command the reader's attention. Rhythms flow, they bounce, they energize the crowd. No black person is seeking explanations beyond "A nutcase will do anything." Hospital Tommy is a master of language. But Tommy is not alone in his skill; even the drunken Porter can draw a crowd. Finally, some of the names Morrison chooses exude rhythm: Empire State (he just stands and sways), Railroad Tommy, Ruth Foster Dead, Ryna's Gulch and Solomon. In the novel's opening scenes the lone discordant note is struck by the white nurse who represents authority. She does not understand the language, she cannot spell, and she has poor manners.

Morrison's black folk survive on their strength, their humanity, their cussedness and their ability to be in touch with the old way. Their collective wisdom sustains Milkman. He comes to appreciate the dynamic of black life stretching back over the generations. Circe, living alone in an old house filled with dogs and defecation, becomes a testament to black survival. She is secure in her knowledge of being superior to her dead mistress. Not yet at the bottom of his own mystery, Milkman misinterprets her existence. He thinks she remains out of love and loyalty. Circe lets him know differently:

> You don't listen to people. Your ear is on your head but it's not connected to your brain. I said she killed herself rather than do the work I'd been doing all my life! . . . Do you hear me: She saw the work I did all her days and died, you hear me, died rather than live like me. Now, what do you suppose she thought I was! If the way I lived and the work I did was so hateful to her she killed herself to keep from having to do it, and you think I stay on here just because I loved her, then you have about as much sense as a fart.

The old folks have a dynamic of their own and it reflects wisdom, humanity, and the life-affirming qualities of black life.

Throughout Morrison's novel female figures appear as carriers of the old way. Men on the other hand tend to move away from the ancient wisdom: they run, make money, and challenge whites in both real and symbolic confrontations. Black women try valiantly to pass on the lesson and the simple wisdom.

> Hi
> The woman looked up. First at Guitar and
> then at Milkman. What kind of word is

that? Her voice was light but gravel
sprinkled. Milkman kept staring at her
fingers manipulating the orange, Guitar
grinned and shrugged, it means hello.
Then say what you mean.
Okay, hello.
That's better what you want?

Later in the conversation Pilate asks Guitar about the silent but staring Milkman. "Do he talk?" Pilate wants to know. When Milkman nervously makes the same greeting mistake, Pilate laughs but says:

You all must be the dumbest unhung Negroes on earth. What
they telling you in them schools? You say "Hi" to pigs
and sheep when you want 'em to move. When you tell a
human being "Hi" he ought to get up and knock you down.

Shamed but still fascinated by Pilate, Milkman began to separate fact from fiction. Unlike the stories he had heard about his aunt, she was not dirty, ugly or drunk. Still most of the lessons of Pilate's pride, freedom, strength, humanity and native intelligence are lost on the young men. Pilate and Circe possess the self-knowledge and wisdom essential for cultural survival but few absorb their teachings.

Morrison does not blindly celebrate the old way but she does imply that it offers freedom and is relatively easy to acquire. Milkman, however, does not complete his transformation to the old wisdom until Guitar murders Pilate. For the first time in his life Milkman had to protect/sacrifice/give to someone he loved. He rose and leaped to confront Guitar in a death struggle. He flew. At last he knew what Shalimar knew: if you surrendered to the air you could ride it. Morrison's novel has come full circle: it opens and closes with a flying motif. Mr. Smith's attempt to fly is doomed to failure: without the ancient knowledge he is simply going to die. Milkman actually flies, and the moment of resolution is hopeful.

Between the two scenes is a sprawling yet tightly structured Pan-African novel. Undergirding the work is the dynamic of black culture stretching from the present to ancient Africa. Those who survive on mostly their own terms are those who keep the faith. Those who will survive in the future must give some attention to preserving the past. Morrison's artistic and nationalist view allows us to validate black culture and reaffirm its adaptive survival power, its creativity amidst oppression, its life-affirming qualities, as well as its ancient wisdom and humanity and its capacity for cultural survival.

RALPH STORY

An Excursion into the Black World:
The "Seven Days" in Toni Morrison's Song of Solomon

What was the basic goal of such desperate people, and what manner of men
and women were these who threw themselves into the ocean "with much
resolution," rather than submit to slavery a long way from home? . . . The
question then arises: after the struggle to break the oppressors' hold upon
our lives is stymied, is suicide another form of battle against that domination?
Thousands upon thousands of Africans—we cannot know the number—took
that path. For many, of course, it was the traditional pathway back to the
homeland, for they believed that death would deliver them to the unseen but
well-remembered shores. . . . Others, countless others, took some new occasion to leap over the side of the vessels.

Toni Morrison's masterwork *Song of Solomon* (1977), perhaps the greatest
novel ever written by an Afro-American, begins with the character of Robert
Smith (adorned with blue wings) jumping from the roof of Mercy Hospital.
To most Westerners, this act of suicide was probably interpreted as just that:
a suicide, which also, for those moderately knowledgeable in Greek
mythology, paralleled the flight of Icarus. Yet Morrison's Smith, an insurance
agent who bids goodbye to the world amidst "roses strewn about," and
before many curious onlookers, was also committing revolutionary suicide—
an idea which most Western readers and even some contemporary Japanese
have a hard time embracing despite the fact that in Japanese culture the idea

From *Black American Literature Forum* 23, no. 1 (Spring 1989). © 1989 African American
Review.

of ritualistic suicide has long been considered both noble and manly (see Mishima). Thus, in one descriptive passage Morrison unites both Eastern and Western trains of thought. More significantly, her novel reveals the complexities of Afro-American life, history, and culture through her creation of a revolutionary group called the Seven Days. This article discusses the Seven Days in Morrison's *Song of Solomon* as a key element in the work's literary development and as a microcosm of the two primary ideological streams which have characterized Afro-American political thought in the twentieth century.

Smith's suicide was linked to his involvement with the Seven Days, a revolutionary group that symbolically and as a literary device makes *Solomon* a truly great novel of magical realism (see Menton). The book clearly reveals the disparate and extremely complex ways Afro-Americans have thought about the quality of their lives; it also reveals what many of them have decided to do about it individually and collectively. In creating the Seven Days, Morrison reaches into the historical black community and its contemporary equivalent to reveal a dissonance which has always characterized the Afro-American world. This dissonance, tension, or Yin-Yang polarity unfolds principally through the relationship between Guitar Bains, spokesperson for the Seven Days, and his friend Milkman Dead, the middle-class protagonist of *Solomon*. Their socioeconomic differences, consequential socializations, and their divergent experiences are a microcosm for the two most distinguishable Afro-American ideological streams and their respective historical advocates, e.g., Malcolm X and Martin Luther King. As Harold Cruse wrote several decades ago, ". . . the present-day conflict within the Negro ethnic group, between the integrationist and separatist tendencies, has its origins in the historical arguments between personalities such as Frederick Douglass and as Martin R. Delany. . . . the emergence of the Malcolm X brand of nationalism proves its persistence, despite the fact that both strains have undergone considerable change and qualification."

Ultimately, however, Morrison's Seven Days transcends this convenient, yet historically accurate, dichotomy of Afro-American ideological streams. For black folk "to love so much they would kill" is a profoundly radical idea yet one which can be clearly discerned in the poetical works of the Black Arts Movement of the late 1960s, especially the writings of LeRoi Jones/Amiri Baraka. Acting out the credo embodied in the title of Huey Newton's work *Revolutionary Suicide*, and indirectly fitting the description for Jones's "The End of Man Is His Beauty," Smith clearly felt that "to fly away" was his only alternative:

> Your world shakes
> cities die
> beneath your shape.
> The single shadow

at noon
like a live tree
whose leaves
are like clouds

Weightless soul
at whose love faith moves
as a dark and
withered day.

With the revolutionary ideas of the late 1960s as a backdrop, the flight of
Robert Smith is not only a death but also a ritualistic hari-kari decision. As a
black man in America, the life he chose as an assassin for the Seven Days, a
group committed to avenging the murders of black people, ultimately gave
him only one way to end his life—by his own hands. And it is surely death
that a black man faces when he murders a white person in America. On a
figurative level, it is much like "death" to be a black American male, who,
without employment, competitive educational credentials, or economic
resources, becomes a statistic. These real men exist, secretly, beyond the
reach or influence of mainstream culture. Much like them but with a political purpose, Morrison's Robert Smith did not believe he would ever achieve
justice, given the nature of American society. Note Guitar's reasoning:

> "Do we have a court? Is there one courthouse in one city in the
> country where a jury would convict them? There are places right
> now where a Negro still can't testify against a white man. Where
> the judge, the jury, the court, are legally bound to ignore anything
> a Negro has to say. What that means is that a black man is a victim
> of a crime only when a white man says he is. Only then. If there was
> anything like or near justice or courts when a cracker kills a Negro,
> there wouldn't have to be no Seven Days. But there ain't; so we are."

In the course of Morrison's meticulously revealing this society, she gives
readers a glimpse of black rage, the certainty of which has, for a variety of
reasons, tended to remain undisclosed. (The urban riots of the 1960s offered
a dramatic piece of public testimony.)

The black community has always been extremely diverse socially,
economically, and politically, yet until recently one would not have been
cognizant of this rather obvious fact—a fact, I might add, purposely obscured
by the media, reduced to insignificance historically by white novelists and
film makers, and avoided by many black writers, social and literary critics,

and would-be political leaders. Only a few black novelists have dared to expose the reality of the inner city, with all its diversity, to readers. Usually, even a single black murderer in a novel (or short fiction) by a black writer has been regarded as shocking. For example, Richard Wright's heroic figure Brother Mann in "Down by the Riverside" (1938) jolted more than a few American readers: "The flare flickered to and fro. His throat tightened and he aimed. . . . He fired, twice. The white man fell backwards on the steps and slipped with an abrupt splash into the water. The flashlight went with him, its one eye swooping downward, leaving a sudden darkness." And Bigger Thomas, in Wright's *Native Son* (1940), shocked an even greater number of literate Americans. Conversely, in the heart of the real black community, the rage of some black folk and their willingness to defend themselves against any attack or to strike back at whites for their hostile actions has always been well known and understood; usually, however, it comes to the fore exclusively amongst black folk and out of the earshot of whites, or even some of those Negroes who are perceived to be loyal to them.

As Ralph Ellison said some thirty years ago, "There is no place like a Negro barbershop for hearing what Negroes really think." The barbershop is the one place in both Morrison's novel and actual black communities where black males speak openly and candidly. In the late 1960s, black barber-shops were also noteworthy for the political discussions which frequently took place within them. Morrison's Railroad Tommy and Hospital Tommy, two more members of the Seven Days, are therefore very realistic and believ-able. Through her creation of the Seven Days and her use of the barbershop as the group's informal meeting place, Morrison delineates a class and race history of Afro-American political thought so accurate that her genius in this particular area has yet to be fully appreciated.

The Seven Days can also be linked back to black secret societies of the nineteenth century, an intriguing consideration, since their existence, unlike that of many groups in the late 1960s, wasn't necessarily documented or even acknowledged:

> In one instance a secret society was organized to overthrow slavery. In 1844 a Moses Dickson, who had for years worked on steamboats running from Cincinnati up and down the Ohio and Mississippi rivers, determined to do something toward securing the freedom of the slaves. In 1844 he and eleven other free negroes met to form an organization for this purpose. After consulting together they decided to take two years to study over and develop a plan of action. In 1846 the twelve met in St. Louis and organized the Knights of Liberty.

Morrison's Seven Days, then, is a group grounded in both contemporary and nineteenth-century Afro-American history. There is, for example, the fact that Robert Smith, the first character we witness in Solomon, is an agent for the North Carolina Mutual Agency, a fictional insurance company very much like the real North Carolina Mutual and Provident Association which conceivably began, as did most black insurance companies, as a secret society.

Morrison's strength, conveyed in Addison Gayle's assertion about the prolific black novelist John A. Williams, lies "in the synthesis of fiction and history." Other comparisons which can be made between the two novelists' work are that Morrison's Seven Days, like Williams' King Alfred Plan in *The Man Who Cried I Am* (1967), gives the novel an intriguing impetus: an unresolved question which, along with Morrison's extraordinary use of black myth and folklore, moves the narrative forward with drive and power, sustaining readers' attention, provoking their curiosity, and generating controversy. The intimacy of the folklore, the characters' names, flying Africans, the quest for Afro-Americans to reconstruct their past, and the Seven Days give this work a fascinating tension as well as an edge of verisimilitude that combine to provide a completely original delineation of black life in the urban American North. In this respect, Morrison is one of the trailblazers of Afro-American literature. *Song of Solomon* fulfills the description Gayle provided for works by black novelists that "require a new look at, and approach to history":

> The new approach to history [i]s necessary for the education of young Blacks growing up in twentieth-century America, a fact recognized not only by such prominent black historians as John H. Clarke and Lerone Bennett, committed to reinterpreting history in line with the black historians, adding to it those nuances particular to the writer of fiction—dramatizing facts, recreating situations and enobling men [and women] and events. . . . [Needed are books which deal] with aspects of the racial past and suggest, in so doing, that time and circumstances demand that black people look inward, for paradigms of positive import.

The device Morrison uses to make *Solomon* resound historically is the series of interchanges between Guitar and Milkman.

The class differences between Milkman and Guitar are made obvious by Morrison early in the novel. Milkman, as a stalwart member of the black bourgeoisie, has lived a life in pursuit of material and sexual pleasure. His "membership" in black middle-class society can even be detected in his hidden disdain for black women of the underclass like Hagar: "He seldom took her anywhere except to the movies and he never took her to parties where people of his own set danced and laughed and developed intrigues among themselves." Guitar, on the other hand, a member of the black working class, has evolved in the opposite direction; he has, by the time both of them have reached their thirties, developed a consciousness that has spurred on his active membership in the Seven Days and simultaneously made him antipathetic to the world from which Milkman hails and the life middle-class blacks like Milkman represent:

> "Look, Milk, we've been tight a long time, right? But that don't mean we're not different people. . . . I know you. Been knowing you. You got your high-tone friends and your picnics on Honoré Island and you can afford to spend fifty percent of your brainpower thinking about a piece of ass. You got that red-headed bitch and you got a Southside bitch and no telling what in between.

It is only a matter of seconds before Guitar really lets Milkman see the differences between them in stark, candid terms:

> "You're welcome everywhere I go. I've tried to get you to come to Honoré—"
> "Fuck Honoré! You hear me? The only way I'll go to that nigger heaven is with a case of dynamite and a book of matches."

Guitar has discovered his mission as a member of the Seven Days. Unlike Milkman, he has come to reject not only the values and attitudes of the black middle class but also the life of the black working and lower classes as well, symbolized by the Southside where "one lived knowing that at any time, anybody might do anything. Not wilderness where there was system, or the logic of lions, trees, toads, and birds, but wild wilderness where there was none." Guitar's organization is "logical" and reasonable, in sharp contrast to the "wilderness" so much a part of "ghetto life." Members of the Seven Days have even transcended ego and the need for glory or martyrdom: "'. . . it's not about other people knowing. We don't even tell the victims. We just whisper to him, "Your Day has come." The beauty of what we do is its secrecy, its smallness. . . . We don't discuss it among ourselves, the details. We just get an assignment. If the Negro was killed on a Wednesday, the Wednesday man takes it; if he was killed on Monday, the Monday man takes that one.'"

The central message conveyed by Morrison's Seven Days via the Milkman-Guitar dialogue is that if more than just a handful of courageous, righteous, and sacrificial black men and women had been willing to "love" enough to avenge the murders of their people, virtually giving up their lives, then the overt and covert oppression of black folk might have ended long ago. "Love" for the Seven Days is like the love of one soldier for a countryman who has died in combat. It forces the reader to consider black people as if they have been engaged in a protracted struggle against superior and unpredictable adversaries: "No Love? No Love? Didn't you hear me? What I'm doing isn't about hating white people. It's about loving us. About loving you. My whole life is love." Ultimately, the challenge Guitar (speaking for the Seven Days) extends to Milkman is that he and his comrades are no longer willing to wait for justice for black people or for the quality of life to improve for the race. The members of the Seven Days have rejected all racial uplift strategies that preceded them and do not see evolutionary progress as meaningful: "'It's not about you living longer. It's about how you live and why. It's about whether your children can make other children. It's about trying to make a world where one day white people will think before they lynch.'" It becomes clear to Milkman that Guitar, as a representative for the Seven Days, will no longer regard his childhood friend in the same manner. Their differences are political and classical and automatically make them frightened antagonists: "Milkman rubbed the ankle of his short leg. 'I'm scared for you, man.'" Guitar responds, "'That's funny. I'm scared for you too.'"

Morrison's intuitive and experiential understanding of the urban, Northern black community is strengthened and enhanced by her consciousness of Afro-American history and culture and the internal and external forces which have swirled within and without its citizenry. Her character Macon Dead, for instance, is representative of the Booker T. Washington school of racial progress through land ownership but updated and made believable by his tangible material success and the practical legacy he tries to give to his son. Dead's individual power is contrasted with the collective strength and heart of the Seven Days, whose members are his antithesis; Guitar and Milkman are also at opposite ends of the class/race spectrum. Guitar belongs to the wider black community, and as his movements throughout the community (from Feather's pool room to Tommy's barbershop to Mary's bar) illustrate, he has accumulated his knowledge of the world and self through conscious thought and worldly experiences. Guitar is *street*; Milkman is *house*. Guitar, moreover, has learned about the tragedy of black life in America from the personal tragedy of his father's murder and from those men who stand in opposition to what Milkman's father, Macon Dead, represents. In short, Guitar joins the Seven Days because of his experiences and his life, as if Morrison were suggesting that it takes just such experiences and tragedies for black men to embrace a revolutionary praxis. Milkman, on the other hand, ends up rejecting his background and the world his father has created for him by setting out to rediscover his racial past—a noble quest but one which is only individually rewarding. Those who form the Seven Days assume a racial position and outlook on their lives as opposed to Dead, Sr.'s class (material) view. They understand their history and know that not even money will prevent their people from being heartbroken:

> ". . . you not going to have a governor's mansion, or eight thousand acres of timber to sell. And you not going to have no ship under your command to sail on, no train to run, and you can. . . shoot down a thousand German planes all by yourself and land in Hitler's backyard and whip him with your own hands, but you never going to have four stars on your shirt front, or even three. . . . Well now. That's some thing you will have—a broken heart." Railroad Tommy's eyes softened, but the merriment in them had died suddenly. "And folly. A whole lot of folly. You can count on it."

Railroad Tommy and the others in the Seven Days have realized they will never be millionaires nor will most of their people. They have, in essence, rejected the "integration of the individual" as a beneficial approach to success for the black masses and instead adopted a more radical and extreme collective posture. Yet unlike Milkman's father, they have an empathy and passion for black people that can be discerned in Morrison's deft recreation of the impact of Emmett Till's 1956 murder on the "Days" as they are gathered in the barbershop:

> In a few seconds it was over, since the announcer had only a few speculations and even fewer facts. The minute he went on to another topic of news, the barbershop broke into loud conversation. Railroad Tommy, the one who had tried to maintain silence, was completely silent now. He moved to his razor strop while Hospital Tommy tried to keep his customer in the chair. Porter, Guitar, Freddie the janitor, and three or four other men were exploding, shouting angry epithets all over the room. Apart from Milkman, only Railroad Tommy and Empire State were quiet.

Morrison, cognizant of how the Emmett Till murder outraged the national black community, uses this historical event to show the racial solidarity of the "Days." She also demonstrates that their actions, though violent, are no more extreme or bizzare than the actions of the two white men who killed the adolescent Till for saying "Bye, baby" to a white female. The "Days" are political murderers who kill, like most zealots, for the love and quest of a greater good for their people. Porter, a member of the "Days" who "cracks up," is described by Guitar as having gotten so depressed and despondent as a result of his mission that he went temporarily berserk: "'It was getting him down. They thought somebody would have to take over his day. He just needed a rest and he's okay now.'" Despite his bizarre behavior, Porter, in the same desperate but compassionate way Guitar talks to Milkman, professes his love for his people: "'I love ya! I love ya all. Don't act like that. You women. Stop it. Don't act like that. Don't you see I love ya? I'd die for ya, kill for ya. I'm saying I love ya. I'm telling ya. Oh, God have mercy. What I'm gonna do? What in this fuckin world am I gonna dooooo?'"

Morrison's unique, omniscient sense of the black community of the urban North is conveyed in her precise and exact rendering of the male figures in the Seven Days. Unlike the black male fiction writers who preceded her, Morrison, in *Song of Solomon*, has not chosen to depict an estranged, disconnected, solitary "native son" who murders or an "invisible man" who runs from the South and goet to the white world to plead his case but ends up in contemporary ambiguity in a basement with 1,369 lights. Instead, Morrison has focused her vision on *the community and its men*— separate, distinct individuals who come together as a collective entity yet remain complex, whole characters. Morrison's global understanding of the black world makes her much like her great predecessors in terms of her grasp of "the people," but she has widened the Afro-American literary tradition by creating a larger-than-life work which embraces black culture, history, and folklore, while simultaneously making the experience of reading her work insightful and inspirational.

MICHAEL AWKWARD

"Unruly and Let Loose": Myth, Ideology, *and Gender in* Song of Solomon

I write without gender focus. . . . It happens that what provokes my imagination as a writer has to do with the culture of black people. I regard the whole
of my world as my canvas and I write out of that sensibility of what I find
provocative *and* the sensibility of being a woman. But I don't write women's
literature as such. I think it would confine me. I am valuable as a writer
because I am a woman, because women, it seems to me, have some special
knowledge about certain things. [It comes from] the ways in which they view
the world, and from women's imagination. Once it is unruly and let loose, it
can bring things to the surface that men—trained to be men in a certain
way—have difficulty getting access to. . . .

—Toni Morrison, "An Interview with Toni Morrison,
Hessian Radio Network, Frankfurt, West Germany"
(conducted by Rosemarie K. Lester)

In several respects, *Song of Solomon* is perhaps the most challenging text
that Toni Morrison has yet produced. The interpretive challenges presented
by the novel have as their primary source the nature of the author's appropriation of the myth around which she structures what has been called a tale
of Afro-American "genealogical archaeology." As Dorothy Lee asserts in her
discussion of the epic qualities of Morrison's text, the author "draws on
specific Afro-American legends of Africans who could fly and who used this

---

From *Callaloo* 13, no. 3 (Summer 1990). © 1990 Charles H. Rowell. Reprinted by permission of
the Johns Hopkins University Press.

marvelous ability to escape from slavery in America; that is, literally to transcend bondage." However, Morrison does not simply "draw on" this myth;
rather, what she offers in the narrative of Solomon's mythic flight is a radically transformed version of this legend which suggests the immense, and in
many respects injurious, changes that have occurred over the course of the
history of blacks in America. Indeed, a careful analysis of the subtle, appro-
priative nature of Morrison's mythic figurations (including what is apparently
a traditional heroic male act of archaeology—its protagonist Milkman Dead's
"archetypal search for self and for transcendence,") reveals her complex
inscription of ideology, or more accurately, ideologies: the afrocentric and
feminist politics that inform *Song of Solomon*.

Comments offered by Morrison in "Rootedness: The Ancestor as
Foundation" appear to corroborate the general critical emphasis on the epic
qualities of *Song of Solomon*. In a discussion of what she views as the Afro-
American novel's destiny to replace the celebrated forms of black expressivity
(blues, jazz, spirituals, and folktales) as a primary locus for Afro-American
cultural wisdom's preservation and transmission, Morrison argues thus:

> the novel is needed by African-Americans now in a way that it
> was not needed before—and it is following along the lines of the
> function of novels everywhere. We don't live in places where we
> can hear those stories anymore; parents don't sit around and tell
> their children those *classical, mythological, archetypal stories* that
> we heard years ago. But *new information* has got to get out, and
> there are several ways to do it. One is the novel. (my emphasis)

Despite its apparent support of an unproblematized reading of her
third novel as a black male odyssey par excellence, Morrison's statement
strongly suggests a dual—and, in some respects, potentially conflictive—
function for the novel, and, particularly, for a purposefully "classical, mythological, archetypal" text such as *Song of Solomon*. These dual functions are: 1)
to preserve the traditional Afro-American folktales, folk wisdom, and general
cultural beliefs, and 2) to adapt to contemporary times and needs such traditional beliefs by infusing them with "new information," and to transmit the
resultant amalgam of traditional and "new" to succeeding generations. While
both of these functions are ideologically charged—they are informed by the
desire to convey to Afro-American readers "how to behave in this new
world"—it is quite easy to see that certain profound conflicts might arise
between the old (the archetypal tales) and the "new."

In fact, what the criticism devoted to *Song of Solomon* has failed to
respond to in an adequate manner where Morrison's employment of myth

and epic is concerned is the author's inscription of the "new." For Morrison's version of the myth of the flying African is in several crucial respects strategically altered in the form of an updated version of the traditional narrative which is "revitalized by a new grounding in the concrete particularities of a specific time and place." That new grounding is represented by the apparent absence on the part of Solomon, the figure in the Morrisonian version who possesses the secrets of flight, of an accompanying sense of social responsibility. The nameless black slaves in versions of the flying African myth such as Julius Lester's "People Who Could Fly," invested with the transcendent power of the word by a young witch doctor, literally rise en masse in response to the plight of blacks weakened as a consequence of working in the heat that made "the very air seem . . . to be on fire." This young witch doctor, who "carried with him the secrets and powers of the generations of Africa," employs these black powers to lead a stirring mass exodus from deep South fields. When the young witch doctor is himself struck by an overseer who recognizes his role in aiding the infirm to "surrender to the air," he instructs "Everyone" to escape: "He uttered the strange word, and all of the Africans dropped their hoes, stretched out their arms, and flew away, back to their home, back to Africa."

What is striking about this traditional version of the myth, particularly in comparison to its updating in *Song of Solomon*, is the communally beneficial nature of the witch doctor's employment of the (liberating black) word. In Lester's version of the myth, tribal wisdom is employed to make possible a group transcendence of the debilitating conditions of American oppression. The young African witch doctor, possessed of the power of flight, employs his knowledge at the appropriate moment—when the representative of white power punishes the weakened and defenseless, and seeks to destroy the bearer of African cultural wisdom—to effect a communal escape from the site of mistreatment and oppression.

Morrison's appropriation of the myth, while it preserves a clear connection to mythology concerning black flight's possibilities, divests the narrative of its essential communal impulses. In *Song of Solomon*, the empowered Afro-American's flight, celebrated in a blues song whose decoding catapults Milkman into self-conscious maturity, is a solitary one; in other words, the discovery of the means of transcendence—the liberating black word—is not shared with the tribe. He leaves his loved ones, including his infant son Jake, whom he tries unsuccessfully to carry with him, with the task of attempting to learn for themselves the secrets of transcendence. The failure of Solomon's efforts to transport Jake along with him, in fact, serves to emphasize the ultimately individualistic nature of the mythic figure's flight. And while the narrative suggests that the offspring of the legendary Solomon do not perceive themselves as negatively affected by his act—they, in fact, construct praise songs in recognition of his accomplishments—his mate Ryna, who bears his twenty-one children, is so aggrieved at her loss that she goes mad. (Her grief, like Solomon's transcendent act, assumes legendary proportions in the history of Milkman's people.)

The conflict between the archetypal and the "new" in *Song of Solomon*, then, is of particular significance where gender is concerned because, as is generally the case in Western mythic systems, including the genre of the epic, Morrison's updated version suggests that masculinity has become a virtual prerequisite for participation in transcendent action. In this respect, Morrison's appropriation differs significantly from Lester's version of the traditional myth where flight is delineated not as an individual, but as a communal act, an act not limited to the biologically male.

An analysis which suggests, either implicitly or explicitly, that the novel's inscription of an ideology of race is privileged over its figurations of a politics of gender cannot capture the complexities of Morrison's mythic narrative. For, despite Morrison's ambiguous claim, recorded in this essay's epigraph, that she writes "without gender focus," her attraction to the "unruly" features of "women's imagination," which can "bring things to the surface that men—trained to be men in a certain way—have difficulty getting access to," inspires her demonstration of certain masculinist features of mythic narrative specifically and of cultural practice generally. The text of *Song of Solomon* serves as a wonderfully appropriate site for a black feminist criticism—for a discourse attuned to the intersections between afrocentric and feminist ideologies.

Such an analysis needs to be preceded, however, by a discussion of the relationship between myth and ideology which might inform our comprehension of their intersections in Morrison, and by a brief exploration of the largely androcentric epic tradition whose masculinist biases the "unruly" black and female author critically revises.

II

The folklorist Alan Dundes has suggested that "myth is a sacred narrative explaining how the world and man came to be in their present form." But if myth, as Dundes argues, possesses an origin-clarifying function, its articulation also provides a means of explaining how man and woman can cope, in a culturally-approved fashion, with difficulties wrought in the present by natural and supernatural forces. The mythic/epic hero's merits, and the quality of his achievements, are measured in terms of what George deForest

Lord calls "the success of the hero in search of himself and his success in restoring or preserving his culture." Consequently, myth's function is to contribute to the maintenance of the norms and values of the culture out of which "sacred narrative" emerges.

Richard Stotkin's recent work illuminates the ideological underpinnings of myth. He defines myth as a "body of traditional stories that have . . . been used to summarize the course of our collective history and to assign ideological meanings to that history," and analyzes the essentially ideological function of myth in the following way:

> the terms "myth" and "ideology" describe essential attributes of every human culture. Ideology is an abstraction of the system of beliefs, values, and institutional relationships that characterize a particular culture or society; mythology is the body of traditional narratives that exemplifies and historicizes ideology. Myths are stories, drawn from history, that have acquired through usage over many generations a symbolizing function central to the culture of the society that produces them. Through the processes of traditionalization historical narratives are conventionalized and abstracted, and their range of reference is extended so that they become structural metaphors containing all the essential elements of a culture's world view. . . . [M]yths suggest that by understanding and imaginatively reenacting the conflict resolutions of the past, we can interpret and control the unresolved conflicts of the present.

Myths, then, are implicitly ideological in their conveyance and advocacy of their culture's belief systems in symbolic forms that are both historically significant and immediately relevant. To use Morrison's phrase, they inform their culture's inhabitants "how to behave" in a time-tested, culturally-approved, manner.

Stotkin's sense of myth's implicitly ideological function of "defining and defending [the society's] pattern of values" accords with Morrison's own formulations concerning mythic narratives. Arguing that fiction "must be political" in order to be of value to society, Morrison insists that novels have always "provided social rules and explained behavior, identified outlaws, identified the people, habits, and customs that one should approve of." Apparently, her interest in myth derives, at least in part, from an awareness of myth's usefulness in the transmission of ideology and in the preservation of cultural wisdom, values, and world views.

Morrison's position as black and female, however, problematizes her relation to myth because of the fact that traditional myths, like most other cultural forms preserved from an androcentric past, tend to inscribe as part of their truth a subordinate and inferior status for women. While a close examination of Morrison's corpus dicourages a reading of her work as radically feminist, clearly the author's novels are infused with a consistently female-centered perspective. Such an ideological stance leads Morrison to confront the sometimes virulently phallocentric nature of traditional Western myths, including Afro-American ones. Indeed, Gerry Brenner's essay on *Song of Solomon* asserts that Morrison ironically applies, and forcefully rejects, the (masculinist) monomythic prinicples delineated by Otto Rank. Brenner's astute perceptions concerning Morrison's comprehension of the sexism inherent in the epic suggest the appropriateness of an analysis of the ways in which the novelist's woman-centered ideology complicates her use of (afrocentric) myth.

Such an analysis is facilitated by the formulations of feminist critic Rachel DuPlessis, particularly her discussion of contemporary women writers' manipulation of traditional myth. DuPlessis, who has argued that twentieth-century women's literature is characterized by manifestly ideological efforts to create narrative strategies "that express the critical dissent from dominant [androcentric] narrative," says of the female confrontation of traditional mythological forms:

> When a woman writer chooses myth as her subject, she is faced with material that is indifferent or, more often, actively hostile to historical considerations of gender, claiming as it does universal, humanistic, natural, or even archetypal status. To face myth as a woman writer is, putting things at their most extreme, to stand at the impact point of a strong system of interpretation masked as representation, and to rehearse one's own colonization or "iconization" through the materials one's culture considers powerful and primary.

Joseph Campbell's discussion in the classic study *The Hero with a Thousand Faces* of women's roles within the male monomyth confirms DuPlessis's assertions concerning female exclusion as subject from sacred narrative. Campbell suggests (although without the sense of censure that informs DuPlessis's formulations) the following:

> Woman, in the picture language of mythology, represents the totality of what can be known. The hero is the one who comes to know. . . . Woman is the guide to the sublime acme of sensuous adventure. By deficient eyes she is reduced to inferior

states; by the evil eye of ignorance she is spellbound to banality and ugliness. But she is redeemed by the eye of understanding. The hero who can take her as she is, without undue commotion but with the kindness and assurance she requires, is potentially the king, the incarnate god, of her created world.

According to Campbell, the informing principles of myth inscribe woman as supplement and object, as a lesser being "redeemed" by the heroic male "eye of understanding," as one who requires male "kindness and assurance" to escape pejorative evaluations of her character and being.

Clearly, Campbell's influential formulations demonstrate the virtual impossibility of an uncritical contemporary female author's employment of traditional myth. For, in his discussion and apparent advocacy, for instance, of the Adamic myth of woman's origins inside man, Campbell validates the phallocentric myth that women's role is to complete—to make whole—the heretofore psychologically fragmented and defeminized male hero. The mythic (and historical) role of the female as supplement, then, reflects androcentric ideology in ways which suggest the utter difficulty and manifest dangers for female writers of employing traditional myths in uncritical ways. To do so is, in DuPlessis's words, "to rehearse one's own colonization or 'iconization.' "

White female wirters who feel altogether excluded from and subjugated by traditioanl Western sacred narratives view these myths' radical subversion as a means of "delegitimating the specific narrative and cultural orders of [the past]." For such writers, among whome DuPlessis counts Adrienne Rich, Sylvia Plath, and Margaret Atwood, the goal of myth's appropriation is both a critique of the phallocentric nature of traditional myth and the creation of possibilities for female-centered myths with woman as hero and subject.

However, for an afrocentric female writer like Morrison who, despite its frequent phallocentrism, sees great value in Afro-American sacred narrative, the employment of traditional myth is problematic because of the necessity of affirming the ideological perspectives of these narratives which clearly demonstrate her advocacy of afrocentric ideology, while simultaneously condemning myth's general failure to inscribe the possibilities of a full female participation as subject in the story of black American self-actualization and cultural preservation.

Its success at navigating between these ideological terrains suggests that *Song of Solomon* neither falls outside of the womanist and afrocentric concerns of Morrison's other 1970s novels, nor does it, as Susan Willis has asserted in a provocative analysis of Morrison's corpus, serve to "reinvent the notion of patrimony that emerges even as [Milkman] puts together his genealogy." To read *Song of Solomon* in terms of its informing ideologies facilitates the reader's discernment of the ways in which the novel offers a disruption of the androcentric sequence of both Western sacred narrative in general, and specifically, of (appropriated) Afro-American myth.

III

Morrison's appropriation of the monomyth is, indeed, quite subtle, a subtlety suggested by the relative lack of extended critical comment about her choice of a male protagonist. Despite the clearly female-centered nature of her earlier novels, *The Bluest Eye* and *Sula*, critics generally have been remarkably untroubled by Morrison's creation of an apparently andro-centric narrative. Such an untroubled response is manifest even in Genevieve Fabre's essay on the novel, despite the fact that this essay begins by situating Morrison in a continuum of black female writers who attempt "to achieve literacy . . . [and] freedom," and argues that "Black women writers call attention to the distinctiveness of their experiences and vision" by composing works "deliberately disruptive and disturbing in their bold investigations [that] are part of a struggle against all forms of authority." Although the essay demonstrates an acute understanding of Morrison's afro-centric and feminist concerns, Fabre proceeds to offer a reading of *Song of Solomon* which concentrates almost exclusively on Milkman's "genealogical archaeology," and virtually ignores the problematics of gender as a major consideration. Fabre's curious reticence about gender in her analysis of Morrison's novel, however, does encourage a crucial question: how does what she calls Morrison's "dramatiz[ation of] an archetypal journey across ancestral territory" really reflect, where it pertains to the insights Fabre offers in her introductory contextualization of the novelist's ideological aims, "the essential significance of [black female] *difference*"?

An answer to this question is not quickly forthcoming, for in addition to what critics have generally read as Morrison's inscription of a priv-ileged maleness in *Song of Solomon*, several of her own comments seem intended to discourage analyses of her work whose orientation is primarily—and limitedly—feminist. In "Rootedness," for example, she says, in response to a question concerning "the necessity to develop a specific black feminist model of critical inquiry": "I think there is more danger in it than fruit, because any model of criticism or evaluation that excludes males from it is as hampered as any model of criticism of Black literature that excludes women from it." Perhaps even more inhibiting to a limitedly feminist reading of *Song of Solomon* are comments she offers to explain the roots of Hagar's ultimately debilitating problems, despite her possession of a wonderously self-actualized mentor—her grandmother Pilate. Morrison says of Hagar:

> The difficulty that Hagar . . . has is how far removed she is from the experience of her ancestor. Pilate had a dozen years of close, nurturing relationships with two males—her father and her brother. And that intimacy and support was in her and made her fierce and loving because she had that experience. Her daughter Reba had less of that and related to men in a very shallow way. Her daughter [Hagar] had even less of an association with men as a child, so that the progression is really a diminishing of their abilities because of the absence of men in a nourishing way in their lives. Pilate is the apogee of all that: of the best of that which is female and the best of that which is male, and that balance is disturbed if it is not nurtured, and if it is not counted on and if it is not reproduced. That is the disability we must be on guard against for the future—the female who reproduces the female who reproduces the female.

Morrison rejects the feminist idea(l) of exclusively female communities as the best means of maximizing possibilities of black female psychic and emotional health. Indeed, the question of (gender-specific) exclusion is profoundly important to Morrison's formulations here, for it serves as her motivation for both assertions about the potential dangers of a narrowly focused black feminist criticism and, in her reading of incidents in *Song of Solomon*, for the ultimate demise of Hagar. Clearly, for Morrison, black female psychic health cannot be achieved without the cooperative participation of both females and males in its creation and nurturance. Indeed, male participation helps to provide the novice female with a sense of "balance" between "the best of that which is female and the best of that which is male" without which gendered and tribal health is, for Morrison, quite unlikely.

Such comments might be read as confirmation of Willis's aforementioned assertion that *Song of Solomon* "tends to reinvent the notion of patrimony." However, the novel's complex employment of afrocentric and feminist ideologies can be more fruitfully read in terms of DuPlessis's formulations with respect to contemporary women writers' efforts to disrupt traditional androcentric narrative sequences and strategies. According to DuPlessis, contemporary women writers' work is committed to "rupturing language and tradition sufficiently to invite a female slant, emphasis, or approach," and to "deligitimating specific narrative and cultural orders of [the past]." I want to argue here that Morrison's appropriations of the monomyth and of Afro-American sacred narrative are motivated by such rupturing, deligitimating impulses.

I will further explore hereafter the sense of narrative rupture and breakage implicit in Morrison's appropriations of the male monomyth, focusing on two crucial aspects of the novel: 1) Morrison's literal breaking of Milkman's male heroic quest with the specifically antithetical story of Hagar's demise, and 2) the particular implications of the narrative of Solomon's flight.

IV

In order to fully discuss Morrison's manipulation of the privileged text of mythic (male) transcendence, I must begin with a brief delineation of the particulars of Milkman's journey. Milkman's quest is undertaken initially to provide him access to gold he believes Pilate has left behind as a means of securing a lasting economic and emotional self-sufficiency. In other words, his quest is inspired by an urge to avoid emotional commitment and familial responsibility:

> He just wanted to beat a path away from his parents' past, which was also their present and which was threatening to become his present as well. He hated the acridness in his mother's and father's relationship, the conviction of righteousness they each held on to with both hands. And his efforts to ignore it, transcend it, seemed to work only when he spent his days looking for what- ever was light-hearted and without grave consequences. He avoided commitment and strong feelings, and shied away from decisions. He wanted to know as little as possible, to feel only enough to warrant the curiosity of other people—but not their all-consuming devotion. Hagar had given him this last and more drama than he could ever want again.

Milkman's journey begins, then, as an effort to gain freedom from obligation to others by taking possession of a familial treasure. Instead of gold, however, what he finds, after a series of episodes which conform to traditional monomythic paradigms for the male hero who has been called to adventure, is a mature sense of his familial obligations, an informed knowl- edge of familial (and tribal) history, and a profound comprehension of tribal wisdom. His newly-achieved knowledge of self and culture is manifested dramatically during the course of an intitatory trial-by-fire in Shalimar in which black male elders invite the bourgeois urbanite on a long, arduous hunting trek, and then leave the novice hunter behind to fend for himself. Forced to use his wits to navigate a forest filled with wild animals, Milkman considers the treatment he has received since his arrival, and, more importantly, the ways he has (mis)treated others. Asking himself, "What kind of savages were these people," and believing momentarily that "he had done nothing to deserve their contempt," a significantly more introspective Milkman recognizes the necessity of abandoning such immature perspectives:

> It sounded old. Deserve. Old and tired and beaten to death. Deserve. Now it seemed to him that he was always saying or thinking that he didn't deserve some bad luck, or some bad treatment from others. He'd told Guitar that he didn't even "deserve" his family's dependence, hatred, or whatever. That he didn't even "deserve" to hear all the misery and mutual accusations his parents unloaded on him. Nor did he "deserve" Hagar's vengeance. But why shouldn't his parents tell him their personal problems? If not him, then who? And if a stranger could try to kill him, surely Hagar, who knew him and whom he'd thrown away like a wad of chewing gum after the flavor was gone—she had a right to try to kill him too.

His achievement of a radically reconceptualized view of self and family, and of his responsibilities thereto, occurs when, near the end of his ancestral quest, he is overcome by a feeling of homesickness as he listens to a group of Shalimar children singing "that old blues song Pilate sang all the time: 'O Sugarman don't leave me here.'" This homesickness is accompanied by, and is, indeed, a function of, a more mature and complete awareness of the factors which motivated his family's behavior. He comprehends, for example, that his mother's eccentricities—including the fact that she nursed him well past an age that such a practice was necessary for his nourishment—are in part the result of "sexual deprivation": "now it seemed to him that such sexual deprivation would affect her, hurt her in precisely the way it would affect and hurt him." Subsequently, he wonders "What might she have been like had her husband loved her?" Further, he begins to understand the source of his father's perversely acquisitive nature:

> As the son of Macon Dead the first, [his father] paid homage to his own father's life and death by loving what that father had loved: property, good solid property, the bountifulness of life. He loved these things to excess. Owning, building, acquiring—that was his life, his future, his present, and all the history he knew.

That he distorted life, bent it, for the sake of gain, was a measure
of his loss at his father's death.

In addition to comprehending the ridiculousness of hating his parents
and sisters, and being overcome with a "thick" "skin of shame" for "having
stolen from Pilate," he turns his thoughts to Hagar, the person whose life his
selfishness has most seriously affected. Wondering why he had not exercised
more sensitivity in ending their relationship, he sees that his egotistical
masculinist treatment of Hagar had extended even to his response to her
hysterical attempts to end his life:

> He had used her—her love, her craziness—and most of all he
> had used her skulking, bitter vengeance. It made him a star, a
> celebrity in the Blood Bank; it told men and other women that
> he was one bad dude, that he had the power to drive a woman
> out of her mind, to destroy her, and not because she hated him,
> or because he had done some unforgivable thing to her, but
> because he had fucked her and she was driven wild by the
> absence of his magnificent joint.

A thoughtful and less self-protective appraisal of his personal history,
motivated by the trials and tribulations that constitute his heroic ordeal and
which include his rejection of an injuriously materialistic perspective, forces
Milkman to comprehend the serious errors of his self-centered ways. Like
the tradtional monomythic hero, he achieves a sense of his identity which is
firmly rooted in his relationship to his family and community. For he has
learned, in short, that he can achieve a sense of self only when he is able to
embrace his unavoidable responsibilities to family and humanity, when he
can recognize and relish a sense of membership with his people. Liberated
from the shallow and selfish perspectives which had previously characterized
him, Milkman has, in short, ended his division from self and tribe and
become whole, has achieved a "coming together . . . into a total self."

Ultimately, Milkman, whose gender permits Morrison to construct the
narrative of his ancestral quest in general compliance with the parameters of
the classical monomyth, is able to perform the culture-preserving service
necessary for the maintenance of his community. In accordance with the
requirements for the successful monomythic hero, he returns to his
Michigan community to share what he has decoded of the sacred narrative's
cryptic lyrics with a family hopelessly divided by decades of mistrust and
perverse mistreatment of one another. Milkman's odyssey confirms the accu-
racy of his father's previous conflation of selfhood and knowledge. Earlier,

when Milkman intervenes in a psychologically and physically violent dispute between his mother and father by striking Macon Dead II, his father says to him: "You a big man now, but big ain't nearly enough. You have to be a whole man. And if you want to be a whole man, you have to deal with the whole truth." Having investigated, in a seemingly thorough manner, his ancestral heritage, Milkman learns a good deal of "the whole truth," which provides him access to what Joseph Campbell calls "the unquenched source through which society is reborn." An achieved sense of wholeness and access to the "unquenched source"—in particular, the history of the Dead clan; more generally, Afro-American culture, and its timeless truths—allows Milkman to embark on the mono-mythic hero's "second task and deed:" "to return to [his 'disintegrating society'] transfigured, and teach the lesson he has learned of life renewed."

Those lessons, however transformative and powerful, cannot alter the most chilling consequence of his former "disintegrat[ed] psyche": his mistreatment of Hagar, and her ultimate death. Concurrent with Milkman's achievement of indispensable awareness of self and culture is Hagar's painful quest to achieve bourgeois American society's standards of female beauty. Indeed, Milkman's and Hagar's gendered situations in a patriarchal system ultimately delimit their journey's very nature and success.

V

Chapter 13 of *Song of Solomon*, which records the circumstances surrounding Hagar's death, offers a literal—and strategic—breaking of the male mono-mythic sequence. The structure of Morrison's novel encourages a contrast between Milkman's (male) monomythic quest for self and community, and Hagar's deathward march toward what Susan Willis has identified as reification. This juxtaposition is, in fact, quite striking. For example, the journeys of both characters are embarked upon as a consequence of their attitudes about bourgeois capitalist values. Milkman, whom Morrison is able to write into the traditional (male) epic quest plot, seeks to escape his environment not because its bourgeois values are oppressive, but because they demand a psychic involvement and sense of empathy for which he is clearly unpre-pared. On the other hand, Hagar's journey to reification and, ultimately, physical death, has its source in her adoption of a patriarchal society's almost timeless figuration of woman as object, in her futile attempt to achieve the bourgeois society's notions of female beauty. Having apparently inherited from her female forbear Ryna the capacity for immeasurable grief as a conse-quence of male abandonment, Hagar concludes, after gazing in a mirror at her own image, that Milkman's failure to love her is a function of her unglamorous, un-Cosmopolitan appearance.

Hagar's female status denies her entry as actor and subject to paradigmatic epic means of transcendence. Consequently, she is denied access to the transformative possibilities of a regenerative necessary distance from a corruptive mainstream American bourgeois value system. Because the mythic black narrative of communal transcendence is no longer extant—and has, in fact, been replaced by an individualistic and androcentric (familial) text—Hagar has no means of achieving a nurturing knowledge of self and culture that would make it possible for her to reject the debilitating tenets of what George deForest Lord calls "a destroyed city, a ruined culture." Hence, she can see possibilities for self-improvement only in the terms that a "ruined" bourgeois American society suggests are proper for her sex. In other words, in a society where female self-actualization is, by and large, impossible outside of the context of an interactive relationship with a man, Hagar's concentration on Milkman's unwillingness to love her is, however injurious, utterly logical. While Milkman comes to a marvelously useful comprehension of history, myth, and nature, Hagar's status as bound, in both the spatial and narrative senses of the phrase, to oppressive domestic plots—a virtual requirement for the abandoned female lover in the Western epic—precipitates a virtual dissociation of sensibility, and an acceptance of the bourgeois society's views of women. This acceptance is reflected particularly in her whole-hearted adoption of its ideas of female beauty.

It is specifically in terms of the image of female mirror gazing that Morrison figures the conclusion of Hagar's grief-inspired aphasia, and her discovery of what she believes is a means by which to rekindle Milkman's interest. When an almost catatonic Hagar sees herself in a compact mirror Pilate holds before her, she is convinced that she has found the source of Milkman's antipathy—her appearance:

> "No wonder," she said at last. "Look at that. No wonder. No wonder" . . . .
> "Look at how I look. I look awful. No wonder he didn't want me. I look terrible." Her voice was calm and reasonable, as though the last few days hadn't been lived through at all. "I need to get up from here and fix myself up. *No wonder!*" Hagar threw back the bedcover and stood up. "Ohhh. I smell too. Mama, heat me some water. I need a bath. . . . Oh Lord, my head. Look at that." She peered into the compact mirror again. "I look like a ground hog. Where's the comb?"

Hagar sets out enthusiastically to achieve the bourgeois society's ideal of beauty. Believing "I need everything" to transform her black difference—what she refers to as her "ground hog" appearance—into the bourgeois society's glamorous feminine ideal, she spends an entire business day "shopp[ing] for everything a woman could wear from the skin out." She purchases, among other things, "a Playtex garter belt, I. Miller No Color hose, Fruit of the Loom panties, . . . two nylon slips," an expensive Evan-Picone outfit, and cosmetics. Hers is a shameless act of commodity consumption, a desperate attempt to make herself into an incontestable example of feminine beauty in order to be worthy of Milkman's love. Her instruments of transformation are soaked and soiled, however, in a downpour of rain, and her efforts to employ these ripped clothes and rain-soaked cosmetics to re-make herself proves far from successful. Hagar understands this when she sees Pilate's and Reba's reaction to her appearance:

> it was in their eyes that she saw what she had not seen before in the mirror: the wet ripped hose, the soiled white dress, the sticky, lumpy face powder, the streaked rouge, and the wild wet shouls of hair. All this she saw in their eyes, and the sight filled her own with water warmer and much older than the rain.

Hagar comes to the bitter realization that her efforts to achieve American society's ideal of female beauty are utterly fruitless. Her brief, painful attempt to compensate for lacking the physical qualities of which she knows Milkman approves—"silky, [penny-colored] hair," "lemon-colored skin," "gray-blue eyes," and a "thin nose"—ends, not with transcendent knowledge of the world as does the male protagonist's epic journey, but, rather, with an awareness that her (ruined) society will never provide her opportunities for the types of transformations necessary to win the love of the man with whom she feels she belongs. Exhausted, and feeling the full hopelessness of her dilemma, she tells Pilate: "He's never going to like my hair."

Morrison interrupts Milkman's monomythic quest, or, in DuPlessis's phrase, breaks the (sacred) narrative sequence, in order to expose phallocentric myth's failure to inscribe usefully transcendent possibilities for the female. This interruption serves to problematize a strictly celebratory afrocentric analysis of Milkman's achievements. Such an analysis fails to permit focus on the clear presence of (female) pain that permeates *Song of Solomon*'s final chapters. Male culpability in the instigation of such pain is evident, for example, in Milkman's revelations about the motivations for his treatment of Hagar. He comes to understand that he "had used her—her love, her craziness—and most of all . . . her skulking, bitter vengeance" to achieve heroic—or what the narrative refers to as "star"—status.

Analyses of Morrison's novel must be attentive to both the transcendent joy of knowledge-informed male flight to the immeasurable pain of desertion felt by females like Hagar and Ryna, whose agony at the loss of Solomon "like to killed the woman" and was so profound at its intensity that "she screamed and screamed, lost her mind completely." Future readings must, in other words, acknowledge that the blues lyrics and the novel encode *both* an afrocentric appreciation of the power and importance of transcendence, and a convincing critique of the fact that, in the updated version of the myth, that power is essentially denied to Afro-American women. Morrison's appropriation of the myth approximates the narrative structures of phallocentric Western myths to the extent that males are figured as actors, while females are aggrieved, deserted, and—because of the culture's and, hence, the narrative form's, masculinist perspectives—permanently grounded objects. The ideological complexity of Morrison's representation of her woman-centered and afrocentric politics is suggested in the lyrics' inscription of transcendence and abandonment: "Solomon done fly, Solomon done gone."

VI

Morrison's delineation in her novel of feminist concerns is perhaps most clearly evident in the (predominantly) female voices of descent that operate in a censurous chorus in the last chapters of *Song of Solomon*. Shalimar females such as Susan Byrd and Sweet are, by and large, remarkably unimpressed by Solomon and by his transcendent act. Susan Byrd, in fact, openly criticizes him for his desertion of Ryna and his offspring. While Byrd recounts to Milkman the provocative aspects of Solomon's mythic flight—she tells Milkman, "according to the story, he . . . flew, like a bird. Just stood up in the fields one day, ran up some hill, spun around a couple of times, and was lifted up in the air. Went right on back to wherever it was he came from"—her narrative focuses primarily on the pain felt by others as a consequence of his desertion. Indeed, it is Susan Byrd who informs Milkman of the derivation of the name Ryna's Gulch: "sometimes you can hear this funny sound by [the gulch] that the wind makes. People say it's the wife. Solomon's wife, crying. Her name was Ryna." In addition to censurious assertions such as "he disappeared and left everybody," she comments further on the ramifications of his leave-taking flight:

"They say she screamed and screamed, lost her mind completely.
You don't hear about women like that anymore, but there used to

be more—the kind of woman who couldn't live without a particular man. And when the man left, they lost their minds, or died
or something. Love, I guess. But I always thought it was trying
to take care of children by themselves, you know what I mean?"

While we might rightly question here the reliability of Susan Byrd's "speculations"—for instance, the song of Solomon is no mere, negligible "old
folks' lie"; further, Hagar's response to Milkman's desertion is of a kind
with Ryna's, and her grief clearly has nothing to do with the difficulty of
single parenthood—certainly the reader can trust her recollections of the
particulars of the mythic narrative. That the reader should trust her view
of the magnitude of the deserted female's pain is confirmed by the reactions
of Sweet and, ultimately, of Milkman, to male acts of abandonment and
transcendence.

Milkman's archaeological act fills him with an "incredible high" under
whose influence he relates to his Shalimar lover Sweet the fact that he is a
descendent of Solomon. Having taken possession of his familial history—he
asserts proudly of the ring shout that accompanies the recitation of the song
of Solomon, "It's my game now"—he says of his forebear: "The son of a bitch
could fly! You hear me, Sweet? That motherfucker could fly! Could fly! He
didn't need no airplane. Didn't need no fuckin tee double you ay. He could
fly his own self!" Unimpressed by the knowledge of Milkman's royal
heritage—after all, as Susan Byrd tells him, "everybody around here claims
kin to him"—Sweet tries to force her lover to consider the consequences of
Jake's transcendent act by asking, "Who'd he leave behind?" Still mesmer-
ized by his status as descendant of such a magical figure, Milkman giddily
responds: "Everybody! He left everybody down on the ground and sailed on
off like a black eagle." It is only when he is forced to confront the consequences of his desertion of Hagar that he is capable of sensitivity to the
socially irresponsible nature of his ancestor's actions, and, further, of his own.

Such confrontation occurs when, upon his return to Michigan,
Milkman is exposed to male flight's significant, sometimes deadly, consequences. Recovering in Pilate's cellar from a blow by his justifiably angered
aunt which had rendered him unconscious, Milkman comes to understand
the tragic ironies of a phallocentric social (and narrative) structure which
fails to permit female access to the culture's sources of knowledge and
power. The narrative informs us of Milkman's revelations: "He had left her.
While he dreamt of flying, Hagar was dying." Milkman, who, despite his
infinite leap in knowledge, clearly still has much to learn, then recalls
Sweet's question about the victims of Solomon's departure, a question
which he had not seriously pondered previously. He begins to see a clear

connection between his act and that of his mythic forebear, the full impact of whose flight he can now understand:

> Sweet's silvery voice came back to him: "Who'd he leave behind?" He left Ryna behind and twenty children. Twenty-one, since he dropped the one he tried to take with him. And Ryna had thrown herself all over the ground, lost her mind, and was still crying in a ditch. Who looked after those twenty children? Jesus Christ, he left twenty-one children! . . . Shalimar left his, but it was the children who sang about it and kept the story of his leaving alive.

It is only at this point, when he learns the painful consequences of the cele-brated male act of flight, that Milkman's comprehension of his familial heritage and the song of Solomon can be said to move toward satisfying completion. Such understanding requires coming to terms with his familial song's complex, sometimes unflattering meaning, and acknowledging both its prideful flight and the lack of a sense of social responsibility in the mythic hero Solomon's leave-taking act.

Song of Solomon, then, is a record both of transcendent (male) flight and of the immeasurable pain that results for the female who, because of her lack of access to knowledge, cannot participate in this flight. In breaking the monomythic sequence, Morrison provides the possibilities for a resistant feminist reading which suggests the consequences of male epic journeys: the death-in-life, or actual death, or the female whose only permissible role is that of an aggrieved, abandoned lover.

Thus, an analysis that foregrounds not only Milkman's archaeological question, but also Hagar's disintegration—in other words, an afrocentric feminist reading of *Song of Solomon*—allows for an interpretation that most closely suggests the complexity of Morrison's appropriation of the epic form and the Afro-American folktale. Such an analysis is necessary, in fact, if we are to comprehend the black and feminist poetics which inform not only *Song of Solomon*, but the author's entire corpus. Rather than reinventing patrimony, Morrison's novel affirms the timeless relevance of the myth's insistence on the importance of transcendent flight as implicitly phallocen-tric in their inscription of a perpetually inferior—non-"heroic"—status for the female.

Morrison's male epic does not represent a break with the female-centered concerns of works such as *The Bluest Eye* and *Sula*, but is a bold extension of these concerns in a confrontation with the tenets of Western literature's most "sacred narrative" form. Like Guitar, who insists that he has earned the right to censurous analyses of the actions of Afro-Americans, Morrison's text asks, in effect, "can't I criticize what I love?" While she dearly wishes to preserve the wonder and wisdom of black culture, Morrison perceives the need to invest the preserved forms of culture with "new information." If cultures generally are not static but are in the process of continual and dynamic development, clearly Afro-American culture, if it is to be valuable in the present as a means of explaining a rapidly changing world in which women are increasingly important and influential actors, cannot continue to produce perspectives which lead to the further creation of narratives that trivialize or marginalize the female. Such recognition does not mean a replacement of afrocentric ideology with feminism, but the creation of spaces that will allow for their necessary and potentially fruitful interaction. In that sense, *Song of Solomon* not only reflects the perspectives of Afro-American culture, but seeks to contribute in significant ways to its transformation.

JAN STRYZ

Inscribing an Origin in Song of Solomon

Toni Morrison's statements concerning her own writing express an aesthetic that repudiates the authority claimed by or for certain literary texts. She self-consciously, habitually "avoid[s] . . . literary references, unless oblique and based on written folklore," she says, "not only because I refused the credentials they bestow, but also because they are inappropriate to the kind of literature I wish to write. . . ." Her writing involves "a compact with the reader not to reveal an already established reality (literary or historical) that he or she and I agree upon beforehand." Expression of the "received reality of the West" involves assuming an authority that is patronizing to the reader. Instead she seeks to "centralize and animate information discredited by the West . . . information dismissed as 'lore' or 'gossip' or 'magic' or 'sentiment.' " Her text "cannot be the authority—it should be the map" and "should make a way for the reader (audience) to participate in the tale." Ultimately, her repudiation of traditional literary authority is designed to bring the reader into an innocent relation with the text: "I want [the reader] to respond on the same plane as an illiterate or preliterate reader would. I want to subvert his traditional comfort so that he may experience an unorthodox one: that of being in the company of his own solitary imagination."

This mirrors her desire for a process of engendering her own text that is similarly innocent: "I sometimes think how glorious it must have been to

From *Studies in American Fiction* 19, no. 1 (Spring 1991). © 1991 Northeastern University.

have written drama in sixteenth-century England, or poetry in ancient Greece, or religious narrative in the Middle Ages, when literature . . . did not have a critical history to constrain or diminish the writer's imagination." With a formal education in literature that concentrated on canonical texts, included a minor in classics, and culminated in a master's thesis on Faulkner and Woolf, though, she is hardly unfettered by a critical literary history. But *Song of Solomon* specifically illustrates how she negotiates the obstacles imposed by the task of freeing her own story from a literary past.

Pilate is introduced in *Song of Solomon* singing the song to which the title refers. But she makes a mistake in the lyrics, substituting "Sugarman" for "Solomon," an apparent displacement of a biblical reference that might seem understandable in an illiterate. Thus the reader compounds Pilate's error with traditional literary assumptions. As Jane Campbell notes, "Morrison lures the reader into expecting a fictionalization of the Biblical song of Solomon but replaces Christian associations with African ones." Pilate's mistake stems from a fragmented oral tradition, not an ignorance of a written text. The recovery of that uninscribed tradition is the project that re-generates identity for Pilate and Milkman in *Song of Solomon* and is the project inscribed within the text itself. So Morrison in this sense produces an "original" written text that fictionally creates its own unwritten source while also affirming the value of unwritten tradition.

Not that the biblical reference is made merely to tease the reader and be abandoned: Morrison says that in *Song of Solomon* she "used the biblical names to show the impact of the Bible on the lives of black people, their awe of it and respect for it coupled with their ability to distort it for their own purposes." Literary reference possesses a serious power that is appropriate to play with in the creation of identity.

The dynamics of such distortion reveal themselves in Pilate's father's selection of her name:

> Confused an melancholy over his wife's death in childbirth, [he] had thumbed through the Bible, and since he could not read a word, chose a group of letters that seemed to him strong and handsome; saw in them a large figure that looked like a tree hanging in some princely but protective way over a row of smaller trees.
>
> He had copied the group of letters out on a piece of brown paper; copied, as illiterate people do, every curlicue, arch, and bend in the letters, and presented it to the midwife.

Macon Dead, Sr. does not merely ignore the traditional meaning of a particular written sign; he redefines writing, allowing inscribed characters to speak
through their own physical characteristics. And his mode of choosing, his
manner of reading, is a creative gesture affirmed even in the face of the
midwife's protests ove the unacceptability of naming a baby daughter after "a
Christ-killing Pilate." For the midwife, the meaning of the name is fixed
within its traditional written context, and that scrap of paper grotesquely
marked should be returned to the "Devil's flames" from where it came. She
represents a fundamentalist viewpoint that sees the impulse to read outside
sanctioned tradtion as potentially dangerous and therefore evil; the name of
an evil can only be safely contained by authority, and to let it loose in the
world may open a sort of Pandora's box. In his literary innocence, Macon, Sr.
does not regard the text as inviolable, however. The present occasion, the
naming of the baby, is the primary context here and determines the word's
present meaning. At the moment he selects it, and even as he physically
copies its form, the name and its referent mirror a mutual innocence.

   Literary associations touch the name only after Macon, Sr. learns of
them, and even then only indirectly, through his implicit reinterpretation of
the biblical story within the context of his own situation:

> " . . . You don't want to give this motherless child the name
> of the man that killed Jesus, do you?"
>   "I asked Jesus to save my wife."
>   "Careful, Macon."
>   "I asked him all night long."

Verging on blasphemy, his statement simply places Jesus' identification as
"savior" in the context of his wife's death; there, the identification collapses.
And since Jesus would not save his wife's life, his retrospective indifference
to preserving Jesus' life would seem merely balancing to him. "Pilate" here
signifies Christ-killer only in the tacit way that Macon's affirmation of the
selection of that name denies Jesus' authority. His second, less innocent,
reading of his selection also thus simultaneously acknowledges and repudiates the textual source of the name.

   Curiously, Macon, Sr. insists on putting the piece of paper back in the
Bible: "It come from the Bible. It stays in the Bible." This act of apparent
veneration for the integrity of the text is rendered ironic by Macon's unconventional reading. Of course the Bible must have symbolic significance for
him, or he would not have consulted it in the first place. But through this act
the name, clearly for him a physical entity and not just either sign or symbol,
remains connected to its physical origin. Pilate the child is thus physically

kept distinct from Pilate the textual entity, even though the placement of the scrap of paper symbolically links her to the text.

Pilate herself must complete the process of naming that her father, in his equivocal relation to the authority of this most patriarchal of texts, could not complete. So after his murder, when she is twelve, she claims the name, removing the scrap of paper with the only thing he had ever written from the book, placing it in a small brass snuffbox that had belonged to her mother, and fashioning the box into an earring that she thereafter always wears. The tactile quality that her father had conferred on the name is retained and extended through this new set of physical associations. "Pilate" becomes in a more immediate sense the name her father gave her at the same time that it is physically distanced from its literary source. Its literal and figurative associations converge in Pilate herself, now that she wears the name in both a figurative and literal sense. Further, containing the name in her mother's snuffbox replaces it within an ancestrally significant space that she creates. Joining the two personal mementos available to her, she breaks the link that still symbolically bound the name to its literary past. Finally, the ear-piercing operation provides the bodily space through which she links herself to her parental "house."

Now she embodies the oral significance of her name, the meaning her father gathered when he first heard from the midwife what he had written: "Like a riverboat pilot?" In danger because a witness to her father's murder, she sets out towards Virginia, where she thinks she might find her father's or her mother's people, stays briefly with a preacher's family, is forced to leave, and departs with a geography book. Again she heads towards Virginia, living a migrant life, finally settling for a time in an island community off the coast of Virginia, where she has a baby. Then,

> when Reba was two years old, Pilate was seized with restlessness. It was as if her geography book had marked her to roam the country, planting her feet in each pink, yellow, blue or green state. She left the island and began the wandering life that she kept up for the next twenty-some-odd years, and stopped only after Reba had a baby.

In the course of her self-inscription, she has adopted her own textual influence, which now marks her. Non-literary, it is not intrusive or directive but merely maps the space over which she can freely play out her narrative. She also becomes a character in an unwritten book here, "planting her feet in each pink, yellow, blue or green state," tracing a fresh story through her action. The sensory and spatial nature of this book provides a field where text and life can enter into a fruitful relationship.

Empty of any temporal dimension, and exempt from participation in any literary tradition, her book provides neither an artificial past nor any clue that will help Pilate weave together the narrative of her own past. She is, in a sense, caught in the dimensions of her own originality. So she moves forward, negotiating the social obstacles raised by her physical oddness, the lack of a navel. This sign of separation from her own physical origins reflects her process of self-birthing, of "inch[ing] . . . headfirst out of a still, silent, and indifferent cave of flesh," the womb of her already dead mother. Physically sealed, self-contained, she seems diabolically unnatural to the members of the black community who discover her difference, and thus the implicit apprehensions of the midwife concerning her name appear fulfilled: She is the embodied name of an evil, a transgressor of both spirit and flesh escaped not only from the proper enclosure of a sanctified text but also from a womb not authorized by nature to produce life. The misreading of Pilate by the community effects an isolation in the present that reinforces her isolation from her past. In fact the name she must conceal now is her family name, for she had learned that "the last name had a bad effect on people." When she did venture "to ask if anybody knew of a family called Dead," "people frowned and said, 'No, never heard of any such.'" Though she bears a metaphoric representation of her ancestry on her person, she cannot read the symbolic contents of the snuffbox any more than her father could its literal one. She is thus sealed off from the present community, from her ancestral past, and so in a certain way from herself.

Both a combined character in and author of her own narrative, she stills the temporal flow of her wanderings by locating her consciousness in the present, gathering her various experiences into herself, and, in processing experience, reinscribing the world in terms of her own character:

> Although she was hampered by huge ignorances, but not in any way unintelligent, when she realized what her situation in the world was and would probably always be she threw away every assumption she had learned and began at zero. . . . Then she tackled the problem of trying to decide how she wanted to live and what was valuable to her. When am I happy and when am I sad and what is the difference? What do I need to know to stay alive? What is true in the world?

Just as her social alienation precipitates this introspection, her double perspective as pariah—outcast within an outcast community—enables her to mirror the black psyche. So through the process of self-inscription, she also inscribes an identity for her community; Milkman, wondering what Reba's last name is, says "I'll ask Pilate. Pilate knows. It's in that dumb-ass box hanging from her ear. Her own name and everybody else's." She employs a specular, not a written, form of recording in taking the measure of the community's character, however, and manages not to violate others with her unusual gaze:

> Her respect for other people's privacy . . . was balancing. She stared at people, and in those days looking straight into another person's eyes was considered among black people the height of rudeness, an act acceptable only with and among children and certain kinds of outlaws—but she never made an impolite observation.

Her "alien's compassion for troubled people," concern with human relationships, and capacities as healer and peacemaker all give a benevolent, even nurturing, tone to the gaze in contrast to *The Bluest Eye*, which concludes that "the loved one is shorn, neutralized, frozen in the glare of the lover's inward eye."

Pilate's visionary look, untainted by common qualities, becomes a vehicle through which she can contain and express the character of the black community while still remaining separate. She functions as a female version of the mythic hero, a literary "original" embodying a maternal stature that goes against conventional conceptions of motherhood to include familiarity with violence, a de-centered home life, physical strength, and individuality. But she goes beyond the role of mere character to function as a figure for the text, specifically an "original" text unrelated to the biblical text from which she derives her written existence. Reading and inscribing the world through the senses, marked by experience, she becomes a lived text. There is a sense of narrative, a temporal dimension to her wanderings, but self-enclosure and emphasis on the present moment subordinate this movement and make the figure Pilate into a representation of form itself, removed from the constraints of the past. Figured again in the snuffbox, the text "Pilate" is not a chaos-breeding escapee of that other box-like enclosure, the sacred book, but its own womb of significance.

But as character she cannot advance the overall plot of the novel precisely because of her ignorance of her past. Placing things in the context of her own present experience, she misinterprets her ghostly father's statements, thereby ironically supplying the pieces that will provide the narrative its impetus. She responds to his "Sing, Sing" by singing. She retrieves what she thinks are the bones of the white man her brother killed when her father's ghost tells her "you can't just fly on off and leave a body."

It requires Milkman, a character concerned with the future but disturbed by and forced to confront retrograde movement, to discover the identity of those pieces. Being forced to look out the back window of his father's car as a child in order to see anything "was like flying blind, and not knowing where he was going—just where he had been—troubled him." His flight South in search of the gold he believes Pilate left behind leads to the resurrection of the family name "Solomon" omitted from Pilate's song, the identification of "Sing" as Pilate's mother, the discovery that the sack she had carried and kept for so many years contained her father's bones. Thus the name blank, which had been mistakenly filled in "Dead" on a registration form by a white man—and so had remained a dead blank, a careless inscription that was actually an erasure, which Pilate's mother said "'would wipe out the past'"—is finally filled with a narrative formed around a song.

Morrison's general efforts to "remove the print-quality of language" in order "to put back the oral quality" and "make the reader see the colors and hear the sounds" are specifically played out in *Song of Solomon*. While this leads to emphasis on experience, it involves more than a return to simple mimesis and representation of reality, though it has been suggested that this quality characterizes current black women's fiction. Slippage of meaning takes place, but not within a system that defines itself exclusively in terms of "writing;" written narrative escapes its own form through the conscious use of writing, through subversion of literary elements and intended meaning by (written) characters within the text. The accidental meaning generated by "preliterate" characters' seeming mistakes in reading the significance of either written or oral texts comprises a visionary writing that would seem by its arbitrary and personal nature to prevent the coherent linkage of its component pieces. But rather than producing a chaotic text, the narrative line curves back towards itself, finds an origin, and so completes a circle, creating closure. Milkman's return to the site of the family name—and the name is inextricable from its site—effects more than just his discovery or even appropriation of the name; it effects his empowerment. But whether the name can contain the significance of the family history, whether the power of that meaning is, rather, located in the physical place, or whether Milkman himself generates meaning and power as a product of his journey, are irrelevant questions. These all exist in a reciprocal relation that liberates the Dead clan from a derivative written existence.

As a first-born son in the family line, Milkman—or Macon Dead III—did not have his name selected from the Bible, as did all the other family members born since Pilate. Free from any association with that particular text, he can recover the names belonging to the oral tradition which the biblical names had supplanted since the family had become "Dead." Further, he transforms the name "Dead" itself. Previously a sign signifying merely a lack of significance, it is incorporated into the body of his own experience at the narrative's end. The leap into "the killing arms of his brother," following the offer "you want my life? . . . Here," is his realization of the legend woven into his ancestral name; the "surrender to the air" that makes possible his dream of flight is enacted within the space that is the face of death. The names "Solomon," "Shalimar," and even "Dead" all at once become his own.

Yet this return to origins involves a crafted sort of innocence. That is, either the accidental generation of a plot that leads the Deads innocently to their origins has a meaningful pattern that suggests the presence of an author or else the reader more innocently assumes that the play of meaning occuring within a closed system—in this case the family and its community— leads naturally to its source. Just as Morrison's craftsmanship simultaneously calls attention to and repudiates the presence of an author in *Song of Solomon*, it echoes the biblical "Song of Songs" in such a way as to deny the authority of the earlier text.

In the course of her writing, Morrison places that preliterate reader she wants as her audience within the text as character: "Whenever I feel uneasy about my writing, I think: what would be the response of the people in the book if they read the book? . . . Those are the people for whom I write." This gesture also creates the illusion of an authorless text, in that the characters become the creators of their own narrative when they are made to function as both actors and readers. Locating the origin of the family name within *Song of Solomon* reinforces this illusion by asserting that the family's own identity and significance are to be found within the story they enact.

The relation between "Song of Songs" and *Song of Solomon* is more notable for structural reasons than thematic ones. In "Song of Songs," the bride begins by addressing her "song of all songs to Solomon" in one variation, which suggests that Solomon may be the bridegroom who answers her. In another variation of the same line, she refers to "the song of all songs which was Solomon's." Perhaps this later interpretation led to the "traditional ascription of authorship to King Solomon," or perhaps the inscription of authorship "may have come about because of several appearances of his name in the text." The overdetermination of the figure "Solomon" is furthered by the confusion of "Solomon" with a place name, "Shalmah," at one point in the text, and an obscure reference to the bride as "Shulammite maiden," a name which "seems related to the Hebrew for Solomon." Thus the figure of the verses' author is represented within the text and seems to emerge from the text. The conflation of the identities of character, author, and site in "Song of Songs" are reminiscent of the similar set of relationships in *Song of Solomon*, and so the association of the novel with the verses reflects and reinforces the integrity of the novel.

In *Song of Solomon* the father's name takes on meaning through a narrative process associated with a male figure and a containment associated with a female figure. Employing an essentialist perspective that accords with Blake's statement "Time is a Man Space is a Woman," Morrison constructs her own black cosmology: "Our cosmology may be a little different as each group's is, so what I want to figure out is how different." She says that change and progress, qualities which "under the guise of civilization to improve things" also "destroy all sorts of things," are important to men. But to this might be contrasted another quality, a "freedom of will," a "self-flagellant resistance to certain kinds of control," and opposition "to accepted notions of progress . . . best typified in certain black males." Her interpretation of the tar-baby image as something that "came to mean the black woman who can hold things together" for her provides a maternal metaphor for the workings of her texts. Disturbed by the childhood story of the tar-baby figure a white man uses to catch a rabbit, she began to explore the image:

> "Tar baby" is also a name, like nigger, that white people call black children, black girls, as I recall. Tar seemed to me to be an odd thing to be in a Western story, and I found that there is a tar lady in African mythology. I started thinking about tar. At one time, a tar pit was a holy place, at least an important place, because tar was used to build things. It came naturally out of the earth. It held together things like Moses's little boat and the pyramids.

Here the method of "fretting" the image is figured in the image itself: appropriation becomes incorporation, a literal bringing into the body of various elements to make something new.

If she articulates the cosmology of the black people withing the bounds of this fiction, the cosmology of her fictional text is reflected here too. Narrative movement reaches a destination that is also an origin and so achieves closure within the field of the text. *Song of Solomon*, even while it repudiates a certain type of "authorized" writing, tells the story of a writing that is not parricidal, a writing that recovers the story of the father and incorporates it into a text that, while engendered and animated by that story, is in its individuality itself original.

DOREATHA DRUMMOND MBALIA

Song of Solomon: *The Struggle for Race and Class Consciousness*

Toni Morrison's literary canon is a testimony to the principles of dialectics: it develops; it is interconnected; it reveals contradictions; and it reflects quantity and quality. Her canon also substantiates the premise that literature is a reflection of the society in which it is produced. *The Bluest Eye*, her first novel, explores the question of what it means to be an African in a racist, capitalist society, in this case, the United States. Specifically, Morrison's interest is in exposing the vicious, genocidal effects of racism on the African child. The major shortcoming of the novel, if measured in light of her developing class consciousness, is the solution proposed for eradicating these effects: racial approbation. Despite its weakness, the question posed by *The Bluest Eye*, "Why am I considered inferior?" and the answer, "Because I am an African born in a racist society," are natural starting points for any concerned African struggling for a solution to her people's plight.

In many ways, *Sula* picks up where *The Bluest Eye* ends. *Sula* reflects the evolutionary process that is the trademark of Morrison's canon: the three whores—the Maginot-Line, China, and Poland reappear as Eva, Hannah, and Sula; Pauline Breedlove is Mrs. Helene Wright; Pecola becomes Shadrack; and Claudia is Sula. Of particular interest is Morrison's change in thematic emphasis from her first novel to her second; Sula searches for self-identity, not group identity, a change that mirrors the developmental stages

From *Toni Morrison's Developing Class Consciousness*. © 1991 Associated University Presses, Inc.

of the consciousness of the African masses. Once the African knows who she is, often her struggle becomes one for individual rights. Unfortunately, this struggle for self-development leads some Africans to see themselves in isolation from their people, from the community that has in fact shaped, protected, nurtured, and guided them. This selfish quest for individual fulfillment is certainly that of Sula. Not responsible individualism, hers is a "socially disintegrative version of individualism, that possessive individualism or sanctified rapacity which is extolled by capitalist societies."

By the time she writes *Song of Solomon*, Morrison seems fully conscious of the relationship between the individual African and his community. Evidently, after writing and considering the dilemmas presented and the solutions posed in *The Bluest Eye* and *Sula*, after witnessing and participating in the historic, valiant struggle waged by Africans in the sixties and early seventies, and after being in contact with and editing the works of conscious, revolutionary Africans such as Chinweizu, Morrison has become more aware of the dialectical relationship between capitalism, racism, and sexism. In *Song of Solomon*, she subordinates sexism to both racism and capitalism, realizing that the exploitation of the African woman by the African man is the result of his national and class oppression. That is, sexism is correctly viewed as the consequence of the African's lack of race and class consciousness. Morrison's awareness of these relationships empowers her to create a protagonist whose survival depends on his development of a people consciousness, which, once gained, permanently alters his view of women. One has only to contrast Milkman's relationship with Hagar and Sweet to appreciate the veracity of this statement. After *Song of Solomon*, Morrison will never again create a male protagonist whose race and class consciousness is so underdeveloped that he exploits and oppresses African women.

In fact, this work marks a qualitative leap in Morrison's consciousness as an African and as a writer (for her, the two are inextricably related) in several other regards: she is more aware of the importance of dialectical and historical materialism; she is more aware of the role capitalism plays in the African's exploitation and oppression; she is more aware of the need to create a protagonist who develops during the course of the novel; and she is more aware of the importance of creating a text that allows theme to dictate structure.

To fully appreciate the qualitative leap that Morrison makes in regard to the nature of the African's oppression in the United States and in regard to her artistic dexterity, her protagonist's growth should be viewed as three distinct yet interconnected developmental stages that lead to his increased race and class consciousness: the preliminal stage, the liminal stage, and the postliminal stage. There are general characteristics peculiar to each as well as particular characteristics associated with the protagonist's heightened consciousness.

In the opening chapters of the novel, Milkman's low level of consciousness in regard to his people's race and class oppression manifests itself in his nickname. Ironically, Macon Dead III acquires it as a result of his extended nursing period, for instead of helping him to become more attuned to his mother and her needs, this lengthy bonding period proves ineffectual in a society that promotes selfish individualism above love and concern for humankind: Milkman is emotionally estranged from Ruth Dead as he is from all women with whom he interacts. As his nickname suggests, he milks women, pilfering their love and giving nothing in return. Even at age thirty-one, he knows very little about women, an ignorance made evident by his inability to distinguish his sisters from his mother. Nor can he conceived of women as human beings, not even his mother: "Never had he thought of his mother as a person, a separate individual, with a life apart from allowing or interfering with his own." Women, in general, have value only as "need providers" for Milkman. Therefore, his act of urinating on Lena becomes an act symbolic of his pissing on all women, Hagar in particular.

It is Hagar who is most exploited. While she genuinely loves Milkman, he loves her solely as a receptacle in which to empty his lust, seldom taking her anywhere except the movies and considering her his "private honey pot." Eventually, even sex with her becomes a bore, being "so free, so abundant." So, as a pimp taking leave of his whore, Milkman pays Hagar for twelve years of service and writes her a thank you letter, reminding her that they are first cousins and self-righteously telling himself that he is performing a selfless act. Like Sula, Milkman—in this liminal stage—shits on those around him, particularly the women of the novel.

Pilate is no exception. From her, as from Hagar, he receives a love both free and abundant. Wallowing in it, Milkman feels for "the first time in his life that he remembered being completely happy." Most important, it is because of Pilate—the pilot—that he is steered in a conscious direction. Through her acknowledgement of, dignity in, and proudness of her African-ness, despite her lack of material wealth, Milkman gets his first lesson in race and class consciousness: "While she looked as poor as everyone said she was, something was missing from her eyes that should have confirmed it." Like Pilate, Milkman must learn to respect his African self and to realize that money does not ensure happiness. Instead of killing the potential savior of his people as does her biblical namesake, Dead Pilate breathes life into Milkman. It is she who first forces him to confront his identity as the living dead who sucks the life force from his people; from her he learns the essence of life. Devouring the fruity, yolky core of life and speaking in a voice that reminded Milkman of little round pebbles that bumped against each other, Pilate is nature personified. She is, in fact, earth mother. What Milkman gives her in return for life is the murder of her daughter and the theft of her father. Significantly, it is not until the Shalimar Hunt, when he learns the importance of whispering to the trees and the ground, touching them, "as a blind man caresses a page of Braille, pulling meaning through his fingers," that Milkman appreciates the life that this earth mother provides him.

It is quite apropos, in light of his surname, that Milkman at first reciprocates Pilate's love with death. Like all the members of the Macon Dead household, he is dead. Even the family car, a spotlessly clean Packard, is regarded by the community as a hearse, a car that cauterizes the ties between the living (the community) and the dead (the Dead family). As the community voice of the novel, the Greek chorus, Freddie's evaluation of the Dead is valid: "A dead man ain't no man. A dead man is a corpse." At this point in his life, Milkman Dead is neither a man (exploiting all women with whom he comes into contact), nor a human being in general. He is both psychologically and emotionally dead.

Additional manifestations of Milkman's low level of consciousness are his overall state of confusion and his association with things behind him. His disconcertedness is best exemplified by his obsession with flying. Yet while he seems bombarded with images of flight and imbued with a natural sense of flying, he experiences feelings of flying blindly. And, of course, he is. Not knowing his past, he is unsure of the future: "Infinite possibilities and enormous responsibilities stretched out before him, but he was not prepared to take advantage of the former, or accept the burden of the latter." Unconscious of the fact that responsibilities are an integral part of life, Milkman lives the limbo life of the living dead, always struggling "to make up his mind whether to go forward or to turn back." His face reveals the confusion he feels, for "it was all very tentative," and "it lacked a coherence, a coming together of the features into a total self." This confusion will last until Milkman immerses himself in the life of his people; it is a confusion symbolized by a short limb because, as the narrator makes clear, this short limb is more the creation of his own mind than an actual fact:

> By the time Milkman was fourteen he had noticed that one of his legs was shorter than the other. When he stood barefoot and straight as a pole, his left foot was about half an inch off the floor. So he never stood straight; he slouched or leaned or stood with a hip thrown out, and he never told anybody about it—ever. . . . The deformity was mostly in his mind.

In spite of Milkman's lack of consciousness, he seems instinctively aware of the importance of the past, for he is obsessed with things behind him. In fact, "it was becoming a habit—this concentration on things behind him." Moreover, he is aware that everyone moves in the opposite direction as he, "going the direction that he was coming from," a suggestion that they already have knowledge of their past, which directs them to their future. However, he is not yet prepared to turn his instinctual awareness into a conscious search for his history.

Not only do the general characteristics associated with Milkman help the critic assess the protagonist's level of consciousness in the opening chapters of the novel, but also particular characteristics in regard to his race and class consciousness prove invaluable clues. In regard to race, the extent of Milkman's consciousness can be gauged by several factors—his relationship with the local community as well as his awareness of national events that affect African people. So isolated is he from his people that he is the last to know about the relationship between Henry Porter and his sister, First Corinthians; he is the last to know about the Seven Days; and he is the last to know about Emmett Till's murder. Once he is aware of these occurrences, he at first shows little concern for all except that which affects him directly, the courtship between Henry Porter and First Corinthians. Milkman is bored by all other events, revealing his complete estrangement from the community. When informed of the vicious murder of the fourteen-year-old Till, a murder which elicted the sympathy of both Europeans and Africans worldwide, Milkman replies: "Yeah, well, fuck Till. I'm the one in trouble." Such statements as this reflect Milkman's need to develop the race consciousness, which will allow him to see himself and other African people as one, having a common identity, a common history, and a common struggle.

The protagonist's class consciousness is just as weak as his race awareness. Believing in his father's capitalist philosophy that to own things is the essence of life, Milkman has little regard for the masses in the community, and, consequently, they have little regard for him. Being one of those masses, Feather throws Milkman out of his pool hall, rightfully associating the young Macon with his father. If Milkman is to establish close ties with the community, he must rid himself of dead weight—that Macon Dead mentality. He must begin to love his people more than his money, which will require that he, like Pilate, commit class suicide: "She gave up, apparently, all interest in table manners or hygiene, but acquired a deep concern for and about human relationships." As for now, Milkman's interest in life is "wherever the party is," and his associations, with the exception of Guitar, are with the petty bourgeois St. Honore crowd.

It is not until Milkman begins to question the people and events around him that his consciousness begins to develop, that he enters the liminal stage of discovery and growth. Although this period of liminality actually begins in chapter 3—"Now he questioned them. Questioned everybody"—it is not sufficiently developed until chapter 5 when he has discovered the answers to crucial questions of identity.

Chapter 5 begins with Milkman's death wish, an attempt by him to renounce all that he has learned thus far because such knowledge brings with it an acceptance of the responsibility of adulthood in general and African-hood in particular:

> Above all he wanted to escape what he knew, escape the implications of what he had been told. And all he knew in the world about the world was what other people had told him. He felt like a garbage pail for the actions and hatreds of other people. He himself did nothing. Except for the one time he had hit his father, he had never acted independently, and that act, his only one, had brought unwanted knowledge, too, as well as some responsibility for that knowledge.

In his determination to renounce all, Milkman patiently, resignedly awaits the vengeful, deadly rage of Hagar, laying in "Guitar's bed face-up in the sunlight, trying to imagine how it would feel when the ice pick entered his neck." Pregnant with images of death—words such as *indifference, silence, fatigue* and *lazy righteousness* are used throughout—this chapter reflects Milkman's readiness to "roll over and die," his readiness to become an egg, easily cracked and easily eaten, because "afterward there would be no remembrance of who he was or where."

Milkman's death wish is a necessary phase in his development, for his confrontation with and subsequent defiance of death teach him both sensitivity and sympathy, allowing him to look beyond self. In actuality, this attempted physical suicide prefaces and prefigures his class suicide. It is in this liminal state, a period of growth though not a full state of consciousness, that, for the first time, Milkman "rubbed the ankle of this short leg," feeling a sensation that is dialectically related to his increased consciousness. To the extent that his race and class consciousness develop, so does his leg develop, for Milkman's belief in his short limb was "mostly in his mind." It is in this liminal state that he feels "a quick beat of something like remorse" when he remembers Guitar's story about a doe, that one should never kill a female deer. Such physical and emotional occurrences are clearly indicative of Milkman's maturing consciousness.

Extending from chapters 3 to 9, from his attempted suicide to his recognition of his wish to live, a wish that brings with it responsibility, Milkman's liminal stage of development can be documented in particular by his increasing race and class awareness. With his newly gained sensitivity, Milkman asks Guitar questions about his best friend's strange behavior: "We've been friends a long time Guitar. There's nothing you don't know about me. I can tell you anything—whatever our differences, I know I can trust you. But for some time now it's been a one-way street." Of course, Milkman, blinded to all people and things except himself, created the one-way street. In point of fact, this occasion marks the first in which he has asked his friend questions that have not concerned the Dead family. Not just questioning his friend's lifestyle, Milkman argues with Guitar about the morality of the Seven Days' philosophy, saying, "But people who lynch and slice off people's balls—they're crazy, Guitar, crazy," and asking, "What about the nice ones? Some whites made sacrifices for Negroes. Real sacrifices." When juxtaposed with "Fuck Till," these concerns in regard to racial issues reflect a different, more sensitive Milkman. They do not, however, reflect a fully conscious protagonist. For Milkman is only questioning the philosophy of people who "sound like that red-headed Negro named X," not proposing an alternative solution for eradicating the oppression of African people.

Milkman's awareness of race is made more poignant by his personal confrontation with the police. Stripped of his dignity, emasculated like millions of other African men throughout the world, Milkman is overwhelmed with shame:

> Shame at being spread-eagled, fingered, and handcuffed. . . . But nothing was like the shame he felt as he watched and listened to Pilate. Not just her Aunt Jemima act, but the fact that she was both adept at it and willing to do it—for him.

This incident helps Milkman to distinguish between those Africans who assume the role of the Uncle Tom or the Aunt Jemima as a way of life and those who do so as a way of survival. While he feels proud of Pilate, who sacrifices her dignity to free him from jail even when he was prepared "to knock her down if she had come into the room while he was in the act of stealing" from her, he feels ashamed of his father, who "buckle[s] before the policemen." And the fact that he sees more dignity and life in the poor Pilate than in the rich Macon increases his class consciousness. That is, the incident crystalizes for him the way in which capitalism, with its emphasis on money and status, affects African people who ascribe to its values: they will always be petty capitalists, puppets "with an accomodating 'we all understand how it is' smile."

This incident with the police is the second that contributes to Milkman's developing class consciousness. The first results from the appearance of a white peacock, symbolizing both the race and the wealth of the ruling class in the United States. Ironically, this peacock appears while Guitar and Milkman are planning to rob Pilate's "gold." Significantly, it is Milkman who first sees it, "poised on the roof of a long low building that served as headquarters for Nelson Buick." Equating both flight and money with freedom, Milkman asks Guitar why a peacock can't fly. His friend replies, "Wanna fly, you gotta give up the shit that weighs you down." Although Milkman is not yet fully conscious of the connection between the diamondlike tail of the peacock and the "gold" he is planning to steal from Pilate, Dead weight that will only impede his search for identity, this incident does contibute to his growing class consciousness.

Milkman's postliminal stage, which marks the height of his consciousness, is characterized by his initiation into a new society, the society of the Shalimar hunters. Like the preliminal and liminal stages, this stage is symbolized by linguistic, psychological, and physical changes. As his race and class consciousness develop so does his language. Irresponsible, individualistic statements such as "Yeah, well, fuck Till," which characterize his preliminality and which symbolize his complete insensitivity to the plight of African people, are replaced by the Africanized voice of collective communion, a communion shared by all living matter. Psychologically, Milkman accepts the responsibility of adulthood and Africanhood: "He had stopped evading things, sliding through, over, and around difficulties." Having learned to respect the natural world more than the material one and having gained the ability to laugh at himself, Milkman has become a psychologically balanced individual:

> There was nothing here [on the Shalimar hunt] to help him—not his money, his car, his father's reputation, his suit, or his shoes. In fact they hampered him. . . . They [the Shalimar hunters] hooted and laughed all the way back to the car, teasing Milkman, egging him on to tell more about how scared he was. And he told them. Laughing too, hard, loud, and long. Really laughing.

After "the pain in his short leg [becomes] so great he began to limp and hobble," physically, Milkman becomes balanced as well: he no longer limps; both legs are equal.

In regard to race, his high level of consciousness is exemplified on two occasions, when he learns of his grandfather's murder and when he participates in the Shalimar hunt. Milkman first learns of his grandfather's murder from Pilate, but he hears these details during a time when his race consciousness is at its lowest level. When he hears of the murder a second time, from Reverend Cooper, he asks, infuriated, why the Danville Africans did not seek revenge: "'And nobody did anything?' Milkman wondered at his own anger. He hadn't felt angry when he first heard about it. Why now?" His anger is aroused on this occasion because of his heightened awareness of himself in connection with other African people. Eventually, this consciousness manifests itself in a sincere love for and understanding of his people, even for the slightly unbalanced Day, who comes to kill him:

> But something had maimed him, scarred him like Reverend Cooper's knot, like Saul's missing teeth, and like his own father. He felt a sudden rush of affection for them all, and out there under the sweet gum tree, within the sound of men tracking a bobcat, he thought he understood Guitar now. Really understood him.

During the hunt, Milkman's class consciousness sharpens as well. Learning the insignificance of money and status when juxtaposed with a true communion with African people, Milkman commits class suicide. While it is true that the seeds of his decision to bond with the African masses instead of those having his wealth and status are planted when he first meets Pilate, his conscious decision to do so germinates from his Shalimar experiences. According to anthropologist Arnold van Gennep, one must undergo several initiation rites prior to being incorporated into a new society. In Milkman's case, these rites are related to his increased class consciousness.

First, the initiate must be stripped of all that is psychologically and physically associated with his old society. This initiation rite entails a physical descent into a cave, an enclosing or engulfing that usually signals a baptism and an imminent rebirth. Milkman experiences both. Entering Hunters Cave with all the material, artificial trappings of capitalist society— a wad of money, an expensive watch, a beige three-piece suit, a "button-down light-blue shirt and black string tie," a snap brim hat, a suitcase with a bottle of scotch, and beautiful Florsheim shoes—Milkman emerges an offspring of nature, with water-ruined suit, soggy shoes, and a broken watch.

Second, the initiate must be cognizant of the mores of the new society. In Milkman's case, he must learn that he cannot exploit the people. He can neither show nor receive gratitude with money. Because humanism is a traditional African principle valued more than money and held in esteem more by the African masses than the African petty bourgeois, Circe, Fred Garnet, and the Shalimar community are offended by Milkman's capitalist behavior:

They looked at his skin and saw it was as black as theirs, but they knew he had the heart of the white men who came to pick them up in the trucks when they needed anonymous, faceless laborers.

Just as important as the principle of humanism, Milkman must learn egalitarianism, the inherent equality of every human being. Prior to the hunt, he thinks himself so superior to the Shalimar people that he sees them not as unique individuals, but as one large anonymous group. For instance, with the Shalimar men in hearing distance, he condescendingly asks the storeowner (whom he only assumes to be Mr. Solomon because he never asks the storeowner his name) if one of the men can help him: "He looked at the men sitting around the store. 'You think maybe one of them could help with the car?' he asked Mr. Solomon."

Third, he must put his newly learned humanistic theories into practice by participating in the rituals of the new society. Milkman does so by agreeing to go on the hunt, a ritual that proves to be a psychological and physical test of strength, allowing him to shed his old capitalist-oriented ideology and replace it with a new people-oriented, nature-oriented ideology. In the true spirit of baptism and rebirth, Milkman rethinks his past behavior and contemplates the new life awaiting him, a life that will allow him, like the men of Shalimar, to commune with all of nature's children:

> It was more than tracks Calvin was looking for—he whispered to the trees, whispered to the ground, touched them, as a blind man caresses a page of Braille, pulling meaning through his fingers.

His new, revolutionized consciousness enables him to confront and to regret his old way of life: "The consequences of Milkman's own stupidity would remain, and regret would always outweigh the things he was proud of having done."

Significantly, it is not until after Milkman has revolutionized his consciousness in regard to race oppression and class exploitation that he sheds his sexist views of women. Prior to this increased awareness, Milkman, as his name suggests, milks the life out of women, giving them nothing in return. As pointed out, so reactionary is his view of women that he has difficulty distinguishing his mother from his sisters and rarely thinks of any of them. Pissing on Lena, squealing on First Corinthians, spying on Ruth, stealing from Pilate, and murdering Hagar—all are evidence of Milkman's low level of consciousness. At the time he commits these acts, he is not aware of the oneness which connects African people, that pissing on Lena is like pissing on himself, that the sexual exploitation and murder of Hagar are the sexual exploitation and murder of himself. As the prophetic Pilate explains to Hagar, all are acts of self-hatred: "How can he not love your hair? It's the same hair that grows up out of his own armpits. The same hair that crawls up out of his crotch on up his stomach."

Not only actions, but also words are early reflections of Milkman's lack of consciousness in regard to women. He tells Hagar, "If you keep your hands just that way and then bring them down straight, straight and fast, then you can drive that knife right smack in your cunt." Such backwards, genocidal acts committed and words voiced against the mothers of his race can only find life in a society the promotes profit above human welfare, the individual above the group. It is this priceless treasure of knowledge that Milkman gains by the end of the novel.

Quite noticeably, his consciousness in regard to women begins to rise when he discovers some of his mother's past and heightens even more after his participation in the hunt. Earlier, Guitar had warned Milkman against exploiting women by relating an incident in which Guitar killed a doe; "A man shouldn't do that." This warning, however, goes unheeded until Milkman takes an active interest in his mother's well-being: "He remembered Guitar's story about killing one. . . . 'A man shouldn't do that.' Milkman felt a quick beat of something like remorse." But like the prickly feeling he gets in his knee, this fleeting sense of sympathy reflects only the beginnings of growth and healing, not the completion of them. Significantly, "He shook it [the feeling of remorse] off and resumed" his old way of thinking, talking, and acting. That is, he proceeds to kill the doe. In this case, when he discovers Ruth at her father's grave site, he kills her with words: "You come to lay down on your father's grave? Is that what you've been doing all these years? Spending a night every now and then with your father?"

It is not until Milkman has stripped himself of the ruling class's views of race (intraracial, in this case) and class superiority that he is able to see women as his equals. This rite of passage is not complete until the Shalimar hunt, during which Milkman first becomes conscious, then ashamed of his exploitation of Hagar, "whom he'd thrown away like a wad of chewing gum after the flavor was gone—she had a right to try to kill him too." It is only after this event that he fully understands the reciprocal nature of human relationships:

> She [Sweet] put salve on his face. He washed her hair. She sprin-
> kled talcum on his feet. He straddled her behind and massaged
> her back. She put witch hazel on his swollen neck. He made up
> the bed. She gave him gumbo to eat. He washed the dishes. She
> washed his clothes and hung them out to dry. He scoured her

tub. She ironed his shirt and pants. He gave her fifty dollars. She kissed his mouth. He touched her face. She said please come back. He said I'll see you tonight.

Perhaps the most significant evidence of Milkman's awareness of the principle of reciprocity as related to women is his commitment to guide Pilate to Shalimar to bury her father's bones, just as she had guided him to bury the Dead in him. In fact, with his revolutionized consciousness—which prizes humanism and egalitarianism—he becomes the pilot, the source of life. Thus, the name "Milkman" is transformed to signify that which is positive, not negative. The protagonist becomes the milkman who is capable of carrying the source of life for those in need. The emphasis here is on the word *capable*, for while Milkman's race and class consciousness develop sufficiently to allow him to recreate self, it never reaches the point where Milkman moves beyond self-healing to "other-healing."

Still, Morrison's creation of a character who must develop both race and class awareness prior to developing an egalitarian and humanistic view of women reflects her own increased consciousness of the dialectical relationship between the African male's nation-class oppression and his exploitation of African women. Such a qualitative leap in her ability to analyze the nature of capitalism empowers her to structure a text that is qualitatively better than the first two. Evidently, Morrison's understanding that an awareness of the particular nature of the African's oppression must precede the development of a viable solution increases her awareness of the dialectical relationship between meaning and structure. The first must dictate the latter. Such a mature understanding of the role of narrative structure is reflected in *Song of Solomon*. The overall text, the chapters, and the sentences within the chapters reflect this symbiotic relationship between form and content.

First, Morrison uses flight as structure for the overall text. *Song of Solomon* begins and ends with unsucccessful flight attempts: Robert Smith's begins the novel; Milkman's ends the novel. Richard K. Barksdale comments on the use of flight as structure when he writes,

> The story that is related about [the characters'] experiences does not have a definable beginning, middle and end. The novel begins with a black man attempting to fly and ends with a black man attempting to fly. In other words, the pattern of narration is circular, not linear.

That the structure is circular suggests the absence of a solution, the failure of the protagonist (and his precursor) to share the liberating knowledge he has gained in order to create an environment free of oppression. That is, the unsuccessful nature of both flights reflects both men's lack of responsibility to the African community. Through their own admission or commission, they reveal their guilt: Smith leaves a suicidal note asking forgiveness; Milkman flies away despite his new awareness that true flight for humanity in general and the African in particular is the ability to fly without ever leaving the ground. Moreover, the facts that Smith's death and Milkman's birth occur almost simultaneously enhance the structural relationship between the two characters and the concept of flight.

Second, Morrison divides her chapters into two parts: the first primarily chronicles Milkman's lack of consciousness in regard to race and class; the second predominantly concentrates on his developing consciousness in regard to them.

Third, the author uses parallel sentences to reflect equal relationships or equal actions. Such is the case when the newly awakened Milkman participates in a ritual of reciprocity with Sweet. Balanced sentence parts are used as well to inform the reader of close relationships between characters. Referring to Pilate and Ruth, Morrison writes: "The singer, standing at the back of the crowd, was as poorly dressed as the doctor's daughter was well dressed."

Morrison's practice of briefly describing relationships, events, and people she is not prepared to discuss adds to the quality of this novel; it is a skillful method of creating a coherent text. At the beginning of the novel, for example, Freddie is referred to as "a gold-toothed man" and Guitar, "the cat-eyed boy." Both names are withheld. This narrative method requires that the reader mentally store the descriptive phrases until the characters are formally introduced. In this way, the reader ceases to be a passive bystander, but becomes an active partner in creating textual coherence by sewing together an earlier section of the novel with a later one.

Additionally, Morrison manipulates time much more skillfully in this work than in her first two. Transition sentences such as "That was the beginning. Now it was all going to end" transport the reader from the past to the present without the nauseating jolt of an air pocket. Such sophisticated use of transitions appears between as well as within chapters. As a case in point, the parental role of Guitar and Pilate in relationship to Hagar serves as the transition device that cements chapters 5 and 6. Chapter 5 ends with Pilate's effort to keep Ruth's mind off Hagar's attempt to kill Milkman:

> Pilate would have moved on immediately except for her brother's
> wife, who was dying of lovelessness then, and seemed to be dying
> of it now as she sat at the table across from her sister-in-law

listening to her life story, which Pilate was making deliberately
long to keep Ruth's mind off Hagar.

Chapter 6 begins with Guitar's effort to take Hagar home after one of her
failed attempts to murder Milkman: "I [Guitar] took her home. She was
standing in the middle of the room when I got there. So I just took her home.
Pitiful. Really pitiful."

Perhaps one of the most significant gauges of Morrison's maturation in
regard to structure is her ability to match form with content. Chapter 13 is
the clearest example of this ability. Coming just after the Shalimar hunt,
during and after which Milkman evidences his heightened consciousness in
regard to race and class, chapter 13 serves as structural proof of Morrison's
theme: "You can never go off and leave a body." Thematically, it picks up in
the middle of chapter 5, detailing the events surrounding Hagar's demise
after Milkman makes his most cruel, race-killing statement concerning the
mutilation of her sexual organs. Milkman's selfish individualism affects all
Africans: Hagar's death in general and the destruction of her reproductive
capability in particular mean the death of future generations of African
people. By placing chapter 13 between ones which evidence Milkman's
development, Morrison reminds the reader that the past must serve as a
useful guide to the future. Thus, even though Milkman does not understand
the full significance of Sweet's question—"Who did he [Solomon] leave
behind"—the reader does. Neither Solomon nor Milkman uses knowledge
responsibly—to forge a better future for their kind.

In structure and in theme, *Song of Solomon* is a more advanced work of
art than either *The Bluest Eye* or *Sula*. Thematically, Morrison understands
that the African in the United States experiences national and class oppression. Additionally, she is aware that the African male's exploitation of the
African female is related to this oppression; that it is, in fact, the result of it.
Such clearsightedness enables her, for the first time, to create a male as
protagonist, one who must first become conscious of himself in relationship
to his people; then and as a consequence, reject the individualistic, vulturistic
class aspirations of his oppressor before experiencing a wholesome relationship with a woman. Structurally, Morrison's consciousness of the importance
of discovering the cause of the African's oppression before proposing a solution empowers her to subordinate structure to meaning.

Yet, in spite of the growth evidenced in her writing of *Song of Solomon*,
Morrison has not yet sufficiently matured to understand that while the African
is exploited both racially and economically, his economic exploitation forms
the basis for his national oppression. In the words of Kwame Nkrumah, while
"capitalist exploitation and race oppression are complementary, the removal of

[the first] ensures the removal of the other." Without such an understanding, she cannot propose a viable solution, the eradication of capitalism. This is the thematic weakness of the novel. By the end of it, Milkman sees himself as an African exploited by capitalism and oppressed by racism, but he offers no solution to this dilemma. Instead, he surrenders to exploitation and oppression. Rather than moving beyond the act of defeatism exhibited by his forefather, he repeats it: Knowing what Shalimar knew, he surrenders to the air.

Thus, it is interesting that Milkman possesses the knowledge, the theory needed to help abolish the exploitation and oppression of African people, needed to revolutionize their consciousness, but he chooses not to use this knowledge as a weapon of change. He fails to make his contribution to humanity. In contrast, Guitar does act, but his is misguided action, for he does not have the knowledge base of Milkman. Both knowledge and action are needed because "practice without thought is blind; thought without practice is empty." Milkman and Guitar must come, that is, fly, together to create the conscious action so desperately needed by African people. And they do, but the conscious, action-oriented offspring they create by such a union does not materialize until *Tar Baby*.

Because they are dialectically related, not only does the theme of *Song of Solomon* indicate the maturation that Toni Morrison must yet develop, but so does the structure. While it is an advancement on the narrative forms of her first two novels, it does not reflect her fullest consciousness of the nature of capitalism. Once she is at her highest peak, Morrison will reject all those structural elements that reflect the injustices of capitalism, in particular the notion that one human being is superior to another. For instance, in *Tar Baby* she will not merely rely on an omniscient narrator, one who knows all despite his lack of involvement. Rather, she will create a structure that allows for narrative contributions from all the major characters. In this manner, she creates a text that is much more socialist in design.

MARIANNE HIRSCH

Knowing Their Names: Toni Morrison's Song of Solomon

That is the ability we must be on guard against for the future—the
female who reproduces the female who reproduces the female.
—Toni Morrison

Wherever human society wishes to move into an articulation, the
Father must discover and humbly observe his limit.
—Hortense Spillers

Why they got two words for it 'stead of one, if they ain't no difference?
—Toni Morrison

The "absence" of fathers permeates feminist stories.
—Sara Ruddick

1
Daddy

In the introduction to her collection of black feminist theoretical essays,
Changing Our Own Words, Cheryl Wall identifies 1970 as a moment of origin
for "a community of black women writing." Novels, autobiographical texts,
essays, and poems which appeared during that year shared thematic focal

---

From *New Essays on Song of Solomon*. © 1995 Cambridge University Press. Reprinted with the permission of Cambridge University Press.

points: "the exploration of family violence, sexual oppression and abuse, and the corrosive effects of racism and poverty." What is more, they envisioned black female characters as survivors—active agents in the struggle for social change. In exploring the texture of familial interactions and in placing women in positions of centrality, however, these texts formed a community which appeared deeply threatening to male readers. As Deborah McDowell argues in the same collection, women's writings that concentrate on the domestic space of home also reveal that space as "the privileged site of women's exploitation." McDowell traces black male critics' responses to these texts, exposing their obsessive desire for the recuperation of the patriarchal family, for the restitution of the father's dominant place. African American women's experiences within the construct of family have been buried, she insists, and only now, since 1970, have women's subordination and victimization within the familial plot begun to emerge into view, thereby frustrating the desires of male readers for unequivocally positive images.

Toni Morrison's novels systematically interrogate a range of familial roles and representations: her project, it would seem, is to define African American family romances in the aftermath of slavery and in the context of twentieth-century economic and social pressures, shaped by racism and sexism. Morrison's narratives penetrate to the subconscious aspects of familial interaction, even as they place family firmly within the space of community and society. Her novels juxtapose the realities of African American family relations to hegemonic family romances, to the dominant mythos of the patriarchal nuclear family in which the ruling culture constitutes the measure of success. In each of her novels, Morrison interrogates that mythos from the vantage point of a socially marginal and economically disadvantaged culture, one whose history radically challenges the very bases on which the mythos of the patriarchal Oedipal family rests. Drawing on multiple mythologies, Morrison's novels refine and redefine the understandings of familial ideology that have dominated during the last thirty years in U.S. culture. Writing of the African American family of the 1970s and 1980s, however, means confronting not only the legacy of slavery and the distortions it performed on all intimate relationships but also the great social and economic pressure in the wake of Lyndon Johnson's "Great Society." It means confronting the stigma of a popularly acclaimed Moynihan report (1965) that labeled the black family a pathological "matriarchy" and failed to claim any public repsonsibility for the realities: massive unemployment and low pay for African American men and women, poor educational opportunities for black youth, the drug culture, and the resulting pressures placed on familial structures. Instead, Moynihan maintained, and others echoed, the black family's "deterioration" could be explained by the rampant sexual debauchery among the black population, by the instability and violence of black men, and by the pathological dominance of black women. McDowell identifies the report as singly responsible for the silences about women's experiences within the family. To write the story of the African American family in the wake of the report and the public images it fostered is always to write against the risk either of perpetuating or of appearing to repress this noxious stereotyping.

In recent years, cultural critics have begun to reveal the racist assumptions that underlie the Moynihan report and subsequent analyses of "the black family," as well as the divergent and incompatible ideologies of family that continue to pertain in the United States. Speaking in particular of the father's complicated role and of father–daughter incest, Hortense Spillers bluntly articulates the methodological difficulties confronting the writer and critic: "We situate ourselves, then, at the center of a mess altogether convoluted in its crosshatch of historic purposes. There is no simple way to state the case, but crudely put, we might ask: to what extent do the texts of a psychoanalytic ahistoricism, out of which the report, the transaction of incest arise, abrade, reveal against the historic scene and its subsequent drama? Does the Freudian text translate in short (and here we would include the Freudian progeny Lévi-Strauss and Lacan among them)?" The notion of "translation" can only begin to describe the methodological quandary, for the very terms "family," "father," and "mother" signify differently in an African American context than they do in a Eurocentric one. The laws of captivity recognized neither maternity nor paternity, Spillers elaborates, but they made the status of paternity particularly distant from the patriarchal domain reigning in the dominant culture: the mostly illiterate African slave father, dispossessed of his culture and subordinate to the "captor father's mocking presence," transmits neither patronym, logos, nor law to his progeny. Paternity is more than, other than, a "fiction"; it is, in Spiller's terms, a "puzzle." What terms, one might ask, are available to the feminist writer and critic who wishes to discuss this "puzzle" in the 1970s, 1980s, and 1990s?

In *The Bluest Eye*, her first novel, published in 1970, Morrison begins her familial interrogations with one of the most deeply suppressed and unsayable issues in familial respresentation, father–daughter rape and incest, but here she is clearly more interested in the daughter's story than in the father's. Although her portrayal of Cholly Breedlove is remarkably gentle and even sympathetic, Morrison focuses less on him than on Pecola herself, on *her* dreams, desires, and disappointments. Cholly's devastating role is to act out more directly the humiliation that society has already inflicted on Pecola. In her next novel, *Sula* (1973), Morrison concentrates even more

single-mindedly on women. From the self-estranged Shadrack, to the abandoning Boy Boy, Jude, and Ajax, the absent Mr. Wright, the incapacitated
Plum, the futureless Chicken Little, to the interchangeable Deweys,
Morrison seems systematically to inscribe the incapacity of African American
masculinity, even as she writes men out of positions of importance in
familial units and women's lives. This is truly a world without fathers. Eva's
three-woman family becomes a model which Morrison will repeat in two
subsequent novels, a female-headed household that manages without men.
Although she is fascinated by this arrangement, Morrison in no way ideal-
izes it. When her central character Sula rejects femininity as defined by
heterosexuality, when she dreams of a life outside maternal identification,
the novel sympathizes with her but clarifies that this rejection is not, in that
context at least, either a viable or a successful choice.

By 1977, with the publication of *Song of Solomon*, however, Morrison
radically shifts the focus of her familial portraits to men. More is at stake
than the choice of Milkman as the male protagonist of her bildungsroman:
it is fathers more than sons who come most clearly into focus. The book's
dedication, simply "Daddy," begins to indicate the import and the implications of this new interest. "Daddy," a child's term of endearment, invokes a
father who is seen from the perspective of the child, not an authoritative
paternal or patriarchal figure. The diminutive "daddy" is the father made
small, made to the size of the child, the father who is nurturing and vulnerable at the same time. Nevertheless, the echo of Sylvia Plath's "Daddy"
reminds us of the father's other side, of his authority, his distance, his
brutality. In Morrison's dedication, "Daddy," on its own, without the "for"
or "to" that is the customary mark of a dedication, amounts more to an
address and an appeal, rather than a gift or presentation. This is a novel
that explores the formation of masculinity, in relation to the process and
the legacy of paternity. And this is an exploration that is addressed to the
father. In no way, however, has Morrison abandoned the thematics of
female familial life. The space between fathers and children, children and
fathers, is still inhabited by women, by mothers, daughters, and sisters: not
only by the magnetic Pilate and her three-woman household but also by
Ruth Foster and her two daughters. Paternal relations are embedded in a
range of other familial interactions, interactions that are dominated by the
problems and the prospects of paternity and that both shape and reflect the
dimensions of the paternal. The novel's project is to work through this
dominance of the paternal and to confront paternal affiliations with other
relational paradigms, so as to discover a balance between the extremes of
familial interaction, between intimacy and absence, closeness and distance.
Its project is to embody the father, to explore the paternal–filial relation-

ship in its bodily manifestation. Its project is to consider the paternal connection to and divorce from the logos and do so in the context of the politics of literacy.

Song of Solomon radically rethinks familial relations and the process of familial transmission. It participates in what Spillers has called the "romance of African-American fiction[, which] is a tale of origins that brings together once again children lost or stolen or estranged from their mothers." Yet this novel adds fathers to mothers and explores the viability of a dual masculine–feminine legacy. Thus, it at once envisions an ideal of hetero-sexual understanding and co-implication and painfully and painstakingly demonstrates the difficulties of reaching that ideal within the circumstances of African American life in the 1960s.

"The fathers may soar / And the children may know their names"—the novel's epigraph raises the novel's central themes: family relations, flight, transmission, origin, knowledge, naming, transcendence, contingency. In its two parts, the epigraph confirms the intersections and interconnections between the structures of the familial (paternity, childhood) and the structures of language and the symbolic (naming and knowing). Even as it highlights paternity, however, the epigraph places it at a distance; controversially it condones and supports this distancing: "The fathers may soar." Morrison disturbingly explains this in an interview: "I guess I'm not supposed to say that. But the fact that they [men] would split in a minute just delights me. . . . [T]hat has always been to me one of the most attractive features about black male life." Morrison continues: "One of the major differences between black men's work and black women's work is that the big scene for black men is the traveling Ulysses scene. They are moving. . . . That going from town to town or place to place or looking out and over and beyond and changing—that's what they do." Masculine flight, literalizing an important theme in the African American literary and cultural tradition, dominate's the text's beginning, middle, and end. But in this text, flight is both escape and evasion, both transcendence and avoidance. I propose, in what follows, to read the novel through the two parts of the epigraph and to explore, in particular, the novel's models of paternity, its complicated negotiations of paternal presence and absence, and the impact of the paternal on other familial relationships.

My own position as a Euro-American feminist critic of this African American text, my upbringing in a patriarchal nuclear family, and my present situation in a "blended" middle-class family should not be disguised. If indeed, as Hortense Spillers suggests, "the African-American text run(s) parallel to that of a Eurocentric psycho-mythology," if indeed the history of the African-American family obliges the critic to scrutinize the very terms she uses to discuss its representations, these factors certainly determine my perspective as a "parallel" one: one that runs next to but that does not unproblematically intersect with that of the text. My engagement with the text, therefore, has to be an act of displacement and an exercise in "translation," an exercise in perceiving the simultaneity of likeness and difference. The present context in which we read Morrison's 1977 text, however—the recent resurgence in public scrutiny of the "black family" and its "problems," of which the most pervasively discussed certainly are the father's "absence," the "parallel" crisis in the Euro-American family, and the antifeminist backlash they have caused—makes an engagement with this novel crucial. *Song of Solomon*, I believe, offers ways in which to read aspects of paternity which have heretofore remained untheorized. In allowing us to explore the myths and realities of paternal "absence," this novel retains its topical significance for male and female, black and white readers alike.

2
"The fathers may soar"

"The Macon Deads exemplify the patriarchal nuclear family that has traditionally been a stable and critical feature of Western civilization. The misery of their daily lives demonstrates how few guarantees that domestic configuration actually carries." Valerie Smith's characterization of the Dead family aptly suggests how, in fact, the nuclear patriarchal structure itself creates the problems it is supposed to resolve. Among the many family portraits in the space of the text, the Deads represent, in fact, the only nuclear arrangement. What "deadens" the Deads, however, is Macon, the father: his single-minded ambition, his unscrupulous greed, his unabashed materialism, his lack of nurturance. Macon is the only father in this novel who is present, home with his family; he is the only father who has neither flown away nor been killed nor killed himself. Yet, ironically, his presence is so overpowering as to disable the other members of his family. The novel's images of paternity vacillate between this crushing presence and a devastating absence, between incestuous closeness and injurious distance.

Macon himself admits that he can speak to his son "only if his words held some command or criticism. 'Hello, Daddy.' 'Hello, son, tuck your shirt in.' 'I found a dead bird, Daddy.' 'Don't bring that mess in the house.'" Macon's relations with his wife and daughters are so unloving as to have made the latter "boiled dry from years of yearning" and the former "dying of lovelessness." But Macon has been concentrating on another aspect of paternity, the one he wants at all costs to pass along to his son as "what's real": the acquisition of property. "Let me tell you right now the one important thing you'll ever need to know: Own things. And let the things you own own other things. Then you'll own yourself and other people too. Starting Monday, I'm going to teach you how." Macon's slippage between owning "things" and owning oneself and other "people" is remarkable, especially for a descendant of slaves. Yet he believes, wrongly, that he inherited his material ambitions from his own father, Macon Dead Sr., the American Adam who out of nothing fashioned the beautiful farm Lincoln's Heaven, who grew "real peaches," and who was killed because his land was in the white farmers' way. Whereas Macon Sr. owned things that "grew" other things, Macon II aspires to own things that "own" other things and people too.

Macon II's misapprehension, a misreading that clearly echoes the distortions of master–slave relations, is crucial, for his distance from the land and from his past, as well as his obsessive search for urban respectability and success, has changed him, unrecognizably, from a "nice boy," to a "stern, greedy, and unloving" man. "Be nice if you could have known him then," Pilate says to Milkman about his father's boyhood. "He would have been a real good friend to you, like he was to me." Throughout the novel, Macon II's paternity is contrasted to that of his own deceased father, Macon Sr., as well as to his own loving fraternal/paternal relation with the young Pilate. "For a dozen years she had been like his own child." "Hadn't been for your daddy, I wouldn't be here today." Macon used to carry the motherless Pilate in his arms to a neighboring farm and then come right back to "work right alongside" his father. What that phrase means about father–son connection, Milkman understands only much later when he hears it from his father's childhood friends: "Milkman thought then that his father was boasting of his manliness as a child. Now he knew he had been saying something else. That he loved his father; had an intimate relationship with him; that his father loved him, trusted him, and found him worthy of working 'right alongside' him." Macon Sr. is the father who cooked the wild turkey better than anyone, who named his farm Lincoln's Heaven, who warmed his orchard with a fire when the spring was too cold, who trained dogs and horses, who sang like an angel as he plowed forty acres. He is the father who could claim the land and make it his. He is also the father who remained in perpetual posthumous contact with Pilate, guiding her through difficult times with wisdom and intimate care. Unlike his own father, Solomon, Macon Sr. does not fly off and leave his family; he sticks by them in daily and close nurturing protection and care. And his protection is neither too close nor too distant: he knows how to "work right alongside" his son without smothering him or leaving him, offering for the novel a paradigm of successful paternal–filial relation. But it is precisely Macon Sr.'s distinctive relation to property which gets him killed. Since he can neither read nor write, since he does not possess the literacy that will legitimate the power of the logos as he has defined it, he cannot truly own the land he nurtures and cares for. Even while he aspired to success in the terms of the dominant culture, that is, ownership and material possession, he wished to inscribe that success with his own mark of difference: he chose nature over the symbolic; he chose to nurture his property rather than to claim it in the terms of the white patriarch's law. The only way the white patriarch can dispossess him of his property, then, is to kill him.

Macon Sr., or Jake as he was called as a child, is himself the victim of paternal abandonment. As a descendant of the fabled Solomon, father of twenty children, Jake was the last, referred to mysteriously as the "only son": he was the one chosen by his father to accompany him on his triumphant flight back to Africa but was carelessly dropped back in the home the father abandoned. Ever concerned about abandonment ("You can't just go off and leave a body," he keeps repeating to Pilate), he builds a stable, beautiful, and fertile home even without the help of his wife. Nevertheless, he does not succeed in keeping it and in surviving. His history of vulnerability and longing, of warmth and care, his unique relation to property, contributes to the picture of ideal paternity offered by Macon/Jake.

Solomon's own paternity receives contradictory interpretations in the space of the text. His flight, a heroic return to Africa, offers his descendants a mythic form of transcendence with which to identify, an admirable and legendary rejection of his slave condition, a revolutionary rebellion. But his flight can also be seen as an act of paternal irresponsibility and abandonment, especially as it echoes the mock-flight of the insurance agent Robert Smith, with which the novel begins: "But anyway, hot stuff or not, he [Solomon] disappeared and left everybody. Wife, everybody, including some twenty-one children. . . . It like to killed the woman, the wife. . . . [S]he's supposed to have screamed out loud for days." As Susan Byrd concludes her narrative about Solomon's mysterious flight, she wonders about Ryna's screams: was she the kind of woman who could not live without a particular man, or was she distraught by having to take care of twenty-one children by herself? In allowing Susan to pose this question, the novel qualifies the option of flight even as it features it—in the novel's epigraph, its beginning, and its end. Heroic soaring is also antiheroic evasion.

These contradictory paternal images come together in another figure we encounter only in various narratives and legends thoroughly the novel: the town's first black doctor, Dr. Foster. Foster nurtures not only his daughter, Ruth, but also the rest of the black population, for he cares for the sick and delivers all the babies. Yet, arrogant and disdainful of his patients, he "flies off" in his own way through his self-destructive and escapist dependence on drugs. Even with Ruth he is unable to find an acceptable delimitation between paternal love and transgressive incestuous closeness. As he welcomes Macon Dead's attentions to his daughter, he thinks less of her than of his own disturbing confusion:

> Her steady beam of love was unsettling, and she had never dropped those expressions of affection that had been so lovable in her childhood. The good-night kiss was itself a masterpiece of slow-wittedness on her part and discomfort on his. At sixteen, she still insisted on having him come to her at night, sit on her bed, exchange a few pleasantries, and plant a kiss on her lips. Perhaps it was the loud silence of his dead wife, perhaps it was Ruth's disturbing resemblance to her mother. More probably it was the ecstacy that always seemed to be shining in Ruth's face when he bent to kiss her—an ecstasy he felt inappropriate to the occasion.

Is it appropriate for Doctor Foster to be delivering his own granddaughters, to be there when his daughter "had her legs wide open?" Was Ruth naked in bed with her dead father when Macon walked in, as he claimed, or was she, as she insists to her son, kneeling in her slip sucking his beautiful fingers, the only part of his body not puffy from ether? As it fails to settle these questions, the novel acts out the confusion between closeness and distance that it tries in different ways to resolve. When she goes off to lie on her father's grave at night, as though to meet a secret lover, Ruth insists that he was the "only person who ever really cared whether I lived or died. . . . When he left [this world], I kept on reigniting that cared-for feeling I got from him." Here, Ruth expresses a daughterly yearning that dominates the novel's filial emotions, the need for continued and close paternal bodily closeness.

The incestuous confusion of distance between Ruth and her father is perpetuated in her relationship with her son and is responsible for his name, "Milkman." It is here that the confusions between closeness and absence which define paternal relations extend to and shape a number of other familial interactions. Ruth's secret and transgressive nursing feels to Ruth not only like "a balm, a gentle touch," but also like an act of magic and creativity. As Ruth's imagination equates nursing with spinning gold, she places herself in a heroic tradition of fairy tales which the novel juxtaposes to the masculine heroism of flight. In "Rumplestiltskin," spinning gold successfully is the miller's daughter's way of staying alive. In outwitting the spirit who helps her and in "knowing his name," she manages to keep her child and to care for him. This is the tradition of domestic heroism with which Ruth identifies but which the public world deligitimates when Freddy voyeuristically and mockingly intrudes on the

mother and growing son. Some appropriate but undefinable balance of closeness and distance is violated during those moments of nursing, a balance no
relationship in the novel except the two Macons' brief and endangered
"working alongside" can successfully reach.

If parent–child relations are subject to the risks of incestuous familiarity, brother–sister bonds are equally endangered in this complicated
father-dominated familial landscape. Milkman comically performs an act of
fraternal transgression when he urinates on Lena and kills her plant,
symbolically making her sterile. Milkman's love for Hagar is doomed
because they are too closely related: "'This here's your brother, Milkman,'
. . . 'That ain't her brother, Mama. They cousins.' The older woman spoke.
'Same thing.' . . . 'Then why they got two words for it 'stead of one, if they
ain't no difference?'" When Hagar's love starts getting boring and flat, it is
because it is too familiar, because she has stopped introducing distance by
refusing. Pilate's questions to Hagar celebrating their similarity could
equally well elicit the opposite for the answers she intends: "'How can he
not love your hair? It's the same hair that grows out of his own armpits.
The same hair that crawls up out of his crotch on up his stomach. . . . It's
his hair too. He got to love it.'" This sameness, beautiful to Pilate and to
Hagar, but unwanted by Milkman, can only be broken by extreme familial
violence, a violence expressed first in Milkman's cold and formal letter of
disengagement, then in Hagar's ritualized and unrealized murder attempts,
and ultimately in Milkman's shocking suggestion to her that she insert the
knife in her own crotch. Indirectly, of course, she does just that when she kills
herself after first attempting to make herself into an object of desire, introducing the objectifying distance of clothes, makeup, and media images
between herself and her incestuous lover.

The transgressive and uncomfortable nature of Milkman and Hagar's
relationship mirrors the marriage of their ancestors Macon Sr. and Sing and
explains the mystery of their legendary history. If Macon/Jake and Sing grew
up together in Shalimar, why did they tell everyone in Pennsylvania that they
met on the wagon of ex-slaves going north? And if Macon/Jake was born in
Shalimar, why did he say he was from Macon? And why was Sing so insistent
that he keep his lugubrious attributed name Macon Dead; why was she so
eager for a new start and a clean slate? Although Milkman raises these questions, his quest yields no satisfactory answers. His quest implies, however,
that their quasi-incestuous upbringing could be the key, that if they were to
establish what may have felt like an incestuous marital bond, it had to be in
secrecy and in a new place.

The great preponderance of incestuous connections in the novel, from
the ancestors to the youngest generation, constitute one side of familial

configuration; escape, distance, and death constitute the other. That "inexorable play of sameness, of identities misplaced and exchanged," that is incest is inadequate as a figure on which to base cultural formation: culture requires articulation and differentiation. But flight is equally problematic, for differentiation must, in turn, be based on connection. Two figures can perhaps serve as objective correlatives, as incarnations, of the contradictory familial images the novel develops: Pilate's smooth stomach and the dead body of Guitar's father. Together they make it possible to think through the gendered nature of relationships, as well as the particular role of the paternal in the vacillation between presence and absence, sameness and difference, which seems to define all intimacy in the text.

When Pilate "birthed herself," she broke her interconnection with the dead mother. Because it is a sign of lack, an absent connection, her absent navel and the absent cord it implies are utterly threatening to everyone around her. No one can come into the world already cut loose. But Pilate has amply compensated for her lack: her father's and brother's nurturing closeness provided her with the intimate bond she missed. When her father is killed, however, she needs artificially to create a bodily connection to him and perhaps, by extension, to her mother. When she pierces her own flesh with the earring which, shaped like a womb and connected to her body like an umbilical cord, contains her name, she repairs the absence of relation that has failed to mark her body. By placing her name in her ear, moreover, she can literally incorporate the father's word, make it flesh.

The body of Guitar's father—sawed in two by a sawmill, with the two halves no longer fitting together—serves as another paradigmatic image in the novel's analysis of relationships. This one, however, is marked as masculine and as paternal; it demonstrates, moreover, the ways in which the family, by way of the father, is embedded in larger social and economic forces. Guitar is permanently shaped not so much by the loss of his father but by the contradictions of his father's death, by the lack of fit: the candy offered the children by the mill owner in exchange for their father, the money offered their mother and her accepting, grateful smile. What is wrong here, what Guitar literally cannot swallow when he rejects candy, is the father's unnatural death in the service of white capitalist patriarchal production and consumption and the intervention of the white industrialist who equates the black male with cash and candy.

The death of Guitar's father, like the murder of Macon Dead II at the hands of the Butlers, points to the social plot which exists outside, but which is interwoven with, the familial. It is the plot of the dominant culture, which is threatened by African American adult masculinity and entrepreneurial spirit. The play of sameness and difference within the black family, then, is always overshadowed and interrupted by another dominant and controlling term: the white patriarch protecting "his" property. It is when he, or his machine, saws the black man in two or shoots him five feet into the air or lynches him that he reestablishes his single authority. But the black man's parts never fit; his body does not stay buried. And the black man's son or daughter needs to try to make sense of this puzzle. Unlike Pilate, Mr. Bains cannot repair the damage done to him. In the vocabulary of this novel, men, especially men who are fathers, are more deeply implicated than women in the larger structures of money and power that interrupt and determine the familial plot. African American paternity, as Hortense Spillers claims, is always dual, divided. The father's familial affiliations, much more so than the mother's, the daughter's, or the sister's, are always subject to the demands of this second, social plot. Sawed in two, shot five feet into the air, black men cannot bring into balance the external social threat with the internal familial needs and demands for intimacy. Macon II demonstrates that this lack of fit applies to middle-class black men as well as to the poor and disadvantaged, just as Guitar's involvement with the Seven Days, all men, demonstrates a different response to the dualities and divisions that characterize African American masculinity. Whatever "doesn't fit" in the familial interactions Morrison portrays, then, is much exacerbated in the position of the masculine and the paternal.

The white patriarch's external intervention in the life of the black family explains perhaps the alternative, Oedipal narrative that lies at the origin of Pilate and Macon II's story: the incident in the cave. Macon's primal murder of the ghostlike old white and white-haired man guarding his sacks of gold indeed reads very much like a "parallel" story to that of Oedipus, as well as like a story of misplaced revenge. It is thus, perhaps, that in Spillers's terms, the Freudian text can "translate." The day after their father was murdered by the Butlers, the two children spend the night hiding out in a cave. Like Oedipus at the crossroads, Macon lashes out rather incomprehensibly at an old man he accidentally meets and kills him unthinkingly. This Oedipus kills not his own father but the white patriarch. He murders the authorial father who killed the black father and who owns the gold and has to guard it against the black father and his children. Like Laius, this paternal figure is the primary aggressor and has a primal guilt for which he must atone. If, unlike Oedipus, Macon never gets the benefit of this murder, however, it is because of Pilate's intervention. This leads to Macon's split with Pilate, his resentment and misunderstanding of her, and his continued yearning for the white man's gold, a yearning he passes on to his son. The daughter/sister refuses to perpetuate father/son conflict even if that conflict has been displaced onto the white father. The daughter/sister understands that the two fathers are interchangeable: although her father was killed by whites, she carries what she thinks are a white man's bones as her "inheritance." But bones are indistinguishable: "I've been carrying Papa?" Pilate incredulously asks after years of a misapprehension which carries no consequence. For her, there is but one paternity and it is a double and divided one. Even though its parts cannot be re-membered, they must be kept close and carried along.

When Milkman mistakes the bones for gold, he demonstrates the difference between the masculine and feminine relations to the social: Pilate is content to keep her unidentified bones in her own separate alternative social space; Milkman, on the other hand, wants the money that will buy him a way into social success. Whereas she has brought the "white" man into her space, Milkman wants to take his place.

As he goes back to the South to search for Pilate's gold, he finds, instead, the legacy of ancestral knowledge handed down, not through his father, but through Pilate herself. Milkman's quest involves learning not only about masculinity and paternity but also about femininity and maternity. He needs to resolve these slippages between material and spiritual inheritance, between literal and figural, between masculine and feminine. He needs to perform the reconciliation of Pilate and her brother. These very slippages, however, illustrate the novel's interconnection between familial structures and its structures of signification which need to be read back into the family. The play of sameness and difference that defines familial interaction defines also the act of naming and the process of representation.

3
"And the children may know their names"

"Everything bad that ever happened to him happened because he couldn't read. Got his name messed up because he couldn't read." In the terms of Lacanian psychoanalysis, the father is the logos, the patronym, the name. He marks the child's entry into the symbolic—that system of signification in which the sign is arbitrary, separated from the referent through multiple substitutions and meditations. It is his status in the symbolic that allows the father to break the relation of sameness and mirroring that at least appears to link the child and the mother. Through this necessary break, the father introduces the child into the culture he makes possible. The father, moreover, represents not only the logos but the law. But what of the father who does not read or write, yet who lives in a culture where writing, as Henry Louis Gates Jr. has shown, is the visible sign of reason and of humanity? What of the illiterate father who is excluded from the law except as its victim?

In Morrison's novel, this father, robbed of his authoritative power by his subordinate social status, attempts, on the one hand, to establish his own paternal authority in the terms of the culture which excludes him and, on the other, to challenge that culture by flying away from it. Solomon flies off to Africa, defying the rationality which undergirds every Western belief system. His own name—Solomon, or lawgiver—gets modulated throughout the novel by its sound, becoming Shalimar, Sugarman, Charlemagne. Yet his name raises the question of whether, if he could, he would be the Lacanian lawgiver, of whether he is "saved" by his oppression. His son Jake attempts to assimilate and to become the patriarch: he accepts the arbitrary name given him erroneously by the drunken white officer, a name which results from a misreading of the columns of the bureaucratic form which has become his identity. And he passes that name down to his son, who will transmit it to his son as well. To name his daughter, he steps into the symbolic through the mediation of the Book, the Bible. He wishes to make his act of naming as arbitrary has he knows the hegemonic system of signification to be. Yet, as he does so, some of his own tradition, where words and things are acquired less arbitrarily—his Native American mother's name is Singing Bird; his uncle's name is Crow—intrudes, complicating the process. Macon II remembers how his father

> chose a group of letters that seemed to him strong and hand-some; saw in them a large figure that looked like a tree hanging in some princely but protective way over a row of smaller trees. How he had copied the group of letters out on a piece of brown paper; copied, as illiterate people do, every curlicue, arch, and bend in the letters, and presented it to the midwife.

In naming Pilate, Macon Sr. chooses a figure that is as nurturing and protective as he is toward her: the larger tree seems protectively to hover over the smaller ones. Every time Macon Sr. attempts to use the symbolic, however, it tricks him. He goes to Pennsylvania because he cannot read the signs for Boston; he names his daughter Pilate because he cannot recognize the name of the Christ-killer; he signs away his right to his land, because the white neighbors exploit his illiteracy. Yet his son, who can read and manipulate the system for his own benefit, nevertheless perpetuates this paternal tradition of naming his daughters arbitrarily after the first word he points to in the Bible: Magdalene and First Corinthians. Pilate herself still follows, though rather more cautiously, her father's naming practice. She gives her daughter, Rebecca, a biblical name but asks someone for some suggestions and chooses one that sounds good rather than one that looks good or the first one her finger hits.

All of the characters' relations to the unreliable and inhospitable process of symbolic substitution are uncomfortable; each feels a more intimate bond with or a nostalgia for a more literal connection to language and naming. Although she can never claim her own act, Ruth unwittingly renames Milkman through her act of nursing, repossessing him from the symbolic, connecting him to her with a stream of milk, an alternative to the ink the fathers, white and black, use to write their children's names. The community engages in a similar act of repossession when they name their street "Not Doctor Street" or the hospital "No Mercy." In Shalimar, Milkman discovers the power of this literal connection between signifier and referent when he meets Sweet. Pilate can also be "pilot"; she can "sing," thereby literally becoming her mother. The nostalgia for the literal is expressed in numerous acts of metamorphosis which are acts of materialization and literalization: Pilate carries her father's memory in the bag of bones, Milkman keeps Hagar's hair, Ruth sucks her father's fingers and lies on his grave, Pilate carries her name in a box in her ear, feeling its connection as she marks/infects her flesh with it.

Empowered by these close material connections, the characters seem to yearn for more authentic, less distant and arbitrary names and words. The bond with the land Milkman achieves during the hunt leads him to fantasize an alternative system of communication outside the symbolic:

> No, it was not language; it was what there was before language.
> Before things were written down. Language in the time when
> men and animals did talk to one another, when a man could sit
> down with an ape and the two converse, when a tiger and a man
> could share the same tree, and each understood the other; when
> men ran *with* wolves, not from or after them.

But analogous to the structure of incest, this literality shares with incest the at once liberatory and deeply problematic challenge to hegemonic cultural structures. As Milkman knows from his own surname, the literal has its own problems; if he rejects the symbolic, then he is already dead, not symbolically deadened by the culture in power, but simply, literally dead. In spite of its pitfalls, the symbolic is, in this novel, the structure that those who are willfully and crucially excluded from it need to confront and come to terms with. But like black paternity, the symbolic in the context of African American culture is also dual and divided: in its fissures, other structures are inscribed and they interrrupt and challenge its single and authorial power. Incestuous literality impedes the progress toward culture; distant mediated symbolization deadens and denies vitality and intimacy. *Song of Solomon* searches for the space between, the space of contradiction which can transform and rede-fine the paternal and, through it, the familial more generally.

How to mediate between the too close incestuous literality of a nonsymbolic nonlanguage and the arbitrariness and uncaring distance that has made the characters "dead" is the project of the novel's quest, the process of "knowing their names." It is a project parallel to and interwoven with the mediation between paternal overpowering presence, on the one hand, and paternal absence, on the other:

> Surely, he thought, he and his sister had some ancestor, some lithe young man with onyx skin and legs as straight as cane stalks, who had a name that was real. A name given to him at birth with love and seriousness. A name that was not a joke, nor a disguise, nor a brand name. But who this lithe young man was, and where his cane-stalk legs carried him from or to, could never be known.

Knowing this young man, this ancestor, is "knowing their names"—a process different from naming or even from renaming. It is a process neither literal as the water stain on Ruth's table, which spreads across the fine wood even as it symbolizes the stain on the family, nor figural as her dead velvet flowers, which have never had an anchor in nature or the real. It is a process that *reads* within the symbolic a connection to a literal which interrupts, disturbs, and challenges its hegemony.

> He read the road signs with interest now, wondering what lay beneath the names. The Algonquins had named the territory he lives in in Great Water, *michi gami*. How many dead lives and fading memories were buried in and beneath the names of the places in this country. Under the recorded names were other names, just as "Macon Dead," recorded for all time in some dusty file, hid from view the real names of people, places, and things. Names that had meaning. No wonder Pilate put hers in her ear. When you know your name, you should hang on to it, for unless it is noted down and remembered, it will die when you do.

Milkman reads throughout his journey; he reads road signs, the song, the name of the father and the mother. As Milkman reads, as he discovers the meanings and the names both, he engages in the process of "knowing their names" as this novel defines it. Through a complicated process of reading, this process modulates literal and symbolic. It does not totally give up literal connection but insists on undertaking the long, exhausting, and necessary journey through symbolic substitution; it reaches Lacanian language by way of slavery's heritage of illiteracy, thus making that heritage useful and powerful rather than disempowering.

"Knowing their names" is a reading process full of dangers and pitfalls, full of misreadings and wrong turns. It is never complete. The arbitrary play of substitutions that is the symbolic and the literal connections of sameness each threaten to explode into violence. How are we to read the numbers game played by the Seven Days? In the absence of legal recourse, they insist on avenging black deaths on the same day and in the same category, little girls for little girls; but that system of literal substitution bypasses any notion of guilt or innocence, and the people who actually die are not the ones who committed the murders; they are their substitutes. And how are we to read Guitar's final fraternal attack on Milkman? Milkman did not in fact cheat the Days; there was no gold. Yet Guitar still insists that he needs to kill him. First, he erroneously and arbitrarily, symbolically, kills Pilate. If he then needs Milkman's life, is it to create a space of distance between them, separating himself from their fraternal closeness? Or is it to kill off that part of himself which is Milkman and skeptical about the Days' project? Is Milkman's intended death as arbitrary and symbolic as the other Days' executions, or is it literally a punishment? Does he, in fact, die, or does he fly, bridging the valley that separates him from his alter ego? The novel does not determine this end for us but remains inconclusive, undecidable, unreadable. Yet it ends in several moments of nurturing and connection, between Milkman and Pilate, between Milkman and Guitar, and between Milkman and Solomon/Shalimar/Sugarman/Charlemagne. Milkman's final leap is not a flight away from home; it is a flight toward his past and toward Guitar. It is a leap into a landscape that responds by literally *saying* "tar, tar, tar," that echoes the cries not for death but for being "am, am, am, am," and "life, life, life, life."

Milkman's quest is the child's quest for his name and for his father's name. It is a journey of substitutions: knowledge for gold for all his possessions, Shalimar for Danville, cars for buses for planes, legs for cars, and so on. As a journey, it is also an act of reading, of understanding the song he has always known, a song the children used to keep their father's story of leaving alive. It is a journey back over his own life, to understand his own misunderstandings, especially his devaluation of the women who nurtured him; Pilate, his mother, Hagar, his sisters. His search leads him back to Jake and Sing, to his father and to Pilate, to thes brother–sister pairs who were so dangerously close as to have been violently separated by death or quarrel. Is his ancestor Shalimar or Solomon or Charlemagne or Sugarman? Whose legacy does he fulfill when he flies at the end, Solomon's or Singing Bird's? These slippages remain important because they define the difficulties of articulation Milkman cannot resolve. What they mark is the fantasy, and in some sense the real-ization, of a dual inheritance, masculine and feminine, a different duality which supports, supplements, and multiplies the fractured and ultimately debilitating duality of the novel.

More than Milkman, the novel's end features Pilate, her loving connec-tion to humanity and her death. Burying her father's bones allows Pilate herself to die. Before she does so, she tries to bury her name and earring, no longer needing its material connection to the past and to the paternal naming practice. But a bird (her mother?) comes to reclaim the earring, and the name, from the father's grave, where Pilate had thrown it. As Milkman sees it, he understands that "[w]ithout ever leaving the ground, she could fly." As Pilate becomes her mother, Singing Bird, Milkman can claim this maternal legacy as well, and he does so when he transforms the song and sings it to Pilate: "Sugargirl, don't leave me here." "'There must be another one like you,' he whispered to her. 'There's got to be at least one more woman like you,'" Milkman wishfully asserts. Is the novel suggesting that he himself is, could be, might be, that other female figure? When Milkman ambiguously and contingently accepts this maternal heritage along with the paternal, the novel re-members the heterosexual bond of transmission that was broken when Sing dies, when Macon leaves Pilate, when he stops making love to Ruth. As it does so, the novel successfully transforms the paternal.

Ironically, however, this heterosexuality does not lead to generation. Milkman, the male protagonist, alone benefits from the lesson learned. Hagar's own quest is only a mock-heroic/tragic version of Milkman's: as she returns from her shopping spree in the rain, she also loses her clothes and possessions, but only to arrive home a ridiculous and suicidal mockery of the sexual object featured by the advertising industry. In spite of their elaborate education, Lena and Corinthians also do not share in the benefits of the knowledge Milkman has been allowed to earn. When Hagar dies, when Lena and Corinthians fail to have children, when Milkman ambiguously leaps and soars, the impossibility of transmission is clarified. The novel has not yet found a way to think beyond the perspective of the child whose invocation, "Daddy," forms its dedication—beginning and end. And although the novel has allowed the male children to know not only their own names but also their mothers' and their fathers', it has not done the same for the female children. It has not yet found a way to share the son's knowledge with the daughter. Although it has deconstructed the dichotomy between the material presence of the mother and the legendary, symbolic absence of the father, it has not yet found a way to incarnate that more embodied yet still comfort-ably symbolic form of paternity. For that, *Song of Solomon* insists, African American masculinity is still too deeply threatened and endangered.

LINDEN PEACH

Competing Discourses in Song of Solomon *(1977)*

As an African-American with a long-standing interest in deconstructing the white frame of reference by which black people have been defined, it is not surprising that in *Song of Solomon* Morrison should appropriate *the* archetype of white American literature: the romance narrative. But although *Song of Solomon* uses a traditional Euro-American mode of narrative, it would be misleading to interpret the novel only from this standpoint. The favoured ontology in the book is distinctly African, embracing black folktales and African legends and giving priority to African values.

Song of Solomon is based around the search of a young black man, Milkman Dead, for his legacy. He has been brought up in a family where his father has shunned his own community, whilst striving to become a small businessman respected by white people. His mother has been ostracised by her husband because he believed he had discovered her in a necrophiliac relationship with her father. Whilst Milkman's early adulthood passes in years of irresponsibility and indifference to the emerging civil rights struggles of the time, his quest for the lost family gold eventually becomes a search for spiritual values and the black ancestry in which he had previously shown no interest and which had been denied also by his father. His spiritual mentor in this search and the guardian of the lore he

From *Modernist Novelists: Toni Morrison.* © 1995 Linden Peach. Reprinted with permission of St. Martin's Press, Inc.

hopes to find is his aunt, Pilate, another member of the family disowned by his father because she is not respectable enough for him.

In the Preface to *The House of the Seven Gables* (1851), Nathaniel Hawthorne asserted that 'when a writer calls his work a Romance, it need hardly be observed that he wishes to claim a certain latitude, both as to its fashion and material, which he would not have felt himself entitled to assume had he professed to be writing a Novel'. A definition of romance, therefore, is difficult almost by definition. However, it is clear that for many nineteenth-century American writers the latitude which Hawthorne claimed for romance included working with folklore, myth and ritual; exploring anti-rational structures and levels of meaning; dramatising the instinctual and the passional. Quite apart from the Puritan and Calvinistic distrust of mimetic representation in the arts, it was inevitable perhaps that a form of writing which embraced the mythical, the instinctual and the anti-rational would aquire a special place, as Toni Morrison herself has argued, in nineteenth-century American culture.

In Morrison's view, romance as 'an exploration of anxiety imported from the shadows of European culture', enabled American writers to confront:

> Americans' fear of being outcast, of failing, of powerlessness;
> their fear of boundarylessness, of Nature unbridled and crouched
> for attack; their fear of absence of so-called civilization; their fear
> of loneliness, of aggression both external and internal.

Song of Solomon is a romance in both the nineteenth-century American sense, and, as we shall discuss later, in the European sense. It has features in common with nineteenth-century American romance: it works with myth, folklore and ritual; and it involves anti-rational structures and levels of meaning. But many of the mythical and folklore elements come from Africa and the anti-rational elements, as we shall see later, arise from an African, and hence African-American, ontology. Krumholz has argued that there is evidence of the influence of two African epics, the Mwindo epic and the Kambili epic. Moreover, the novel is not concerned with the fears of white America; the fears are those of black America—of the dissolution of black culture and the erosion of black sensibilities by the pursuit of white values. Myth, folklore and ritual are the essential means of reclaiming the black cultural heritage in opposition to the white construction of blackness.

White America's construction of blackness is, to a considerable extent, a response to the white fears which Morrison outlines. As she points out, one of the most important strategies by which white Americans confronted those fears was the transference of 'internal conflicts' to black slaves, 'conveniently bound and violently silenced black bodies':

> What rose up out of collective needs to allay internal fears and to rationalize external exploitation was an American Africanism—a fabricated brew of darkness, otherness, alarm, and desire that is uniquely American.

The impact of this 'fabricated brew of darkness, otherness, alarm' is well illustrated in one of the most famous white romances of the nineteenth century, Mark Twain's *The Adventures of Huckleberry Finn* (1884). Misunderstood quite often as the story of a boy's moral awakening or as a piece of escapist, freedom-of-the-river fantasy, its full complexity has also been missed by those who have seen it as a polemic against slavery or as an indictment of white society. The real subject of the book is European-America's fear of black America and the final part of the novel makes explicit the white fear of losing control. Mrs. Hotchkiss's increasingly exaggerated estimate of the number of negroes involved in freeing Jim is an indicator of this, as is the whites' reaction in wanting to skin every negro in the place. The warning left on the door of the hut significantly hints at a larger issue than the freeing of one slave: 'Beware. Trouble is Brewing. Keep a sharp lookout'.

In *Song of Solomon*, the way in which white people project such fears on to blacks is evident in the murder of Till who is also a victim of white fears of the sexuality of the negro: as we explained in the introduction, he is alleged to have whistled after one white woman and is accused of sleeping with others. In the novel, the black men who adopt or seek to adopt white, middle-class values do so within a context of entrenched, white power in a society which is frightened of them and which eventually denies them. The novel unfolds against a backdrop which describes how Not Doctor Street arose as a name for Mains Avenue because the whites refused to sanction the black name of Doctor Street. Moreover black people tended to refer to the Mercy Hospital as No Mercy Hospital (it was not until 1931 that the first pregnant black woman was allowed to give birth in a ward instead of on the steps) and when a black person, Reba, wins a prize as the half-millionth customer of Sears and Roebuck, it is not publicised.

From her reading of nineteenth-century American romance, Morrison argues that the subject 'on the "mind" of the literature of the United States', as texts such as *The Adventures of Huckleberry Finn* demonstrate, was the 'highly problematic construction of the American as a new white man'. Within this context it is ironic, and maybe deliberately so, that in *Song of Solomon* Morrison produces a work which uses American romance conventions to explore the appropriation of white, middle-class American values by African-Americans.

II

Despite its traditional emphasis upon initation, renunciation, atonement and release through ritual divestment, the experiment with the quest narrative in *Song of Solomon* through Milkman's search for his legacy is determined by its radical content. For example it is unclear at first that Milkman is the central character. In many respects he is an unlikely hero; for much of the novel he is uncommitted, unimaginative and draws inaccurate or inappropriate conclusions. But then this is a novel which expresses the limitations of any one view and which in its very structure suggests that to elevate any individual to the status of a hero or any one point of view to the level of myth is reductive.

Each voice in the novel appears to provide only its own fragmented version of the truth—the text literally dramatises the gap between telling and what is told. In fact the way in which the narrative appears to eschew chronological development and linear structure suggests that this fragmentariness is at the heart of the novel's worldview. But through the interplay between different viewpoints, concepts such as community, authority, commitment and individuality, for example, are subjected to scrutiny.

Song of Solomon, like all of Morrison's work, gives priority to ambivalence and discrepancy, eschewing the tendency of Western, Aristotelian philosophical tradition to give credence to single, unified meaning, confident in its modes of ordering and classification. The same story, as Genevieve Fabre argues, is picked up in different places, retold and expanded into further complexity. For example, Milkman's father, Macon Dead, explains the tension between himself and Milkman's mother, Ruth, to Milkman, alleging that Ruth had an unhealthy fixation for her father and he for her which culminated in Macon finding Ruth in bed with her deceased father, 'naked as a yard dog, kissing him' with his fingers in her mouth. Ruth's own version portrays herself as a lonely person who needed the support of her father: 'It was important for me to be in his presence, among his things, the things he used, had touched. Later it was important for me to know that he was in the world'. She accuses Macon of trying to kill Milkman and of killing her father by removing his medicine. Ruth now appears starved of affection by her father who was more interested in winning the respect of white people and acquiring a big house than in loving her as a father should. As a woman, she is driven to take her dead father as a clandestine lover, lying at his feet in the cemetery, because her husband has refused to make love to her in the twenty years they have been married. Each retelling of a story in the novel, as here, raises new questions suggesting that any one version of anything inevitably generates fresh interpretations.

As we shall see, *Song of Solomon* is a dialogical novel, a hybrid of multiple motifs and allusions. Medieval romance motifs are combined, for example, with biblical references and classical allusions. Black folklore, realism and the supernatural are woven together and in the Circe episode realism seems to collapse altogether beneath the weight of fabulation.

The priority which the novel gives to Milkman's journey should be placed, then, within the larger, fragmentary nature of the narrative as a whole. The numerous discourses which surround his journey have more importance in the novel than in the traditional romantic quest, accounting for the fact that it is some way into the novel before Milkman emerges as the central character. It is not simply a matter of Milkman's journey dominating the second half of the novel and the first half of the novel serving to provide a preparation for the hero's quest as Lee argues. Milkman emerges as the hero of the narrative at the same time as a hierarchy of values begins to emerge from the competing discourses of its first part.

Much of our understanding of Milkman's journey is teleological. The journey is from the North dominated by urban, white middle-class values to the black South and it is the latter which reveals the former fully for what it is. Milkman travels by plane, by bus and then by foot—emblematic of the way in which he sheds layers of his former cultural identity. The journey to Circe's home, the house of the servant who saved Pilate and Macon after their father was killed and who bears the name of Odysseus's guide to the lower world, is made difficult as much by his city clothes as by his ineptitude. Gradually, he loses his clothes, watch, suitcase and shoes, symbolising the white cultural values he has absorbed and assimilated at the expense of black values. The loss of the watch is especially significant because Milkman loses the Western concept of time which is essentially linear as opposed to a traditional African concept of time which is cyclical.

There is an additional element to all of this: the various competing discourses of the first part of the novel are within Milkman himself. His quest resolves the conflicts between North and South, male and female, white and black within his own psyche. In doing so, certain discourses which have been silenced emerge and become dominant in his spiritual-physical makeup.

The white peacock encountered by Milkman and Guitar as they seek to steal Pilate's gold suggests, as Lee points out, that in order to fly, the black person must reject the imposed white sociocultural baggage. White peacocks are usually only found in captivity, implying that the white cultural tradition is itself a captivity. Milkman admires the peacock's strut—epitomising those blacks who imitate whites and assume white cultural values, such as Macon Dead in his Packard car and Ruth's father, acquire a similar kind of social strut. Ironically, Milkman realises that the peacock can fly no better than a chicken. Guitar's response encapsulates the problem:

> 'Too much tail', Guitar replies. 'All that jewelry weighs it down. Like vanity. Can't nobody fly with all that shit. Wanna fly, you got to give up the shit that weighs you down.'

Hagar learns a similar lesson the hard way in repeating Pecola's mistake in *The Bluest Eye*. She comes to believe that voguish clothing and cosmetics will lift her skyward, but in the rain they literally fall to the streets. Giving up 'the shit that weighs you down', as Guitar puts it, involves considerable personal growth, self-awareness and personal pain. Hagar, like Milkman who was overnourished on breast milk, is a victim of obsessive love; she has not been able to develop sufficient inner strength and resilience. In this respect, the disintegration of her cosmetics in the rain symbolises the fragility of her own personality.

After the hunt in the South, Milkman acquires knowledge of himself, the community and Guitar. The decision to eat the heart of the slain bobcat, as Lee demonstrates, is redolent of the traditional ritual by which hunters internalised the courage of the prey. The description of the way in which the heart comes from the body 'as easily as a yolk slips out of its shell' reminds us of Guitar's point that Milkman is a shell which has to be broken.

This narrative of escape from the Dead household—dead in the spiritual sense as well as in name—is a story of growth reinforced by the interjection of the account of Corinthians, Milkman's sister. In becoming the 'amanuensis' of Michigan's Poet Laureate, Corinthians becomes an ornament within the elegant emptiness of a home where there is no passion. In this respect, Henry Porter's verse, with which he seeks to woo her, is an improvement upon the celebrated poetry. The relationship which Corinthians establishes with him moves from one based on hatred because of the shame she felt, to one in which she becomes a 'grown-up woman'.

III

The ways in which *Song of Solomon* gives more priority to the competing discourses within it than to Milkman's journey as such, which is where Lee places the emphasis, reflects its African-American concerns. The hero of the traditional quest is usually the child of distinguished parents. Milkman's ancestors are distinguished but in non-traditional ways; his own father, Macon Dead, Jr, is a grotesque fairy-tale character whose lust for gold has made him one of the most affluent and most hated black property owners. However, his name epitomises how much his fixation with white-defined respectability has cost him in personal, social and spiritual terms even though his accumulation of wealth is part of his attempt to overcome oppression, prejudice, poverty and lack of a formal education. It is Guitar who makes explicit the connection between the imposed name, Dead, the appropriation of white values and a more generalised and pervasive white control: 'White men want us dead or quiet—which is the same thing as dead . . . They want us, you know, "universal", human, "no race consciousness".' This is further embodied in the car Macon drives with a winged woman on its bonnet, 'riding backward like flying blind', and in the way in which the black community calls the vehicle 'Macon Dead's hearse'. The counterpoint to the figure on the bonnet of the car is the way in which Corinthians spreadeagles herself across Porter's antiquated vehicle; flying to save herself. Significantly the first trial which Milkman has to undergo in the South in second half of the novel, a fight in a general store in Shalimar, Virginia, is started because the local people are offended by his money and sense of privilege: 'They looked at his skin and saw it was as black as theirs, but they knew he had the heart of the white men who came to pick them up in the trucks when they needed anonymous, faceless laborers.' The importance of this motif within the novel is underscored by Macon's ironic naming of his daughter, First Corinthians, since it is in St. Paul's First Epistle to the Corinthians that personal pride, vanity and ambition are attacked.

In the traditional quest, the hero takes revenge on his father and achieves rank and honours. Milkman, in a process which begins when he strikes his father, eventually frees himself from his father's obsessive capitalism and discovers that he is a descendant of Solomon Sugarman, a progenitor of 21 children, renowned for his ability to fly—commemorated in a nursery rhyme and in the naming of his launching site, Solomon's Leap. Here the novel does not simply parody the European quest narrative, it also draws on the African concept of the mythological hero and betrays the importance which African culture traditionally attaches to the ancestor. In 'Rootedness: the Ancestor as Foundation', Morrison describes ancestors as a 'sort of timeless people whose relationships to the characters are benevolent, instructive, and protective, and they provide a certain kind of wisdom'. The title *Song of Solomon* suggests the biblical song of ancestral wisdom and from the beginning the novel is presided over by the figure of

Milkman's forefather. Indeed, it has the epigraph: 'The fathers may soar / And the children may know their names'. As Segy argues:

> The mythological hero who represented special valor because of his exceptional services to the tribe in the legendary past was regarded as a model, the embodiment of the best of human potentiality. As descendants of his hero, the living through identification with him derived a special tribal pride which was the basis for their ethnocentrism.

Song of Solomon is framed by the African-American vernacular tradition of the flying African. The song which Pilate sings to accompany Milkman's birth is a variant of this Gullah folktale of the ancestor who flew back to Africa to escape the trap of slavery and Milkman's leap at the end of the novel aligns him with Solomon. The importance of this kind of identification with ancestors in African culture is again stressed by Segy:

> He experienced with being part of the mythical past. He was able to identify himself with that which was presented to him as permanent and sacred reality. Because of this identification he was able to step out of his ordinary, egocentered daily life. His individual life was depersonalized, elevated.

However, even this concept of sacred reality represented by the ancestor is open in this particular instance to different lines of interpretation. In abandoning Ryna, Solomon is identified with a number of male characters in the book who abandon women, including Jake Solomon, Macon Dead and Milkman himself. Here, as de Weever points out, the text expounds the potentially dangerous routes out of life, away from the need for commitment and stability, implicit in the Greek myths of Icarus and Daedalus and the folktales of the flying African.

The novel also develops the traditional focus upon ancestry in African culture in an African-American context through its emphasis on the significance of naming. The reclamation of true identity is crucial to black people who in slavery were named by others. As Guitar explains to Milkman: 'Niggers get their names the same way they get everything else—the best way they can'. Ironically, a drunken Union army officer working for the Freedman's bureau put the name of Macon's father's birth place and the fact that his father was dead in the wrong place on the registration form. The fact that Macon, Jr, has inherited this false name highlights the way in which he is a grotesque distortion of his father. His father's real name was Jake, but his son is more like his biblical namesake, crafty and patriarchal. For Jake, property was not mere property, but the symbol of a bond between the land and the community. The man who appears to Macon, Jr, after his father has been killed by the white Butlers reminds him of his father—indeed he might be the father's ghost. In fact, he is the ghostly distortion of Jake which Macon is to become. The old white man hoarding the gold in the cave to which the apparition takes Macon is an adaptation of a stock situation from the traditional quest, gold being hidden in an ogre's cave. Although it cannot be interpreted solely in this light, the borrowed motif draws attention to itself: offering a parody of the whiteness which Macon is to assume.

Of course Milkman's own nickname has ignominous origins; because his mother breastfed him for much longer than normal it was given to him by Freddie, the janitor, who likes to believe he is a friend of the family. The name serves to exacerbate the tension between Milkman and his father. Although Macon doesn't understand the origins of the name he recognises that it sounds 'dirty, intimate, and hot' thereby reminding him of his wife's abnormal fixation for her father and the passion which he denies in himself and in his children. His son's name compounds the shame of his own name:

> Surely, he thought, he and his sister had some ancestor, some lithe young man with onyx skin and legs as straight as cane stalks, who had a name that was real. A name given to him at birth with love and seriousness. A name that was not a joke, nor a disguise, nor a brand name.

In the traditional European quest either during or before pregnancy there is usually an omen against the birth which seems to endanger the father. Milkman is compared before he is born to a little bird and he is the first child born in Mercy Hospital. His birth accompanied by Pilate's Song of Sugarman is also marked by the insurance salesman's leap from the top of the hospital. But once again it is important not to see the circumstances of Milkman's birth only as an appropriation of a European literary convention. The circumstances around Milkman's birth serve to emphasise key myths. The myth of the flying African is appropriated as is the sacredness of the ancestor. Singing is an essential part of the Gospel church and Pilate's 'powerful contralto' suggests that the events which are occurring are in some way sacred. The song proves to be a significant clue in Milkman's identification of his forefather.

IV

In the European romance narrative, the main geographical element is provided by the lands through which the hero travels on his quest. However, *Song of Solomon* presents us with an ideological geography, as it were. There are three overlapping zones in which people live and which have been created by the white political system. As Guitar tries to explain to Milkman:

> 'No Geography? Okay, no geography. What about some history in your tea? Or some sociopolitico—No. That's still geography. Goddam, Milk, I do believe my whole life's geography.'

The three zones as portrayed in the novel reinterpret the geography of the USA in terms of a sociopolitical dialectic: a black centre which is also a disenfranchised community, a zone which is a white zone, and a zone between them which allows for entry into the white zone but to a limited degree only. Indeed, the sociospace occupied by Macon Dead is the overlap between the white and black zones. It is a no-person's land as exemplified in his walk down Fifteenth Street:

> Scattered here and there, his houses stretched up beyond him like squat houses with hooded eyes. . . . now they did not seem to belong to him at all—in fact he felt as though the houses were in league with one another to make him feel like the outsider; the propertyless, landless wanderer.

By contrast, Milkman's entry into the community occurs in the black heart of the South in the fight in the general store provoked by the way in which Milkman has black skin but 'the heart of the white men who came to pick them up in the trucks when they needed anonymous, faceless laborers'. The zones are fluid, of course; political pressures from within can change them as can individual heroes. This is what Guitar, through violence, purports to do even though he operates in the tradition of the trickster and other ambivalent, archetypal figures who, by challenging the hero, push him toward his destination.

The legacy which Macon hopes his son will inherit is the one built by power and property in order to move the boundaries so that the family will one day become integrated with white society. In Europe, social status has traditionally been assessed in terms of land which, passed on through generations, signifies power and elitism. White America's puritan heritage gave the nation a sense of election through predestination, an ethic which confirmed the importance of the individual in building the nation's economic prosperity. In America, property and money translated as success through work became an index of a person's spiritual and moral value. In the nation's ideology, wealth was not associated with greed or exploitation but with the exploitation of inner personal resources. Material poverty became an indicator not of a social problem, but of individual spiritual poverty. The effect of this ideology on Macon Dead is evident in the way in which he is ashamed of Pilate, fearing that the white men in the bank on whose support he is dependent and whose respect he seeks may discover that she is his sister.

We are never told exactly why Robert Smith fails to fly at the beginning of the novel, but we suspect that it is because he is too removed from his heritage, which is also Macon Dead's failing. For some time, Macon believes that gold will set him free. Milkman repeats this mistake and when he enters the cave to find the gold his father has told him about there is a significant absence of light.

If we overstress the elements of the European romance narrative in this novel we might overlook the African myths which also determine the structure. Macon Dead, Jr, is a version of a character, Anaanu, from a very old West African folktale which found its way into America as Brer Rabbit and which is the basis of *Tar Baby* (1981). In one version of the original story, for example, Anaanu is a trickster spider who escapes famine by faking death and at night eats his fill. Macon, like Anaanu, chooses dispossession in order to achieve material gain. Anaanu's pretence at being dead is a form of disguise and Macon, too, in denial of his sister, Pilate, and his family adopts a pretence. Both Anaanu and Macon give up their place within the community for personal gain. Morrison develops this West African folktale within a particular American context and within the frame of the Euro-American quest story.

The European romantic quest has been readily employed in white American literature to explore ways in which the American dream of spiritual greatness has become a dream of material greatness. Whilst this transformation has been treated with considerable bitterness in some white American texts, others which employ the quest motif, such as F. Scott Fitzgerald's *The Great Gatsby*, stop short of condemning the desire for wealth even though they expose the corrupting influence of it in particular examples. Gatsby himself epitomises the American ideal of the self-made man and the capacity in America for people to make their own identities. In becoming Jay Gatsby, James Gatz escapes from his own origins and his naïve quest is linked to Arthurian legendary heroes such as Sir Galahad and Sir Percival and the quest for the Holy Grail. The grail which is Gatsby's quest is a romantic notion of perfect femininity—eventually exposed as false—based on the outward appearance of a corrupt and degenerate system. Gatsby's creation of himself and his quest are compared in the novel to frontier versions of the concept of the self-made man—as a boy, Gatsby made notes on self-improvement on a fly leaf of a copy of *Hopalong Cassidy* and his career begins when he meets Dan Cody, a relic of an earlier America—in order to demonstrate the corruption of the original dream.

In *Song of Solomon*, Morrison combines a number of mythologies so that each acts as a critique of the others. Up to a point, Macon Dead epitomises the white American concept of the self-made man, but, unlike Gatsby, he did not choose his own name. Unlike Gatsby, Macon Dead, Jr, comes to experience a rejecting society and the past which is corrupted in his quest is not a white heritage. In *The Great Gatsby* the dream can only be achieved by overturning any larger sense of moral responsibility for others. In Morrison's novel, although Macon Dead, too, can only realise his quest by eschewing any moral responsibility for others, he also rejects his black cultural heritage:

> Macon Dead dug in his pocket for his keys, and curled his fingers around them, letting their bunchy solidity calm him. They were the keys to all the doors of his houses (only four true houses; the rest were really shacks), and he fondled them from time to time as he walked down Not Doctor Street to his office. At least he thought of it as his office, had even painted the word OFFICE on the door. But the plate-glass window contradicted him. In peeling gold letters arranged in a semicircle, his business establishment was declared to be Sonny's Shop.

The fact that his office is situated on Not Doctor Street compounds the irony in this passage because the name is symbolic of black resistance. The name of the previous black occupant of the premises reminds Macon and the reader of the past which he can never fully eradicate. The previous name suggests that the shop was at the centre of the community whereas Macon's use of the premises as an office for his property business implies a greater emphasis on the pursuit of individual wealth and success at the expense of community.

The tension between Macon's and Ruth's aspirations for their son is part of a larger discourse within *Song of Solomon* around internal difference in the black community. Macon has little regard for university education and Ruth's aspirations for her son to enter university focus on the status which the medical degree will bring her as well as him, epitomised in the silver-backed brushes engraved with his initials, the abbreviated designation of doctor. The coincidence here again suggests how Milkman, like many black people, is not in control of his own destiny and this is bound up in the fact that he has been unable to choose his own name. The novel suggests on many levels that whereas black people become part of the American middle class they do not have the same licence as Gatsby, for example, to create their own identities which is the ideology on which the American middle-class pursuit of prosperity is founded. Thrown into confusion concerning his identity, Milkman's examination of his face before the mirror, his firm jawline and splendid teeth, reminds us significantly of the way in which slaves were examined in the marketplace and of a history with which black people still have to struggle.

V

Milkman's true inheritance, black cultural identity and ancestry, is provided by the women and particularly his aunt, Pilate. Although the epigraph mentions only the forefathers in the novel and the book is dedicated to 'Daddy', Morrison creates a space in which the women may be recognised and may assume importance. In many respects, the women are locked out of the soulless, material-oriented, patriarchal world in which the men—Macon Dead and Dr Foster—are locked. Pilate—'Christ Killing Pilate'—has the worst possible name as Fabre points out. Yet she understands the power of naming; the only name her father wrote hangs in a little box from her ear. She becomes quite literally Milkman's pilot or guiding force. She challenges his indifference and initiates him into the legacy of which black womankind are the guardians, a legacy of wisdom and beliefs. Pilate's lack of a navel associates her with Eve, source of innocence, and, paradoxically, of primal knowledge.

Pilate's perfect, soft-boiled eggs symbolise a balance of which Macon and herself seem separated spheres. Whilst Macon appears to follow and exaggerate the side of Jake which wants to own property and which values the status so accrued, Pilate embodies the spiritual and community-oriented part of him. Pilate's own home contrasts significantly with Macon's. Ruth and her daughter make fake roses and the only confirmation Ruth can find of her existence is the ugly spreading watermark left on the dining-room table from a bowl which once held fresh flowers. When Lena eventually wakes to what is happening to her, the outburst recalls Guitar's condemnation of how white people want black people quiet and 'dead': 'I was the one who started making artificial roses . . . I loved to do it. It kept me . . . quiet. That's why they make those people in the asylum weave baskets and make rag rugs. It keeps them quiet. If they didn't have the baskets they might find out what's really wrong and . . . do something. Something terrible.' Her hesitation before she can bring herself to say the word 'quiet' underscores its significance, for her and for her whole family, as well as the pain in the realisation. The phrase 'something terrible' is set apart and as such highlights the fear whites have of blacks who rise up against their confinement. In the description of the suicidal leap at the outset of the novel, roses occur along with wings and song as specific images, each of which eventually provides this multi-layered text with a sense of coherence around the subjects of freedom, spirituality, life-in-death, the value of myth and the role of the ancestor: 'The sight of Mr Smith and his wide blue wings transfixed them for a few seconds, as did the woman's singing and the roses strewn about.'

Pilate's house is filled with the smell of nature with which she is associated, of the forest and of blackberries. Of course her association with nature is another indicator of how she has taken after the positive side of Jake's character, reminding us of the love he had for his peach trees and his ability to make his crops increase and multiply. When Lena turns her anger against Milkman for the way he has ignored them she draws attention to the dying maple tree. Significantly Morrison herself has pointed out, in Jaye and Watts, that none of Gatsby's people achieves a fulfilling life in the natural environment, suggesting the importance which she attaches to this aspect of her characters such as Pilate.

However, as we suggested earlier, this is a complicated novel not easily reducible to binary opposites. Pilate is a character in the novel of whom we can also be critical. Her rootlessness is symbolised by the rocks which she carries, each one a remembrance of a place to which she has been and, like the name she carries in a box and her bag of bones, they symbolise her search for a place of belonging. Some critics have emphasised not her symbolic strengths but her general passivity, and indeed the passivity of most of the female characters compared with the male characters, and have seen this as confirming the male bias in the epigraph to the novel.

It would be wrong to see Pilate, as some critics have, as a totally negative character for such an interpretation would ignore the way in which the women are seen as the guardians of worthwhile knowledge which the men have to acquire. As Nancy Walker has pointed out, the white romance in America usually embodied a dream of escape that is both peculiarly American and identifiably masculine. Historically, the political and physical experiences of settling and exploring a wilderness required powers that have commonly been granted to men rather than women. However *Song of Solomon* casts women in a better light than the men: Macon Dead, Ruth's father and Milkman himself are selfish, uncaring people. Macon Dead is ruthless with delinquent tenants, wants to own people and worships wealth.

Ruth's father is seen as a 'miracle doctor' by whites, but, obsessed with caste, he does little for blacks. Milkman deserts Hagar and most of the men violate family bonds.

VI

At the heart of the reclamation of a non-Western worldview in *Song of Solomon* is a concern with a preconscious mode of awareness encapsulated in myth. Of course myth may be perceived in mythologising cultures as a means of preserving the wisdom of precedents based on ancestral laws—precedents which often connect ancestral pasts with cosmogonic events. The title of the novel itself reminds us of Solomon's song of ancestral wisdom. But myth may also be preserved as the poetic verbalisation of the unconscious and preconscious. In fact *Song of Solomon* offers a complex model of the unconscious which is close to that which Segy claims is characteristic of mythologising cultures. Pilate and Macon would seem to represent the separating out of the two spheres of the unconscious which Segy identifies. Pilate's own sensibility and creative existence give expression to an inner truth derived from her grasp of a supreme reality beyond her everyday existence, a sense of the wholeness of the order of things. She appears motivated by what Segy would refer to as her 'ontological natural self', a psychological self as it exists before the conditioning of the environment. Macon and Milkman are motivated by an unconscious which has been shaped by the circumstances of their lives and the 'pre-reflective awareness' which Pilate appears to possess has been falsified by interpretation, as is demonstrated by Milkman's repeated failure to ask the right questions. In the book reclaiming the black legacy involves reclaiming a mythological and pre-reflective awareness and all this might appear simply romantic. Distrust of logical thought and empirical rationalism emerged in America in the 1950s and 1960s as part of a counter-establishment culture which led many white American writers to experiment with hallucinogenic drugs and philosophies in search of alternatives to Euro-American models of conceptualising the world. Yet this recurring preoccupation among certain American writers of the 1950s and 1960s was underpinned by perceived differences between Western and non-Western worldviews summarised by Segy:

> It is possible to trace present-day Western civilization to Socratic, Platonic, and Aristotelian concepts predicated upon man's intellect, his logical thought processes, which evolved into a pragmatic, scientific, materialistic outlook. The African

cultures followed another path similar to the spiritual teachings of the Hebrew prophets, Buddha, Lao Tzu, or Jesus, and produced another way of life based upon man's spiritual needs, a socio-religious, well-ordered, communal (and not individualistic) integrated way of life.

Song of Solomon is different in its concern with states of consciousness from the eclecticism of white American literature of the 1950s and 1960s which fused early nineteenth-century European romantic thought with non-Western philosophy. Morrison's novel is concerned with reclaiming and not simply discovering the priorities of a culture founded upon different philosophical and spiritual principles from those of the West. As Wilentz argues, African values are privileged in the novel, as exemplified by Pilate who illustrates the role of the African female ancestor in transmitting familial and cultural knowledge; she makes the potion to improve Macon and Ruth's sex life. Indeed, Milkman's acceptance of myth and the supernatural stems from his acceptance that Pilate is without a navel, and it is this openness, though it takes him 20 years to act on it, which separates him, as Wilentz says, from his father.

Song of Solomon has a moral self-confidence which is not to be found in many contemporary white American novels. Bigsby has gone so far as to see the post-Second World War black writer as the exponent of a liberalism which the white American novel has rejected. This moral self-confidence derives from the belief that there are available truths concealed beneath illusion and falsehood and, as Bigsby claims, this is surely a liberal presumption. But Bigsby fails to locate the source of the narrative's assertion that there are truths to be realised in the reclamation of the priorities of a non-Western culture. His thesis seems to shoehorn the novel into a white liberal tradition to which it simply does not belong:

> And, in terms of black writing, self-perception frequently comes to the protagonist in a visit to the underworld, in a mock death, a dive down into the underground of self and society alike . . .

What Bigsby says here is clearly applicable to *Song of Solomon*, but he does not recognise the romance formula in his own survey of black fiction and, more seriously, how the black novel subverts the romance genre. Bigsby discusses the black protagonist in terms of alienation and estrangement more appropriate to the way in which protagonists in novels by white writers felt cast adrift on the irrepressible new:

> This is perhaps why so many black novels are set in that past
> which is part tangible and part mythic; a usable past which can
> be turned to the purpose of locating a self which had been cut
> adrift in an American environment it could not define and
> whose direction it could not deflect. It is a past, too, which must
> be set against that projected by white historians . . . For the
> black writer, as for the Jew, the past is to be claimed, the impli-
> cations of an alienated self to be denied, a tradition of moral
> responsibility to be accepted.

Despite the good points which are made here, Bigsby's use of 'claimed' rather
than 'reclaimed' is significant. For there is insufficient recognition that we
are dealing with more than just a past. The novel is concerned with the
mythologising nature of black as opposed to white culture and of the differences between black and white concepts of moral responsibility.

Nevertheless, Bigsby is right to assert that there is something
refreshing about the strength of the moral assuredness of African-American
fiction after the emphasis of the non-liberal white novel upon 'cosmic
conspiracies, fragmented layers of experience whose coherences are contingent, a self which is either a distorting mirror or a transparent membrane
offering a pathway to ultimate nirvana . . . ' . Certainly, *Song of Solomon* does
not present the nihilistic vision of many postmodern works that behind every
construction of so-called truth lies only another construction. Nor does it
abandon the notion that individual projects are worthwhile for the individual
and the community simply because all human projects are constructed and
inevitably limited although it does submit them to scrutiny. Macon Dead's
project, for example, is obviously very limited. So too in a different way is
Guitar's involvement with the Seven Days. Guitar, like Milkman, wants Pilate's
gold. But, like Milkman before he realises his true legacy, Guitar's project
courts death even though the name ironically echoes creation in the Book of
Genesis. Arguing for a programme of indiscriminate retaliatory murder
of whites in revenge for the murder of blacks, Guitar can love black people in
the aggregate, but he cannot love individuals nor give sufficient weight to individual responsibility. Bent on revenge in the name of love, he is divided against
himself rather like his father, sawn in two parts at the saw mill.

The concept of individual moral responsibility in this novel is not the
same as that to be found in white American liberal novels. The moral vision
underpinning the narrative fuses recognition of the black cultural legacy and
the reclamation of its priorities, including a community-oriented sense of
responsibility, with a reclamation of a mythological cultural framework. In
order to fly Milkman has to recognise the importance of his cultural legacy

and acquire a commitment towards the wider black community. In the early part of the novel Milkman tries to avoid commitment. Indeed, his name suggests infancy and the egocentricity of a young child from which Milkman has to develop. Overnourished by his mother's milk, he fails to grow until the interjection of Lena's accusation that he has victimised others with his egotism. Within this context, Pilate's explanation as to why she has kept the bag of bones with her makes Milkman ashamed that he has betrayed his mentor who presided over the 'miracle' of his birth. His relationship with Sweet in the South is an indicator of his growth: he is able to enter a reciprocal relationship which culminates in a joyous swim in a spring, symbolising baptism and rebirth.

The black cultural heart of the South is a mythic and perhaps finally an unconvincing counterpoint to the North. The superiority of the men in the South is indicated, as Lee has explained, by their names, the names of poets, kings, and men of God: Omar, King Walker, Luther, Solomon, Calvin Breakstone. They possess a 'pre-reflection awareness' of the kind embodied by Pilate. Milkman observes incredulously that the men and their hunting dogs speak to each other in:

> . . . it was what was there before language . . . And if they could talk to animals, and the animals could talk to them, what didn't they know about human beings? Or the earth itself, for that matter.

The importance of belief over fact (the world of science) is evidenced in the sack of bones which Pilate carries. In the end it does not matter whether the bones are of her husband (as she tells the police) or of a murdered white man (as she believes) or of her father (as Milkman informs her). The bones are a symbol of an obligation to a past event and to a relationship.

Song of Solomon then is a novel which, although it appropriates the characteristics of the European romance formula, cannot be seen only in those terms. It is a dialogical novel in which the same incident or character is seen from different viewpoints and in which competing discourses are highlighted. Although concepts such as community, commitment, authority and individuality are thereby subjected to scrutiny, a hierarchy of favoured positions emerges in the course of the text which have their origins in African-American culture. Over-emphasising how the novel appears to provide an ironic version of the European quest might lead the reader to underestimate how its experiment with the romantic quest form is determined by black concerns, African myth and aspects of an African ontology.

BERTRAM D. ASHE

"Why don't he like my hair?": *Constructing African-American Standards of Beauty in Toni Morrison's* Song of Solomon *and Zora Neale Hurston's* Their Eyes Were Watching God

"How can he not love your hair? . . . It's his hair too. He's got to love it."
"He don't love it at all. He hates it."

This last declaration, uttered by a feverish, distraught, dangerously mentally ill Hagar Dead to her mother Reba and her grandmother Pilate comes midway through one of the most heart-wrenching scenes in Toni Morrison's *Song of Solomon*. In the passage, grandmother, mother, and daughter discuss whether Milkman, the novel's central character, "likes" Hagar's hair. By the time the scene has ended, it doesn't matter that Pilate has offered credible reasons why Milkman couldn't not love Hagar's hair—"'How can he love himself and hate your hair?'" Pilate asks—Hagar is certain that Milkman is only attracted to women with distinctly European features and insists, with deadly finality, "'He's never going to like my hair.'" Ultimately, all Pilate can say in reply is, "'Hush. Hush. Hush, girl, hush.'"

African-Americans, with their traditionally African features, have always had an uneasy coexistence with the European (white) ideal of beauty. According to Angela M. Neal and Midge L. Wilson, "Compared to Black males, Black females have been more profoundly affected by the prejudicial fallout surrounding issues of skin color, facial features, and hair. Such impact

From *African American Review* 29, no. 4 (Winter 1995). © 1995 Bertram D. Ashe.

can be attributed in large part to the importance of physical attractiveness for all women." For black women, the most easily controlled feature is hair. While contemporary black women sometimes opt for cosmetic surgery or colored contact lenses, hair alteration (i.e., hair-straightening "permanents," hair weaves, braid extensions, Jheri curls, etc.) remains the most popular way to approximate a white female standard of beauty. Neal and Wilson contend that much of the black female's "obsession about skin color and features" has to do with the black woman's attempting to attain a "high desirability stem[ming] from her physical similarity to the white standard of beauty."

But just whom do African-American women hope to attract by maintaining this "high desirability"? While there is some debate as to whether the choice of one's hair style automatically signifies one's alliance with, or opposition to, white supremacy, anecdotal evidence clearly points to the straightening of black hair as a way to fit, however unconsciously, into an overall white standard of beauty. What is often overlooked, however, are specific black-male expectations where black-female hairstyles are concerned.

In much the same way that men gravitate toward certain styles, behaviors, and attitudes that are more likely to attract attention from women, male "likes" must rate, on some level, as at least a consideration when a female hair style is chosen. Of course, the reasoning a woman employs while choosing a hair style ranges much further than simply trying to attract some man. Above all, no doubt, women wear their hair in a style that pleases them. However, as Erica Hector Vital put it in a recent article about cutting off her dreads and retaining a short, natural style, certain

> Toni Morrison characters, such as Hannah in Morrison's *Song of Solomon*, Sula in a novella of the same name, and the girl-child Pecola of *The Bluest Eye*, all fall prey to dishonor and grief without the presence of the mothering voices to grant the essential reminders: Don't let your slip show, don't sneak off with the neighborhood boys, don't forget to do your lesson, don't be a fool with your hair. . . . no man likes a bald-headed woman.

While Vital did go on to cut her dreads—as she certainly should have, since that was her preference—one of the questions she asked herself in those final moments in the barber's chair was, "what will the brothers think?" This consideration of the black male's "likes" is not always on the surface, but, like the black male's regard for the black female's "likes," it is there, subterranean.

Morrison and Zora Neale Hurston, in their works, engage the black female's struggle between her own hairstyle preferences and the female hairstyle preferences of the black male. These two authors offer dissimilar but compatible discussions of not only the black female's encounters with the white-female standard of beauty, but also the black female's difficulties negotiating her black-male partner's conception of that standard. Morrison, in *Song of Solomon*, critiques the ideal by creating two characters who fall on opposing sides of the white-beauty construct. Pilate Dead, who wears her hair closely cropped, represents "Nature . . . [as she] energetically work[s] against the allure of outward appearances." Pilate's granddaughter Hagar, on the other hand, "fantasizes a persona that she imagines will make her more desirable to her projected lover, Milkman." Hagar's imagined "persona" is one that will include "silky copper-colored hair," because Morrison primarily uses hair in *Song of Solomon* to draw Pilate and Hagar as opposites where the white standard of beauty is concerned. Eventually, by revolving these opposites around Milkman, the novel's central character, Morrison devises her own African-American standard of beauty, an alternative to the white-beauty ideal.

Hurston, in *Their Eyes Were Watching God*, also examines the black-female response to the white-beauty ideal, but in a markedly different manner. While both Pilate and Hagar have dark skin and "kinky" hair, Hurston gives her central character, Janie Crawford Killicks Starks Woods, all of the attributes of the white-female standard of beauty. Janie's features conform to the black version of the white ideal, including those Neal and Wilson designate as the most important: light skin and long hair. Although Janie enjoys possessing these features, she refuses to allow her light skin and long hair to separate her from the Eatonville community. Indeed, much of the novel concerns Janie's struggle against the community's attempts to place her, because of her features (particularly her hair), on a social level that is above and apart from the community. In Janie, Hurston creates a character who subverts the "history of differential treatment" traditionally accorded those of her skin color and hair texture.

The person in the community primarily concerned with blocking Janie from the community's full acceptance is her second husband, Joe Starks. Determined to force Janie to acknowledge her "difference," Joe insists on separating her from the Eatonville townspeople by keeping her in a "high, ruling chair." Like Morrison, Hurston privileges hair as the battleground of Janie and Jody's fight over access to the Eatonville community.

The first thing Janie does is let down her hair.

In one of the most powerful scenes in *Their Eyes Were Watching God*, Janie confronts Joe Starks, as he lies in bed dying:

> "Listen, Jody, you ain't de Jody ah run off down de road wid.
> You'se whut's left after he died. . . . You done lived wid me for
> twenty years and you don't half know me atall. And you could

have but you was so busy worshippin' de works of yo' own hands, and cuffin' folks around in their minds till you didn't see uh whole heap uh things yuh could have."

When Janie says that Joe didn't know her "atall," she is referring to the way he stymied her repeated attempts to become an integral part of the Eatonville community. It is quite possible that she is also telling him he didn't understand the importance she placed on her hair. A telling moment occurs shortly after Joe dies, when Janie walks to the dresser and looks at herself in the mirror:

> She tore off the kerchief from her head and let down her plentiful hair. The weight, the length, the glory was there. She took careful stock of herself, then combed her hair and tied it back up again.

Then she "starche[s] and iron[s] her face . . . , and open[s] up the window and crie[s], 'Come heah people, Jody is dead. Mah husband is gone from me.'" In this scene, Janie's hair is exhibited as a lasting symbol of her freedom and her self-esteem. Hurston is careful to show that Janie's examination of her hair/self-esteem is more important than immediately announcing her husband's death.

Hurston makes it clear very early on that hair is going to be a primary issue in Janie and Joe's relationship. It was Janie's hair that first caught Joe's attention. As Joe walked up the road,

> He didn't look her way nor no other way except straight ahead, so Janie ran to the pump and jerked the handle hard while she pumped. It made a loud noise and also made her heavy hair fall down. So he stopped and looked hard, and then he asked her for a cool drink of water.

Not only is Hurston careful to identify Janie's hair as the catalyst that brings Janie and Joe together, but she continues the hair references during their brief courtship. When Joe is trying to convince Janie to leave Logan Killicks, Janie's first husband, he refers to her hair to help persuade her:

> "You come go wid me. Den all de rest of yo' natural life you kin live lak you oughta. Kiss me and shake yo' head. When you do dat, yo' plentiful hair breaks lak day."

Hurston loads allusions to Jody's interest in Janie's hair into their meeting and courtship, so it is not surprising that Janie's hair becomes an issue during their marriage.

Ironically, although Janie tells Joe on his death bed that he didn't know her at all, where her hair is concerned he may have known her only too well. Recognizing that Janie's hair was vital to her self-esteem, Joe made sure he kept her hair under his control. Throughout their twenty years of married life, Joe insisted that Janie keep her hair tied up when she was around the store and the post office. Although "this business of the headrag irked her endlessly, Jody was set on it. Her hair was NOT going to show in the store." Janie and Joe were locked in a power struggle over her hair, and for twenty years, Joe won out. Because Joe was aware that Janie's hair symbolized her "self," Joe began to communicate to the people of Eatonville that he "owned" Janie's hair as a means of demonstrating that he, in effect, "owned" Janie. And the public got the message. In the following passage, which occurs just after Joe becomes mayor of Eatonville, some of the townsfolk are sitting around talking, wondering if the power Joe wields as mayor extends to his home. The passage reveals the depth of the community's interest in Janie's hair as a feature that sets her apart from the other townswomen:

> "Ah often wonder how dat lil wife uh hisn makes out wid him, 'cause he's uh man dat changes everything, but nothin' don't change him."
>
> "You know many's de time Ah done thought about dat mahself. He gits on her ever now and then when she make little mistakes round de store."
>
> "Whut make her keep her head tied up lak some ole 'oman round de store? Nobody couldn't git me tuh tie no rag on mah head if Ah had hair lak dat."
>
> "Maybe he make her do it. Maybe he skeered some de rest of us mens might touch it round dat store. It sho is uh hidden mystery tuh me."

Joe "make[s] her do it," because he is, indeed, afraid that one of the other men might touch Janie's hair in the store. One night he catches one of the men standing behind Janie, "brushing the back of his hand back and forth across the loose end of her braid ever so lightly so as to enjoy the feel of it without Janie knowing what he was doing," and Joe subsequently orders Janie to tie up her hair around the store: "That was all. She was there in the store for him to look at, not those others."

The tying up of Janie's hair is clearly an exertion of power on Joe's part. Not only does he seek to send a message to the men of the town, through Janie's hair, that Janie is for him and him alone, but in the process he also sends a message to Janie that her hair is not hers to wear the way she wants.

Her hair, like everything else in their lives—and, virtually, everything else in the town—belongs to him. The lack of freedom for Janie's hair, then, becomes for her a symbol not only of Joe's domination, but of her lack of freedom to join Eatonville's social circle. Joe wants to close Janie off from the world of the porch, where checkers, the "dozens," and folktales are shared among the towns-people, and his desire to separate Janie is exhibited by his insistence that she tie up her hair. Janie, conversely, wants to "let her hair down," and become part of the community. Although she manages to insert comments into porch discussions every now and then, for the most part Joe keeps her "tied up" and closed off from porch conversations.

S. Jay Walker identifies Janie's marriages by the predominant symbols that emerge from those marriages. Her marriage with Killicks might be regarded as the kitchen era, and is characterized by the apron Janie flings away when she runs off with Joe. Her marriage with Joe is symbolized by the "headrag" he forces her to wear. Janie's third marriage, with Tea Cake, is the porch era, when Janie's freedom to travel and join porch conversations, contends Walker, is represented by overalls. After Joe's burial, Janie's freedom from her marriage to him is only complete when she "burnt up every one of her head rags and went about the house the next morning with her hair in one thick braid swinging well below her waist."

Joe's manipulation of Janie's hair must be viewed in the proper context. Certainly there are other men in the town who are interested in Janie (and in her hair) and would no doubt be tempted to try to control Janie the same way Joe did. For example, the envy the men feel later in the book when Tea Cake beats Janie on the muck is a strong indication that, although only certain men get the chance to attempt to dominate Janie, there are many more who would like to try:

> Being able to whip her reassured [Tea Cake] in possession. No brutal beating at all. He just slapped her around a bit to show he was the boss. Everybody talked about it the next day in the fields. It aroused a sort of envy in both men and women. The way he petted and pampered her as if those two or three face slaps had nearly killed her made women see visions and the helpless way she hung on him made men dream dreams.

Sop-de-Bottom sums up the men's feelings when he says, "'Tea Cake, you sho is a lucky man. . . . Uh person can see every place you hit her.'" The irony of the above passages is that, although Janie is trying to fight through Joe's control so that she can join the black community, it appears that the over-whelming majority of the men in the community would have attempted to control Janie in much the same way Joe did. The exception (to a certain extent) is, of course, Tea Cake.

Joe's weakness, his need to control Janie, becomes even more obvious when he is compared with Tea Cake. Although Tea Cake does beat Janie, demonstrating the "controlling" aspect of his personality, he clearly has a more balanced persona than Joe does. Hurston uses Janie's hair to illustrate this balance. Early in their courtship, Janie wakes up to find Tea Cake combing her hair. Janie (understandably, after what she's been through with Joe) questions his behavior, asking, "Why, Tea Cake? Whut good do combin' mah hair do you? It's mah comfortable, not yourn." Tea Cake replies, "'It's mine too. Ah ain't been sleepin' so good for more'n uh week cause Ah been wishin' so bad tuh git mah hands in yo' hair. It's so pretty.'" Instead of requiring Janie to tie her hair up as Joe has done, Tea Cake runs his fingers through it, saying, "'It feels jus' lak underneath uh dove's wing next to mah face.'" Tea Cake is expressing his love by glorifying in Janie's beauty. He is loving her as she is—not trying to make her into a creation of his own.

Hurston effectively uses Janie's hair as a window through which her readers can view the differences between Janie's husbands. Even Killicks was fascinated with Janie's hair, and Hurston uses that fact to show the deterioration of their marriage: "Long before the year was up, Janie noticed that her husband had stopped talking in rhymes to her. He had ceased to wonder at her long black hair and finger it." Hurston holds the attraction to black female hair up as a mirror, and the ensuing reflection, in Joe's case, illuminates his need to dominate his woman.

Unfortunately, it's all too common for men in this country to use hair as a site at which to control women. J. M. Lewis's study is primarily concerned with the way white American females are charged with removing "dirty" hair from their bodies—from pubic areas, on legs, under arms, between eyebrows, etc.—or else be accused of violating the cultural ideal of femininity. Lewis accurately pinpoints the hierarchical implications of body hair when he points out that, if U.S. culture considers body hair "dirty," then it would make more sense to encourage males to remove what the culture has proscribed as unclean, since they have so much more of it. Although Lewis's thesis centers on body hair, the conclusions drawn can be expanded to include hair that appears on the head as well:

> It is suggested that the U.S. practice of female body hair removal behavior expresses an underlying concept that the female is anomalous in regard to well-defined categories. She is problematic as a full adult member of the human species. This chronic adjunct placement of the female leads to a female exclusion principle

embedded in the cultural perception of gender, species, and sexual maturity. The female applies for membership by subscribing to an ideological superstructure of femininity. The anomalous treatment of females and their linkage to males for identity is deeply embedded in U.S. culture and can be demonstrated in other cultural structures such as in the language and legal system.

It could be said that Janie tried to "apply for membership" in Joe's view of the "cultural ideal of femininity" by adhering, however reluctantly, to his demand that she keep her hair tied up. But the question remains: Where did Joe get his idea of what "ideal" femininity should be? Although *Their Eyes Were Watching God* is comprised only of black characters, the events of the novel are rendered in the context of the overall white-controlled society. Joe, as characterized by Hurston, embodies many of the negative aspects of that society. Clair Crabtree sees Janie's relationship with Jody as being a "form of servitude," with the headrag providing "an ironic counterpoint to the portrayal of Starks as a progressive entrepreneur, for his insistence on covering her hair suggests his need to belittle Janie, despite his protestations of her high stature as a lady." It is exactly the hierarchical stratification implied in Lewis's study that is at work here. Jody's efforts to suppress Janie by way of his insistence that she keep her hair tied up is an attempt to enforce the hierarchy he is emulating from the white superstructure.

In the same way Hurston uses Joe as an example of mock-white-male dominance, she uses the relationship between Janie and Mrs. Turner, a black woman who runs a restaurant "on the muck," to illustrate the enormous impact white-controlled society has on all-black communities. Hurston devotes all of Chapter 16 to Janie's and Mrs. Turner's conversation, the theme being white society's image of beauty. Here, along with skin tone, Hurston uses hair not only as a primary illustration of Mrs. Turner's unqualified support of the white-female image of beauty, but also to show Mrs. Turner's attempt to get Janie to join her in that support.

The narrator describes Mrs. Turner as "milky" and possessing a flat behind, but adds,

> . . . Mrs. Turner's shape and features were entirely approved by Mrs. Turner. Her nose was slightly pointed and she was proud. Her lips were an ever delight to her eyes. Even her buttocks in bas-relief were a source of pride. To her way of thinking, all these things set her apart from Negroes.

Hurston also allows Tea Cake the opportunity to describe Mrs. Turner, and, not surprisingly, his description is less gentle: "He claimed that she had been shaped up by a cow kicking her from behind. She was an ironing board with things throwed at it." Also, Mrs. Turner's hair is described by Tea Cake as "'jus' as close tuh her head as ninety-nine is tuh uh hundred!'"

But it is Janie's hair that attracts Mrs. Turner. Janie's "coffee-and-cream complexion and her luxurious hair" make Mrs. Turner want to associate with Janie, even if Janie is, in Mrs. Turner's words, married to "a man as dark as Tea Cake." Mrs. Turner is obsessed with "'lighten[ing] up de race,'" saying, "'Ah can't stand black niggers. Ah don't blame de white folks from hatin' 'em 'cause Ah can't stand 'em mahself. 'Nother thing,'" she continues, "'Ah hates tuh see folks lak me and you mixed up wid 'em. Us oughta class off.'" Because of Janie's light skin and long hair, Mrs. Turner tries to get Janie to act as if she's above other blacks. Mrs. Turner even equates straight hair with intelligence as she attempts to get Janie to meet her brother: "'He's real smart. Got dead straight hair.'"

Janie's reaction to Mrs. Turner's racial bias, however, indicates that, although Janie's hair is vital to her self-esteem, her racial identity is intact. Janie refuses Mrs. Turner's invitation to "class off" by saying, "'Us can't do it. We'se uh mingled people and all of us got black kinfolks as well as yaller kinfolks.'" Then she asks, "'How come you so against black?'" When Mrs. Turner replies, "'Who want any lil ole black baby layin' up in de baby buggy lookin' lak uh fly in buttermilk?'" Janie is perplexed:

> Mrs. Turner was almost screaming in fanatical earnestness by now. Janie was dumb and bewildered before and she clucked sympathetically and wished she knew what to say. It was so evident that Mrs. Turner took black folk as a personal affront to herself.

Hurston's narrator takes the last two pages of Chapter 16 to explain Mrs. Turner's behavior, summing up Mrs. Turner's racial attitude by acknowledging that

> . . . she didn't cling to Janie Woods the woman. She paid homage to Janie's Caucasian characteristics as such. And when she was with Janie she had a feeling of transmutation, as if she herself had become whiter and with straighter hair. . . .

Hurston is very direct in her characterization of a woman who is thoroughly influenced by the white power structure:

> Mrs. Turner, like all other believers had built an altar to the unattainable—Caucasian characteristics for all. Her god would smite

her, would hurl her from pinnacles and lose her in deserts, but she would not forsake his altars. Behind her crude words was a belief that somehow she and others through worship could attain her paradise—a heaven of straight-haired, thin-lipped, high-nose boned white seraphs. The physical impossibilities in no way injured faith. That was the mystery and mysteries are the chores of gods. Beyond her faith was a fanaticism to defend the altars of her god. It was distressing to emerge from her inner temple and find these black desecrators howling with laughter before the door. Oh, for an army, terrible with banners and swords!

It is obvious, from Hurston's sixteenth chapter example, that Joe and Mrs. Turner are not so much acting on, as reacting to, Janie's hair as they view it through white society's ideal of beauty.

Lewis contends that part of the white cultural ideal of femininity is the large amount of value placed upon the "youthful beauty concept" and argues that, if a white female is to retain her culturally prescribed femininity, she must be relegated to a "non-adult or child-like appearance." Late in *Song of Solomon*, Milkman's estranged lover Hagar seeks to achieve just such a "youthful beauty" in her attempt to win Milkman back to their formerly loving relationship.

Shortly after Milkman writes Hagar a "thank you" note ending their relationship, Hagar decides to murder him. The "thank you" hurt Hagar, but she only becomes murderous when she spots Milkman sitting in Mary's, smiling at and talking to a woman whose "silky copper-colored hair cascaded over the sleeve of his coat." Later, when she finds out that she can't bring herself to kill Milkman, she decides to become the woman with the copper-colored hair, reasoning that the copper-colored ideal is what Milkman really wants in a woman. When Hagar's reasoning is viewed within the context of Lewis's contention that females must "subscribe to an ideological super-structure of femininity," it isn't surprising that Hagar would think that the one thing that could return Milkman Dead to her is a perfect head of hair.

"'No wonder. No wonder,'" Hagar reasons as she attempts to determine the reason that Milkman won't love her. "'I look like a ground hog. Where's the comb?'" After a frantic search for the comb, along with her first bath in days and a trip to the beauty shop, Hagar is intent on winning Milkman back by dressing in stylish clothes and making her hair attractive to him. It is certain that she's attempting to let her hair work its magic on him, but it is also obvious that she's submitting to the power males have over women and their hair. Michael Awkward directly addresses Hagar's attempted transformation in "'Unruly and Let Loose': Myth, Ideology, and Gender in *Song of Solomon*." (Although the title of Awkward's essay refers to Morrison's attraction to the "unruly" features of imagination, "unruly and let loose" could just as easily refer to a black woman's recently freed head of hair.)

Awkward argues that, while

> Milkman comes to a marvelously useful comprehension of history, myth, and nature, Hagar's status as bound, in both the spatial and narrative senses of the phrase, to oppressive domestic plots . . . precipitates a virtual dissociation of sensibility, and an acceptance of the bourgeois society's views of women. This acceptance is reflected partially in her wholehearted adoption of its ideas of female beauty.

Awkward's perceptive analysis is only partially correct. While Hagar is certainly attempting to adopt the bourgeois ideal of female beauty—the "silky hair," the "penny-colored hair," the "lemon-colored skin," and the "gray-blue eyes" of the black girls Milkman accompanied as a child on family excursions to Honoré Island—it is a particularly male-driven sense of female beauty that the bourgeois women adopt. In other words, the Honoré girls wear their hair the way they do to attract men—as well as to fulfill their class expectations.

Perhaps the most compelling argument to support the contention that Milkman had de facto control over Hagar's hair is contained in Awkward's assertion that Morrison purposely interrupted Milkman's quest so he could accept the blame for Hagar's death:

> This interruption serves to problematize a strictly celebratory afrocentric analysis of Milkman's achievements. Such an analysis fails to permit focus on the clear presence of (female) pain that permeates *Song of Solomon*'s final chapters. Male culpability in the instigation of such pain is evident, for example, in Milkman's revelations about the motivations for his treatment of Hagar. He comes to understand that he "had used her—her love, her craziness—and most of all . . . her skulking, bitter vengeance" to achieve heroic—or what the narrative refers to as "star" status.

Milkman is taking the blame for mistreating Hagar, and part of that blame must extend to the way she feels about her hair. Even if Milkman can't be held fully accountable for Hagar's perception of how he'd prefer his woman's hair, his power over her as a male lover is such that he is culpable, as Awkward has suggested, to a certain extent.

Hagar eventually concedes to this power when she gives up her quest to make the hair the one attraction that Milkman cannot resist. Hagar's hair hasn't been manipulated physically, as in Janie's struggle with Joe, but it has been manipulated psychologically. Hagar is trapped between her own African physical features and the white-female ideal of beauty. She is perfectly aware of the priority men like Janie's first two husbands (and the man who was observed stroking Janie's hair in the store) place on female hair, and Hagar is also well aware that she doesn't quite measure up. That awareness, among other things, leads to her death.

Hagar's attempt to appeal to Milkman through what Guerrero calls "the consumer system . . . , [using] a mad list of commodities and beauty treatments in order to transform herself into the objectified spectacle worthy of male attention and romance," is in marked contrast to Pilate's reaction to a similar dilemma years earlier. Pilate, like Hagar, reached a point where she had to come to terms with something that was interrupting her relations with men: the fact that she was born without a navel. All it took was a few horrified reactions to lead her to hide her smooth stomach. She did manage to have a relationship with one man (and from that union came her daughter), but she was only able to sustain the relationship by keeping direct light off her midsection. She refused to marry her lover because she felt she couldn't keep him in the dark forever; eventually, she left the island where they met. As Morrison writes,

> Having had one long relationship with a man, she sought another, but no man was like that island man ever again either. After a while, she stopped worrying about her stomach and stopped trying to hide it. . . . It isolated her. Already without family, she was further isolated from her people, for, except for the relative bliss on the island, every other resource was denied her. . . . Finally, Pilate began to take offense.

Pilate took stock, just as Janie did after Joe died: "Although she was hampered by huge ignorances, but not in any way unintelligent, when she realized what her situation in the world was and would probably always be she threw away every assumption she had learned and began at zero."

Pilate, as a young woman, was facing the same crossroads that her granddaughter would face thirty-four years later. The critical difference is that, while Hagar caves in to what Michael Awkward calls "the bourgeois society's views of women" by "shamelessly" pursuing that society's feminine ideal, Pilate takes a different route: "First off, she cut her hair. That was one thing she didn't want to have to think about anymore." In an action that recalls the scene just after Jody dies in which Janie stands before the mirror and lets down her hair, here Pilate appears to do just the opposite—cutting her hair instead of undoing it. But, psychically, the end result is the same: Both women release their hair. They deal with a turning point in their lives by putting their hands up to their head and making a positive change, a change symbolic of their newly found freedom. In Pilate's case, the shedding of her hair, and its baggage, signals her independence from anyone who would reject her because of her navelless stomach, or for any other reason. Lewis writes that a female who willfully violates the cultural norm "challenges the category of gender." But, unlike Hagar, Pilate doesn't attempt to emulate the "cultural ideal of femininity." Instead, after cutting her hair, Pilate looks within for answers:

> . . . she tackled the problem of trying to decide how she wanted to live and what was valuable to her. When am I happy and when am I sad and what is the difference? What do I need to know to stay alive? What is true in the world?

Pilate's independence, like Janie's, is permanent. In the same way that Janie never had to keep her hair tied up again, Pilate keeps her hair short. Hagar, on the other hand, is portrayed throughout the novel as a woman whose hair, like her life, is difficult to control. Morrison subtly uses hair to foreshadow the Pilate-Hagar opposition when Ruth, Milkman's mother, goes to Pilate's house to confront Hagar, who is trying to kill her son. In a flashback, Ruth recalls going to see Hagar thirty-one years earlier. Pilate is sitting on a chair, and Reba is cutting Pilate's hair with barber's clippers, keeping it short. Hagar, however, is "four or five years old then. Chubby, with four long braids, two like horns over each ear, two like tails at the back of her neck." Morrison, using hair as a metaphor, reinforces Pilate's independence/short hair by contrasting it with devil-like imagery ("horns" and "tails") to describe Hagar's growing murderous obsession. A few pages later, moving back to the present, Ruth wonders how "that chubby little girl weighed down with hair [could] become a knife-wielding would-be killer out to get her son." Besides the "devilish" hair connotation and the way Hagar is "weighed down" by her hair, Morrison portrays Hagar's physical gestures as evidence of her imbalance. When Ruth warns Hagar, "'If you so much as bend a hair on his head, so help me Jesus, I will tear your throat out,'" Morrison once again uses Hagar's hair as telling description:

> "You're botherin me," [Hagar replies to Ruth]. Hagar was shouting and digging her fingers in her hair. It was an ordinary gesture of frustration, but its awkwardness made Ruth know that there was something truly askew in this girl.

Morrison, using hair as a common denominator, compares Pilate and Hagar—and clearly Hagar comes up lacking. Most important in the comparison is the way Pilate refuses to allow her hair to be manipulated by anyone: She controls her own hair by cutting it herself. Not only is this a liberating act signifying her independence, but it effectively signals her determination not to be manipulated through her hair, or in any other manner.

Morrison's placement of Hagar and Pilate as opposites is most clearly seen in Milkman's reaction to them. At the same time Hagar is disintegrating in a futile attempt at material growth, Milkman is gaining a family history and an awareness of life outside of his own down in Virginia. Milkman's connection with Solomon, his great-grandfather who flew back to Africa, is the catalyst that frees him to see his former self-centered ways.

The central relationship Morrison uses to show Milkman's evolution from selfish to selfless is his connection with Sweet, the woman he stays with in Shalimar. After being bathed by Sweet, Milkman offers to bathe her. She demurs, saying the tank is too small and there isn't enough hot water left. But he persists, saying, "'Then let me give you a cool one.'" The following passage demonstrates Milkman's growing ability to give and take, instead of just take:

> He soaped and rubbed her until her skin squeaked and glistened like onyx. She put salve on his face. He washed her hair. She sprinkled talcum on his feet. He straddled her behind and massaged her back. She put witch hazel on his swollen neck. He made up the bed. She gave him gumbo to eat. He washed the dishes.

Milkman, as a result of his spiritual awakening, is in a position to see just how badly he has treated Hagar. Again, Morrison uses hair as a way to illustrate this awakening.

When Milkman returns to Pilate's house to tell her of his findings in Virginia, she breaks a bottle over his head, knocking him unconscious. Milkman comes to in a dark cellar where, unbeknownst to him, a green-and-white shoebox of Hagar's hair rests nearby. Milkman tells Pilate about his revelations, and that significant scene ends with Pilate's wondering what to do with the box of Hagar's hair:

> "If I bury Papa, I guess I ought to bury this too—somewhere." She looked back at Milkman.
> "No," he said. "Give it here."
> When he went home that evening, he walked into the house on Not Doctor Street with almost none of the things he'd taken with him. But he returned with a box of Hagar's hair.

The box of hair symbolizes Milkman's inner unity, and also serves as what Chiara Spallino calls "Pilate's tribal punishment: [that] he will always keep a box of Hagar's hair as a reminder of his guilt."

There is another significant reason for Milkman to keep Hagar's hair, however. Morrison has set up two diametrically opposite viewpoints concerning black-female hair: On the one side is Hagar, who is "weighed down with hair," whose hair is "like a thundercloud," and whose "profile [i]s hidden by her hair." Hagar has proved susceptible to the bourgeois society's view of how women should look and what will attract a man. Pilate, conversely, exhibits the ultimate symbol of independence when, "First off, she cut her hair" and thereafter, "kept her short hair cut regularly like a man's." Milkman, then, is charged not only with keeping Hagar's ill-fated head of hair to atone for his sins, but also with choosing between Morrison's symbolic comparison of hair- (and life-)styles.

In the final scene of *Song of Solomon*, Pilate and Milkman go to Shalimar to bury Pilate's father. Then Pilate dies in Milkman's arms after she's been shot. Earlier, Milkman has admitted that "the consequences of [his] own stupidity would remain, and would always outweigh the things he was proud of having done. Hagar was dead and he had not loved her one bit." Now, with Pilate's death at hand, Milkman has his final revelation, and is able to understand which of the two women he prefers:

> Now he knew why he loved her so. Without ever leaving the ground, she could fly. "There must be another one like you," he whispered to her. "There's got to be at least one more woman like you."

Milkman, on both the surface level and the symbolic level, has made his decision. Charged with choosing between Hagar, with her allegiance to the white ideal of beauty, and a woman like Pilate, who has rejected a pursuit of that ideal, he opts for a woman who lives outside of the expectations of the white cultural norm.

With this affirmative choice, Morrison, through her use of hair imagery and its effect on black males, proffers an alternative to the white cultural ideal of beauty. Morrison's two-part alternative ideal of African-American beauty is symbolized, first of all, by the short, kinky hair of Pilate. Morrison's African-American ideal is not based on the hot-combed, straightened hairstyles that were attempted by Hagar and actually carried off by the middle-class girls on Honoré Island. Morrison, in her heroic portrayal of Pilate, argues for an African-American hair aesthetic that aligns itself with that of the indigenous African woman. Juliette Bowles has pointed out that women in traditional West African cultures were "pleased by the bristling, intricate texture of their hair," even if these African women rarely grew what has become known as the "Afro" or "natural" in Western culture. Certainly, Morrison is not suggesting that short, kinky hair is the only "correct" way for African-American women to wear their hair. But Morrison does offer Pilate's closely cropped hair as symbolic of the pleasure both African women and men historically took in traditionally kinky black hair.

The second part of Morrison's African-American cultural ideal of beauty is based on racial identity. While Hagar was making a futile attempt to assume the white ideal of female beauty, Pilate and Reba tried in vain to make her understand that Milkman did, indeed, like her hair as it was. Malin LaVon Walther points out that Pilate, while trying to convince Hagar of her own innate beauty, "connects hair as an attribute of beauty to racial identity":

> "How can he not love your hair? It's the same hair that grows out of his own armpits. . . . It's all over his head, Hagar. It's his hair too. He's got to love it. . . . He don't know what he loves, but he'll come around, honey, one of these days. How can he love himself and hate your hair?"

Walther correctly contends that Morrison

> redefines female beauty by demanding that it be grounded in racial identity. Blacks must love and desire racially authentic beauty, rather than imitating other races' forms of beauty. To do anything less is to deny oneself. For Milkman to love Hagar's hair is to love himself and his racial heritage.

Indeed, Morrison has a lesson for Milkman, as well. It is only through the self-discovery of his journey that he comes to make an informed choice between Hagar and Pilate. His symbolic acceptance of an alternative African-American beauty ideal is, in many ways, instructive to black-male readers who view the white standard of beauty as the only "ideal" and attempt to convince their wives or girlfriends that European hairstyles have no alternative. Morrison's novel-length transformation of Milkman is a subtle suggestion that, if other African-American males were to attempt a similar process, they, too, could take a critical, informed look at the white-beauty ideal.

Hurston's alternative to unconsciously adopting the white cultural ideal of beauty is exhibited in the reactions of Janie Woods. By employing her racial consciousness, Janie struggles against her husbands in order to join the greater black community, and resists Mrs. Turner's attempts to get her to "class off." Janie happens to possess the physical attributes of white-female beauty, but they aren't important to her in the same way that they are important to Killicks, Joe, and Mrs. Turner. Certainly, she enjoys her long hair, as does Tea Cake, albeit not because it represents a connection to white-female beauty, but because it is hers. Janie's "'We'se uh mingled people'" comment suggests her understanding that African-Americans have no need to privilege light skin color and straight hair over dark skin and "kinky" hair. Indeed, Janie's assertion that "'all of us got black kinfolks as well as yaller kinfolks'" confirms her stance. Hurston has managed to create, in Janie, a character who has the physical attributes of white-female beauty but can still effectively demonstrate the destructiveness of the white-controlled society's impact on blacks.

Taken together, Morrison's and Hurston's alternative ideals of black-female beauty cover the spectrum of African-American female physical expression. Long-haired Janie and short-haired Pilate both exist as viable models for black-female readers. For black-male readers, Milkman's transformation and Tea Cake's loving attitude toward Janie are equally as viable—notwithstanding Tea Cake's troublesome "whipping" of Janie. Neal and Wilson prescribe, as therapy, a short list of readings, including W. E. B. Du Bois's *Dusk of Dawn*, Gwendolyn Brooks's *The Tiger with White Glove*, and Morrison's *The Bluest Eye*. Neal and Wilson feel that these books might act as a way to "affirm Blacks and their cultural experiences." Unquestionably, *Their Eyes Were Watching God* and *Song of Solomon* would be welcome additions to this list. As Neal and Wilson assert, "The Black woman [will] begin to realize that the white standard of attractiveness is not suitable for her own life," and the African-American man will realize that the white standard is not suitable for what attracts him. "Beauty is not skin deep or feature wide," continue Neal and Wilson, "but encompasses a Black woman's feelings about herself, her carriage, her style, and her heritage. True Black beauty is a synthesis between physical and personality attributes."

JAN FURMAN

Male Consciousness: Song of Solomon

When asked during an interview if she thinks her novels are evolutionary, Morrison responded that she believes they are: "from a book that focused on a pair of very young black girls . . . to a pair of adult black women, and then to a black man . . . is evolutionary." The black man Morrison speaks about is the subject of her third novel, *Song of Solomon* (1977). (*Song of Solomon* greatly enhanced Morrison's literary reputation and broadened her reading audience. It was a Book-of-the-Month Club selection—the first, it has been widely noted, by a black writer since Richard Wright's *Native Son* in 1940— and a year after its publication 570,000 copies were in print.) Ajax and Cholly, the men who took shape in previous novels, were drawn in outline and may be viewed as previews of the more-detailed male characters in *Song of Solomon* and in later novels. In *Song of Solomon*, Morrison scrutinizes friendship, marriage, family, and relationship to community, primarily (but not exclusively) from men's points of view. Such scrutiny is driven by Morrison's belief that a man's experience of life is different from a woman's. Maleness "tends to be inherent," she believes, in spite of "eighty percent of the literature" to the contrary. Morrison realizes that her comments may be "astonishing" to some and that male and female roles may be learned, but she still holds to an idea of masculinity. Based on her observations of two brothers, a father, and sons, she concludes that men have "different spatial

From *Toni Morrison's Fiction.* © 1996 University of South Carolina Press.

requirements than girls," they relate "to architecture and space differently"; her sons "were attracted to danger and risk" in a way she was not, and on the "question of dominion" men, she says, have "a definite need to exercise dominion over place and people." They "desire to control" in a way that women do not.

Milkman Dead's major conflict of values in the novel exemplifies, to some extent, gender-determined perspectives: as a son he feels immense pressure to embrace his father's affection for things. But Morrison, as an artist concerned with dimensions of spirituality, offers Milkman an alternative to the pursuit of material success: spiritual fulfullment. Milkman, as one would expect, chooses spirituality, and in explicating his judgment, Morrison retraces her precise boundaries of freedom and responsibility for the individual. Like other Morrison characters who would be spiritually free, Milkman must be willing to resist all narrow definitions of the self and take responsibility for the tough choices he makes.

Macon Dead, Milkman's father, has lost this essential freedom; he has traded it for wealth under the mistaken belief that "money is freedom. . . . The only real freedom there is." Macon advises his son to "own things. And let the things you own own other things. Then you'll own yourself and other people too." But despite his thinking so, property does not elevate Macon above other blacks or earn him respect from whites. In truth, blacks do not hold him in high esteem; they merely fear his ruthless exercise of power, and corrupt whites respect not him but his money. A lifetime of acquiring property, collecting rents, and making deals has rendered Macon a greedy, self-absorbed, unforgiving (and unforgiven) man who is incapable of showing love or receiving it. Hating his wife, Ruth, ignoring his daughters, Lena and First Corinthians, and disowning his sister, Pilate, are the sum of Macon's family connections. Even the one relationship—with Milkman—which promises to humanize him is contaminated by their scheme to steal the gold that he thinks his sister possesses. Family for Macon is just another category of personal wealth. His Sunday drives in the new Packard with Ruth and Milkman in the front seat and Corinthians and Lena in the back are merely parades of possessions. The lifeless metallic form of the Packard, which the people in the community dub "Macon Dead's hearse," is a looming symbol of the dead relationships and feelings of the people inside.

At age thirty-two Milkman is his father's son. The macho rebellion of adolescence has been replaced by a self-indulgent callousness and a tacit acceptance of his father's way. Collecting Macon's rents, partying with bourgeois blacks who spend silly hours imitating the leisure of whites—these anchor Milkman's life, "which was pointless, aimless, and it was true that he didn't concern himself an awful lot about other people. There was nothing he wanted bad enough to risk anything for, inconvenience himself for." As it is with his father, family for Milkman is a burdensome afterthought. His interactions with them—all women—is mostly an exercise in male preroga-tive. In fact, he had never really "been able to distinguish them [his sisters] from his mother." Once he had knocked his father into a wall for hitting his mother, but that was less a display of regard for his mother's welfare than a startling instance of arrogance. The younger man had bested the older and, in doing so, felt a "snorting, horse-galloping glee as old as desire." Coming to his mother's defense is a singular instance for Milkman. More typical of his filial tie to her is the unresponsiveness revealed in a "dream" that he relates to his friend Guitar. In Milkman's vision Ruth is in the backyard garden planting tulip bulbs which immediately sprout "bloody red heads" that grow tall and menacing. Eventually, as Milkman watches from the kitchen window, the smothering plants suffocate his mother, who was "kicking to the last." When Guitar asks, "Why didn't you go help her?" Milkman's uncomprehending retort is "what?" Attending to others has never seemed necessary or beneficial to Milkman. As his sister Lena observes, Milkman's has been a thoughtless life of self-gratification: "You have yet to wash your underwear, spread a bed, wipe the ring from your tub, or move a fleck of your dirt from one place to another. And to this day, you have never asked one of us if we were tired, or sad, or wanted a cup of coffee. . . . You are a sad, pitiful, stupid, selfish, hateful man. I hope your little hog's gut stands you in good stead, and that you take good care of it, because you don't have anything else." Lena's accusations shock Milkman into a necessary but unfortunately shallow self-examination, and the conclusions he reaches illus-trate his profound shortsightedness: he will find the gold his father thinks Pilate stole from a cave in Pennsylvania and declare his independence. With enough money he would be free of all human obligations. Such thinking reveals Milkman's incredible conceit. His soul, like his mirror image, lacks "coherence, a coming together of the features into a total."

In many ways Milkman's journey from his home in Michigan to Penn-sylvania to Virginia and back home conforms to the classical male monomyth of the heroic quest. In this structure the hero's adventure takes him on a journey beset with mortal danger but a journey which, in the end, brings him nobility and great honor among his people. Of course, Morrison does not faithfully, nor with a straight face, appropriate the monomyth paradigm to her own story and character. She admits that *Song of Solomon* is her "own giggle (in Afro-American terms) of the proto-myth of the journey to manhood." She feels that "whenever characters are cloaked in Western fable, they are in deep trouble." One kind of trouble is the customary designation of male narrative as more imperative than female narrative. Morrison would, no doubt, decline to identify her novel with a narrative tradition so antithetical to her aesthetic, which makes her consistently attentive to women's narratives even in a text like *Song of Solomon*, which is primarily devoted to men's experiences. Instead, then, of blithely conceiving Milkman's journey in terms of the traditional hero's, Morrison satirically calls attention to the limitations of the traditional quest by making Milkman less heroic and more human. Not a classical hero, Milkman is a contemporary black man lost to his community, family, and, most important, lost to himself. His true quest is not for fortune or honor but for his humanity.

Every phase of his search for gold brings Milkman closer to these truths. In Danville, Pennsylvania, Fred Garnett, a passing motorist, teaches Milkman that not everyone is motivated by financial gain. When Milkman offers him money to pay for a Coke and a ride from the country into town, Garnett shakes his head in disgust and disbelief. Milkman learns that one man can give another "a Coke and a lift now and then" without expecting payment. Reverend Cooper's stories about "old Macon Dead," Milkman's grandfather, about Lincoln's Heaven, the farm that he worked and loved, about the old man's son, Macon Dead, Jr., who "worked right alongside" his father, reveal for the first time to Milkman the powerful balm in the phrase, "I know your people!" As he listens to the old men's recollections of the past, "He glittered in the light of their adoration and grew fierce with pride." These experiences in Danville begin to unravel Milkman's webbing of indifference just as the difficult country terrain where he searches for the gold spoils the superficial finery of his clothes. By the time he returns to town, Milkman has experienced, in the river stream where he loses his balance and falls in, the first baptismal to a new life. His three-piece suit and Florsheim shoes are soiled and torn, his "heavy over-designed" watch is splintered, the minute hand broken as if to signal an eruption. In the country he comes face to face with his limitations. "He had no idea that simply walking through trees, bushes, on untrammeled ground could be so hard. Woods always brought to his mind city parks, the tended woods on Honore Island where he went for outings as a child and where tiny convenient paths led you through." But here Milkman is alone, far from a town, in a place where his father's money is irrelevant. Here he must chart his own course. And that course must be one that takes him away from old paths of insolence, greed, and vanity toward new paths of spiritual enlightenment. Milkman still has far to travel. The journey so far has brought him to an appreciation of family and hard work that he did not have before, but buried treasure continues to make a slave of him. He does not yet know that money cannot buy the kind of freedom he needs.

This insight is not available to Milkman until the second phase of his journey in Shalimar, Virginia. Pilate may have gone there, he thinks, and buried the gold. In this small southern community with no commerce or industry, what is left of Milkman's flashy affluence is insolent to the people who live there: his casual willingness simply to buy a car to replace the broken one he bought the day before, the insult of locking his car against the men he has asked for help, calling them "them," not bothering to give his name or ask theirs. "He was telling them they weren't men . . . that thin shoes and suits with vests . . . were the measure." The possum hunt, however, that Milkman is goaded into joining changes all of that. Finally, stripped of everything except his watch (and he will soon lose that), dressed in brogans, army fatigues, and a knit cap, Milkman, like the other hunters, must take his measure against the laws of nature. Survival depends upon penetrating the darkness, transversing the rocky terrain, interpreting the dogs' barks, anticipating his prey, sending wordless messages to his companions.

Milkman is not up to this work, and he is nearly conquered by fatigue and fear. But with these trials come flashes of genuine insight (not the shallow self-examination of a few weeks earlier). He now realizes that the black men of Shalimar are more than the sum of the money they might earn in city factories or from rent collections. Their primordial link to the earth, to animals, and to each other inspires Milkman's respect. For "if they could talk to animals, and the animals could talk to them, what didn't they know about human beings? Or the earth itself, for that matter." Since he can do none of these, Milkman must acknowledge his own glaring limitations in this place:

> There was nothing here to help him—not his money, his car, his father's reputation, his suit, or his shoes. In fact they hampered him. Except for his broken watch, and his wallet with about two hundred dollars, all he had started out with on his journey was gone: his suitcase with the scotch, the shirts, and the space for bags of gold; his snap-brim hat, his tie, his shirt, his three-piece suit, and his shoes. His watch and two hundred dollars would be of no help out here, where all a man had was what he was born with, or had learned to use. And endurance. Eyes, ears, nose, taste, touch—and some other sense that he knew he did not have.

Milkman's reveries have a domino effect, toppling one illusion after another: money is not freedom, but enslavement; independence means submitting himself to people in his life, not escaping them. He confesses and repents of his shameful retreat from relationships—refusing any involvement in his parents' problems, using Hagar's love and then throwing it "away like a wad of chewing gum after the flavor was gone," betraying Pilate, the one who had saved his life and then loved him unconditionally. Alone, without the accoutrement of his vanity, the old personality gives way to make space for a new spirituality so expansive that only "the whole entire complete deep blue sea!" will contain its volume.

In Shalimar, after the hunt, a transformed Milkman engages a woman's generosity with his—for the first time in his life and without hesitation. Sweet, "a nice lady up the road a ways," takes Milkman in, bathes his sore body, and tends his hurts. In return Milkman gives her a cool bath, rubbing and soaping her "until her skin squeaked and glistened like onyx." He washes her hair, massages her back, makes her bed, washes her dishes, and scours her tub. His unselfish attentions to Sweet are a striking contrast to his inattention to the other women in his life, especially his cousin, Hagar, and a lock of Hagar's hair in his wallet will be a persistent reminder that she died forlorn, with the sound of his spiteful words resonating in his wake. When he was a little boy making the obligatory Sunday drives with his father, mother, and sisters, Milkman had disliked kneeling on the front seat and looking out the back window in order to see anything. "Riding backwards made him uneasy. It was like flying blind and not knowing where he was going—just where he had been." Yet, now he must do just that. In order to move forward with his life, he must review where he has been.

That is the heroic journey for Morrison's characters: to press towards knowledge for its own sake. Morrison holds Milkman responsible for his transgressions, but she also forgives him. "He was not in a position to do anything about [them] . . . because he was stupid," she says. In the future he can "do better, and don't do *that* again." It is important to Morrison that her characters "have revelations, large or small."

The new Milkman is a striking contrast to the other male characters in the novel, who are not transcendent. Macon Dead and Guitar Bains are shaped by ugly circumstances over which they have no control. Each (over)reacts to his helplessness with a compulsive and unremarkable will to conquer. Macon's greedy obsession with owning things and people is a mutated version of his love, as a child, of the land and his family. Belonging to the earth, working with his father, caring for his sister, and earning respect and admiration from the black community define Macon's childhood. His father's violent death at the hands of powerful white men who take his land change love to obsession. "Owning, building, acquiring—that was his life, his future, his present, and all the history he knew. That he distorted life, or bent it, for the sake of gain, was a measure of his loss at his father's death." Proprietorship consumes Macon and alienates him from family and community, leaving no room for spiritual values like love, compassion, kindness, tolerance. He loves only the keys to buildings that he carries in his pocket and that he fondles often and reassuringly. Morrison offers them as a symbol of his empty victory.

Similarly, when Guitar's anger over white brutality against blacks impels him to join the Seven Days as their Sunday man, the anger inside implodes, and he becomes what he hates—a murderer. Like Macon, Guitar is a victim of his experience. Although he is a self-declared avenger of his people, the love of black life is eventually twisted into a love of power. That power gives him, he thinks, authority which he uses to kill indiscriminately—white and black.

Guitar and Milkman are opposite sides of a single fabric, and Morrison constructs their friendship from the threads of male life—street fights, barbershop talk, pool hall banter, sexual conquest, adventure—just as she constructs Nel and Sula's friendship from the threads of women's lives. Guitar's wild courage excites the sheltered Milkman. Guitar is older than Milkman and street-smart. He protects Milkman, he initiates him to street life, and he does not blame the son for the sins of the father. As Guitar reminds a friend who refuses to serve beer to the underaged Milkman for fear of Macon's retaliation, "You can't blame him for who his daddy is."

As the easy laughter of their adolescent intimacy gives way to conflict that throws their differences into stark relief, Morrison uses the space to examine black militancy, not in the service of advocacy, but as a way of characterizing the spectrum of black response to white violence in the 1960s. Some, like Milkman, convinced themselves that white oppression of blacks did not concern them. Others, like Macon Dead, turned white hatred into self-hatred and in turn directed that hatred toward their own people. Diametrically, Guitar and the Seven Days, enraged by the lynchings, the burnings, the murder, respond in kind. For them the white hatred precipitates acts of black love. "What I'm doing ain't about hating white people," Guitar tells his friend, "It's about loving us. About loving you. My whole life is love." In pledging his "whole life" to the universal love of all black people, Guitar cannot claim a more personal love of wife, children, friends. The secrecy of his work isolates him and precludes intimacy. Eventually, the appealing interplay between street wisdom and hard-edged generosity that defines Guitar gives way to brooding paranoia.

The complementing differences in Guitar's and Milkman's personalities that make each part of a whole are not the differences that eventually divide them. They become competing personalities, unrecognizable to each other. As Milkman journeys toward self-discovery and cultural identification, Guitar travels a parallel road toward psychic disintegration and cultural alienation. The belonging and understanding that Milkman recovers on the hunt in Shalimar are lost to Guitar, who once shared the camaraderie of the hunt as a child. But now in the woods he feels not brotherhood but murderous hostility. He is diseased with "white madness"—the bizarre executions of total strangers. Black crimes are not freakish in that way, according to Morrison. Blacks commit crimes "in the heat of passion: anger, jealousy, loss of face, and so on." (Even the Seven Days, though their crimes are deliberate and premeditated, fall within some broad boundary of legitimacy since their work is a response to aggression.) But stalking Milkman and killing Pilate, whose healing, ancestral guidance he rejects in favor of street justice, place Guitar outside all boundaries of rationality and morality. There can be no moral authority in killing for gold or for pleasure.

In a role reversal, as their journeys come to an end, it is Milkman who draws closest to achieving genuine universal love. His final leap from the rock is not the theatrical miscalculation of a disillusioned man wearing blue silk wings that opens *Song of Solomon* but a hard-earned conviction that, like Pilate, he has enough courage to face any episode of life—even death. When Milkman first gleans these truths, he longs to share them with Guitar, but he can only mourn Guitar's loss. Like Nel and Sula's, Milkman and Guitar's breakup is irreparable.

To his credit Milkman empathizes with his friend and with his father and is able to forgive their transgressions. Indications are that he even forgives Pilate's murder. "You want my life?" Milkman calls out to Guitar in the aftermath of the shooting. "You want it? Here." Milkman's tearful offer of himself, even in the service of Guitar's corrupt need, would seem to suggest that Milkman has evolved to the point that he values love more than he values the physical world. Many readers decry what they believe is the deliberate ambiguity of Morrison's conclusion, which does not explore Guitar's guilt and/or remorse and does not resolve Milkman's feelings: does he leap toward Guitar in anger or in love? But understanding what may appear ambiguous requires remembering Morrison's commitment to readers participation in making meaning by leaving "spaces" in the text. She explains that "into these spaces should fall the rumination of the reader and his or her invented and recollected or misunderstood knowingness." Each reader interprets the text in terms that reflect her experiences. Even with that stipulation to readers, however, Morrison does explain that in the final scenes Guitar recognizes Milkman's transformation "and recalls enough of how lost he is . . . to put his weapon down" and perhaps rises up to meet Milkman's gesture of love with a comparable one. Ultimately, however, there is always something more "interesting at stake than a clear resolution in the novel" for Morrison. She is more occupied with her char-acter's survival and with the "complexity of how people behave under duress— . . . the qualities they show at the end of an event when their backs are up against the wall." Milkman's response under duress is to accept what Pilate already knew—that there is no reason to fear death if the spirit is freed in life.

Milkman's unfettered spirit is marked by a dream about flying, Morrison's metaphor for the unconventional life of spiritual freedom. In Sweet's bed he dreams "about sailing high over the earth. . . . Part of his flight was over the dark sea, but it didn't frighten him because he knew he could not fall." As a child Milkman had longed for physical flight, and his discovery at age four that "only birds and airplanes could fly" had made him lose "all interest in himself." The result is a dull, unimaginative childhood that stretches into a pointless, indifferent adulthood. Flying remains a literal conception, impossible to achieve except on his first airplane ride, where "in the air, away from real life, he felt free." Freedom in an airplane "away from real life" is illusory, however. Milkman does not yet know that it is the spirit which must soar. As the insurance agent Robert Smith discovers, in modern times, believing in literal flight is a mental aberration that leads to certain death on the street below. In Michigan, Milkman is wedded to the streets where he estimates his worth in the marketplace in terms of money and commodities. Milkman is like the peacock he chases at the car lot, moored by the weight of his own finery. Guitar could just as easily be describing Milkman when he observes that the peacock has "too much tail. All that jewelry weighs it down. Like vanity. Can't nobody fly with all that shit. Wanna fly. You got to give up the shit that weighs you down." In Virginia, Milkman "gives up" the vanity acquired on Not Doctor Street when he accepts the timeless rhythms of men and animals in the woods.

Flight, the free fall, consistently means freedom, independence, unconventionality, self-knowledge for Morrison. In *Song of Solomon* flight also evokes the American folk tradition. Solomon's song is Morrison's version of the flying African myth about enslaved Africans who escaped slavery in the South by rising up and flying back to Africa and to freedom. In adopting and adapting the myth, Morrison becomes the modern griot, reciting stories from the past to a new generation. And her novel serves an essential function as cultural artifact. Myths are forgotten or misunderstood, Morrison thinks, because people in transit move away from the places where they were born and from the culture bearers who remain in those places. The flying myth is her example of one that is misunderstood by those who can relate to it in Western classical terms only. But Morrison wishes to restore its tutorial power for black people. As she says:

> If it means Icarus to some readers, fine; I want to take credit for
> that. But my meaning is specific: it is about black people who

could fly. That was always part of the folklore of my life; flying was one of our gifts. I don't care how silly it may seem. It is everywhere—people used to talk about it, it's in the spirituals and gospels. Perhaps it was wishful thinking—escape, death, and all that. But suppose it wasn't. What might it mean? I tried to find out in *Song of Solomon*.

When Milkman realizes that the children's song "Solomon done fly, Solomon done gone / Solomon cut across the sky, Solomon gone home" is about his great-great-grandfather Solomon, who had such powers, he rejoices: Solomon "didn't need no airplane. He just took off; got fed up. All the way up! No more cotton! No more bales! No more orders! No more shit! He flew, baby. Lifted his beautiful black ass up in the sky and flew on home." Milkman is exhilarated, but Morrison is cautious. African myth is not less vulnerable to contamination than Western fable. Solomon flew off, and Morrison asks, "Who'd he leave behind?" What about the wife and twenty-one children that he left here on the ground?

With that question Morrison's novel about male consciousness signals her ongoing delineation of women's concerns. Solomon flies off, and Ryna, his wife, is left to take care of the children. Her cries of protest and anguish are still carried on the wind more than a century later for Milkman to hear. In the third generation Milkman and Hagar reenact this tragedy of abandonment. When Milkman leaves, Hagar loses all capacity to think rationally, and she dies, as the euphemism goes, of a broken heart. Milkman dreams of flying as Hagar is dying. As always, however, Morrison intimates that matters of freedom and responsibility are not so easily settled. Milkman is, without a doubt, culpable. He has been callous and careless. But does Hagar's love for him give her the right to demand his love in return? Morrison answers no. Guitar reminds Hagar that "love shouldn't be like that." Love is not possession. "You can't own a human being." And most important you cannot love someone more than you love yourself. Hagar, who "wanted to kill for love, die for love," has not learned these lessons. Guitar calls her one of those "doormat women" whose "pride and conceit" amazes him. Hagar will not or cannot save her own life because she does not value herself outside the narrow limits of Milkman's love. Her frantic efforts to make herself over to fit the popular image of female beauty continues Morrison's recurring invective against the tyranny of such an image. Morrison's description of the carnival of smells, colors, and textures at the cosmetics counter in the department store where Hagar goes is a tour de force of the seductive influences of commercial marketing strategems:

The cosmetics department enfolded her in perfume, and she read hungrily the labels and the promise. Myrurgia for the primeval woman who created for him a world of tender privacy where the only occupant is you, mixed with Nina Ricci's L'Air du Temps. Yardley's Flair with Tuvache's Nectaroma and D'Orsay's Intoxication. Robert Piquet's Fracas, and Calypso and Visa and Bandit. Houbigant's Chantilly. Caron's Fleurs de Rocaille and Bellodgia. Hagar breathed deeply the sweet air that hung over the glass counters. Like a smiling sleepwalker she circled. Round and round the diamond-clear counters covered with bottled, wafer-thin disks, round boxes, tubes, and phials. Lipsticks in soft white hands darted out of their sheaths like the shiny red penises of puppies. Peachy powders and milky lotions were grouped in front of poster after poster of gorgeous grinning faces. Faces in ecstasy. Faces somber with achieved seduction. Hagar believed she could spend her life there among the cut glass, shimmering in peaches and cream, in satin. In opulence. In luxe. In love.

Hagar is bound for disappointment as the promises of cosmetic beauty are washed away with the scents and powders in a pouring rain on the street outside the department store. Morrison's work is a warning shot for those who would be victim to a false standard of beauty like Hagar and like Pauline Breedlove before her. Morrison's heroic characters must resist; they must be transformed, not cosmetically, but internally by their own humanity, and like Milkman they must take responsibility for their own lives. Milkman's journey shapes his metamorphosis so that by the novel's conclusion he has achieved freedom and accountability. Intuitive, compassionate, forgiving, generous, he knows that "if you surrendered to the air, you could *ride* it."

Pilate is the other heroic character in *Song of Solomon*. Her journey to self-knowledge having been completed, she knows, from the beginning of the text, what Milkman discovers in the end, and as her name suggests, Pilate is Milkman's spiritual guide throughout his passage. During Milkman's infancy and even before, she shields him from Macon's angry attacks, and later, during Milkman's adolescence, she catalyzes his course of self-discovery. In her presence, at age twelve, he discovers a woman, who without property and social position, is taller and wiser than his father. That "was the first time in his life that [he] remembered being completely happy." Pilate's stories about her life on the farm, about her father's bravery, about her brother's love, and her refusal to adopt the meaningless rituals that occupy most people—these counter Macon's stories about conquest, ownership, and dominion. Macon's declaration to his son that "Pilate can't teach you a thing you can use in the world" proves false, for Pilate alone teaches him the true meaning of flying without ever leaving the ground. Pilate's is not the selfish flight of Solomon, who leaves everyone behind. Pilate teaches Milkman that "you can't fly on off and leave a body." When Milkman leaves Hagar, it is Pilate who locks him in her cellar upon his return, forcing his dawning realization that Hagar is dead, that "it was his fault and Pilate knew it." His punishment by Pilate's reckoning is to carry with him "something that remained of the life he had taken." That evening Milkman returns home with a box of Hagar's hair as a healing reminder that with freedom comes responsibility.

Pilate, of course, is one of Morrison's ancestors, one of the timeless people who dispatch their wisdom to others, who consciously or unconsciously initiate others into the ways of African-American culture that give life continuity and intent. Out of place in "the big northern city" Pilate embraces more natural rhythms like those of the women of Shalimar who walk the road without purses, "bare-legged, their unstraightened hair braided or pulled back into a ball." Pilate has little need for the creature comforts of "elaborately socialized society." In deciding early in her life whom she wanted to love and what was important to her, Pilate has given up interest in manners and money but has "acquired a deep concern for and about human relationships."

Ancestral, mythic, free, Pilate embodies memorable traits of character that give form to the major theme of Morrison's work: spiritual transcendence. Born without a navel, which evidences the common birth of one human from another, Pilate seems ageless, immortal. As a natural healer whose "compassion for troubled people" and "respect for other people's privacy" are her passport, she has no fear of life. Neither does she have the familiar terror of death: "she spoke often to the dead [and] . . . knew there was nothing to fear." At the end of her life, Milkman wonders if there is another like Pilate. "There's got to be at least one more woman like you," he whispers. As ancestor Pilate bears a major share of the novel's work in passing on cultural knowledge to Milkman and to the reader.

All of Morrison's novels mirror the characters, language, folklore, mythology of African America. In *Song of Solomon*, Morrison nudges cultural memory by examining the importance in the black community of names and naming. Names of places and people are routinely appended, denoting some exploit or episode or special skill or talent or notoriety. Names have meaning; names tell stories: Ryna's Gulch, Solomon's Leap, Not Doctor Street—once called Doctor Street (its official name is Mains Avenue) by blacks in honor of the first black man to practice medicine in the city who lived and died on Doctor Street. When the white city legislators posted notices in businesses on the streeet reminding residents of the avenue's official name, Southside residents deliberately and unceremoniously took up Not Doctor Street, a name which signaled their inventive resistance to any oppression. Milkman (whose name is one old man's idea of humor) considers the import of black men and women knowing their names:

> Names they got from yearnings, gestures, flaws, events, mistakes, weaknesses. Names that bore witness. Macon Dead, Sing Byrd, Crowell Byrd, Pilate, Reba, Hagar, Madgalene, First Corinthians, Milkman, Guitar, Railroad Tommy, Hospital Tommy, Empire State (he just stood around and swayed), Small Boy, Sweet, Circe, Moon, Nero, Humpty-Dumpty, Blue Boy Scandinavia, Quack-Quack, Jericho, Spoonbread, Ice Man, Dough Belly, Rocky River, Gray Eye, Cock-a-Doodle Doo, Cool Breeze, Muddy Waters, Pinetop, Jelly Roll, Fats, Lead-Belly, Bo Diddley, Cat-Iron, Peg-Leg, Son, Shortstuff, Smoky Babe, Funny Papa, Bukka, Pink, Bull Moose, B.B., T-Bone, Black Ace, Lemon, Washboard, Gatemouth, Cleanhead, Tampa Red, Juke Boy, Shine, Staggerlee, Jim the Devil, Fuck-up, and *Dat* Nigger.

To know one's name is to own it, to insist upon claiming its history. Milkman learns to accept his name as a testimony to the loneliness that kept his mother nursing him until he was old enough to dangle his legs to the floor. Jake keeps and owns the unfortunate name given him by an illiterate white man and passes that name on to his son, who passes it on to his son. Pilate keeps "her own name and everybody else's," Guitar thinks, in a brass box attached to her ear. Perhaps she understands as Milkman does that "when you know your name you should hold on to it, for unless it is noted down and remembered, it will die when you do." As Morrison explains it, the gold of Milkman's search "is really Pilate's yellow orange and the glittering metal of the box in her ear" containing her name. In the opening epigraph of *Song of Solomon*, Morrison reminds that "the fathers may soar / And the children may know their names." Each generation is obliged to remember and pass its knowledge on to the next.

GARY STORHOFF

"Anaconda Love": Parental Enmeshment in Toni Morrison's Song of Solomon

> I think that if people put so much emphasis on family and children, it
> is because they live in great isolation; they have no friends, no love, no
> affection, nobody. They are alone; therefore they have children in order
> to have somebody.
>
> —Simone de Beauvoir

Like Simone de Beauvoir, Toni Morrison criticizes parents who enmesh
themselves with their children. De Beauvoir condemns the contemporary
family as an inadequate solution for "the problems generated by an evil
society," but Morrison's view of family relations depicted in her novels is
considerably more textured, since she is interested in the etiology and the
consequences of enmeshment. By emphasizing the contextual dimensions of
her family dramas, the interpersonal family patterns that develop intergen-
erationally, Morrison extends her sympathies to all her characters, even the
most seemingly undeserving ones. Yet the family as interpersonal system has
been largely neglected in studies of Morrison, even in *Song of Solomon*,
perhaps her most ambitious multigenerational text.

From the perspective of psychological criticism, the dominant critical
discourse has been resolutely Freudian. As Eleanor Branch writes, "There is

From *Style* 31, no. 2 (Summer 1997). © 1997 *Style*.

no question . . . that Milkman's story is, in part, centered on the resolution of Oedipal issues." The psychoanalytic critic's attention is most often directed to Milkman's antagonism toward his father, or his obsessive relationship with his mother, or his apparent inability to love another woman. But too exclusive a focus on "Oedipal issues" leads invariably both to an oversimplification of the complex generational relationships within the family and to a diminution of the reader's sympathies that Morrison attempts to evoke for her characters. If a character's behavior is conceived of in solely intrapsychic terms—of unconscious properties and drives residing exclusively in the self—critical discussion leads to unequivocal moral judgments for or against the characters. The clinical tension between the self and the family is intensified by an exclusive focus on either the individual (i.e., intrapsychic clinical theory) or the family (interpsychic theory). The Oedipal Complex as a theoretical orientation, as Knapp suggests, oversimplifies because it does not address the self-in-family. Without mapping systemic operations of the families depicted in the novel, it is therefore inevitable for the critic to choose sides in the novel's Family Feud, creating simplified dichotomies of villain and victim, good living and bad living, "Northern" and "Southern" personalities, and materialistic versus "aesthetic" families.

If the critical focus shifts emphasis from the intrapsychic to the interpersonal or social dynamic, we discover that *Song of Solomon* is a portrait of enmeshment—the suffocating bond parents occasionally create with their children that Morrison calls "anaconda love." Song dramatizes a variety of relational constructs that lead to parental enmeshment. The novel contrasts Macon Dead's and Ruth Foster's families of origin to reveal why they overinvolve themselves in Milkman's life, as they attempt to recapitulate childhood patterns in their own family. Morrison, however, does not privilege Pilate's unconventional, matriarchal, marginalized family unit over Macon and Ruth's conventional, patriarchal, bourgeois nuclear family, as critics often claim. Neither Pilate's nor Macon's family is functional; both sets of parents seek to fuse with their offspring to satisfy their own emotional cravings. Understanding the web of family dysfunctionality increases an appreciation of each character's complexity and of the novel's ambitious thematic design.

I
A "Nice" Place: Lincoln's Heaven as Macon's Lost Governor

The Dead family is organized by brutality and violence, most notably Macon Dead's wife-beating and his abuse of his children. Macon is easy for the reader to despise, for he seems created to elicit distaste and contempt. He is the stereotypical landlord, evicting widows and orphans because they are behind in their rent. He consumes himself with the outward symbols of wealth and elegance, buying the finest cars while the rest of the African-American community in his city suffers dire poverty. He reinscribes within his family the discourse of slavery when he tells Milkman, "Own things. And let the things you own own other things. Then you'll own yourself and other people too." It is no surprise that most critics see him as the novel's villain.

A literal interpretation of Macon's actions is sufficient to categorize him as such. Yet this moralistic reading contradicts Morrison's stated intention, for she herself defends Macon in interviews and commentary. Macon also justifies himself, telling his son Milkman: "I am not a bad man. I want you to know that. Or believe it" Understanding Macon's statement depends upon recognizing the system of relations he has helped create in his family, and of the dynamics of his family of origin. The context of the Deads' domestic violence reveals that Macon's brutality is embedded in a family organization used to sustain and preserve the family's unity. Macon's violence is a symptom of fundamental processes operating within his family's system.

In analyzing the patterns of disturbed families, Gregory Bateson writes that "any self-correcting system which has lost its governor . . . spirals into never-ending, but always systematic, distortions." For Macon's family of origin, Lincoln's Heaven, the farm where he grew up, is a systemic "governor," a structural mechanism that establishes each member's relational identity within the family. Lincoln's Heaven is for both Pilate and Macon a site of domestic concord and cooperation, as they work with their father, Jake. Their family prospers as does the farm itself, and the interaction between all family members is harmonic and cooperative. With the loss of this mechanism in their childhood, both Pilate's and Macon's characters "spiral" in complementary trajectories.

Lincoln's Heaven is not simply where Macon grew up, but a symbolic space. It represents a psychological anchor, a social site where different generations cooperate freely and generously, and where two sexes confront each other as equals. It was, says Macon, "nice." As an adult, Macon seeks to recover that paradise lost. His aggressive actions as an adult are paradoxically intended to establish himself as a replication of his own father, and his home as a duplicate of the farm of his youth. His father-identification, indeed, takes the form of reconstructing Lincoln's Heaven: "he would re-create the land that was to have been his."

When the governor was in place in his youth, when his father owned the land free and clear, Macon was a "nice" and "good" person, a devoted son and brother. Because Macon's mother died giving birth to Pilate, Macon is parentified as a four-year-old child, and must assume the role of Pilate's dead mother, carrying her to the fields and tending to her in Macon Sr.'s absence: "At one time she had been the dearest thing in the world to him." In fact, he thought of her as "his own child." As Pilate tells Milkman, "Macon was a nice boy and awful good to me. Be nice if you could have known him then. He would have been a good friend to you too, like he was to me." While reminiscing with Milkman about the farm, Macon seems to undergo a psychological transformation as he speaks: "His voice sounded different to Milkman. Less hard, and his speech was different. More southern and comfortable and soft."

Superficially, his violence—which contradicts his deeply felt sense of "responsibility" to his family—appears to issue from Macon's greed, his domineering sexism, and his acceptance of "white" middle-class values. But seen from a systems perspective, Macon's abuse has its psychological origin in his family of origin. We learn little of his father Jake's personality, but one briefly narrated incident requires close examination to discover the covert psychic themes of Macon's family of origin. His beloved wife dead, Jake must name his daughter and, to the midwife's horror, writes "Pilate":

> "You don't want to give this motherless child the name of the
> man that killed Jesus, do you?"
> "I asked Jesus to save my wife."
> "Careful, Macon."
> "I asked him all night long."
> "He did give you your baby."
> "Yes. He did. Baby name Pilate."

His choice of "Pilate," then, is his act of rebellion, his retaliation against God for what he perceives as cosmic injustice. Clearly, Jake has choices—expressing faith, for example, or resignation, or despair—in reacting to his personal tragedy. Jake's response implicates his children in his battle against God; in doing so, he unknowingly makes his reprisal a corporate event. Beyond their awareness, the children are made complicitous in his rebellion. In Macon's presence, he angrily strikes back at what he perceives as divine injustice by giving his daughter "the name of the man that killed Jesus"—in effect, sharing with his children his sense of cosmic entitlement and his Luciferian rage when he suffers tragic loss.

Lincoln's Heaven is another vehicle for Jake's self-assertion, this time against a viciously racist society. Symbolically, the farm consolidates two opposing but complementary forces: self-aggrandizement and self-dispensation. Lincoln's Heaven is for Jake's family a symbolic nexus of self and community, two spheres that the farm, created through Jake's labor, connect. First, the farm represents material evidence of Jake's self-assertion and personal achievement, despite the overwhelming odds against him. For Macon, Lincoln's Heaven symbolizes his father's superb self-actualization in a racist society: "[H]e had one of the best farms in Montour County. A farm that colored their lives like a paintbrush and spoke to them like a sermon. 'See? See what you can do?'" The farm epitomizes the self independently shaping and controlling the obdurate world. "We got a home in this rock, don't you see! Nobody starving in my home; nobody crying in my home, and if I got a home, you got one too!"

If owning Lincoln's Heaven permits pride in the self, it also ties Jake to his community. Ownership offers Jake and his children the opportunity for self-giving within the family circle, and for extending generosity and joy to African Americans. The farm serves as a communal vehicle for Jake's rebellion against racial injustice, since the success of Jake's farm allows the community to participate in his rebellion vicariously. As Susan Blake writes, Jake affirms community "at the expense of the white folks." This is at least partly why Jake's farm becomes a locus of communal pleasure in the county, where people enjoy "real peaches like they had in Georgia, the feasts they had when hunting was over, the pork kills in the winter . . . and Sunday break-of-dawn fishing parties in a fish pond that was two acres wide." But peaches and fishing parties are not the only reasons the farm is a community center; Jake's success represents a symbolic settling of scores, a statement against white supremacy.

The farm also stabilizes and strengthens domesticity. The children learn reciprocal care-taking on the farm. Pilate bakes cherry pies for Macon, while Macon watches over Pilate. Since their mother is dead, their father is their only parental model; he is, in a sense, a Janus-like figure, embodying both self-empowerment and involvement of others in his own emotional and psychic designs. While Lincoln's Heaven continually reinforces Jake's heroic nature, at the same time it provides a context for Pilate and Macon's collaboration and mutual support.

As a vanished psychological space rather than as the literal theft of land, the farm's loss and the trauma of Jake's murder will plague Macon and Pilate throughout their lives. The trauma of loss intitates the "spiraling" in both children. Macon's brutality begins when the governor—the totality of opposing symbolic meanings that Lincoln's Heaven reconciles within the family of origin—disappears with the murder of his father. As Macon says, "Something went wild in me . . . when I saw him on the ground."

Macon restates the psychic themes of his family of origin through his acquisition of real estate. By creating a real estate empire, Macon asserts himself, for his business represents both his rebellious self-assertion and his accomodation to the patterns he learned from his father. But without "the lost governor" regulating his actions, Macon spirals out of control. Thus, the relationships with people that his ownership could possibly generate result in perpetual conflict because he fails to recreate in his own property the full complexity of the farm's symbolism. That is, for Macon, ownership of "things" signifies only his own self-aggrandizement and his combat against a highly personalized sense of injustice. He is, as it were, "split off" from the communal dimension that his property could serve for him (as property once served for his father). He cannot conceive of the possibility that his private property provides: that he can balance self-aggrandizement with generosity and cooperation within his community and can work cooperatively with other family members.

Instead, he is feared as a tyrant by his community and his own family. Instead of conceptualizing injustice as the racism his community confronts daily, Macon personalizes injustice. And like his father, Jake, he retaliates. But while Jake's battles were cosmic, Macon's targets are pathetic. Instead of rebelling against God or the white establishment, Macon battles the widow who cannot pay her rent. His facing down Porter (who is armed with a shotgun) recall his father's courage, but not his vision.

Macon, then, represents one pole of the family dynamic—powerful self-aggrandizement through material possession. Pilate, the "raggedy bootlegger," represents the other opposing but reciprocal pole (generosity through self-abnegation). Acting in compensatory balance with Macon, Pilate renounces the world excessively just as Macon excessively grasps for it. Because she never knew her mother, her personality characteristics derive solely from Jake. Like Macon, she resembles her tall, dark father. Her ability to cook soft-boiled eggs and her renowned wine-making echo Jake's farming prowess. Her love of the natural world, implied by her "fruity" odor, suggests Jake's peach trees. Like her brother Macon, Pilate attempts to recreate the security and love she enjoyed as a child on the lost farm, but fails because she too is oblivious to the balancing, harmonizing aspects of her original family's governor.

A chronic pattern of conflict beteen Pilate and Macon—organized around the possession or dispossession of property—acts as a conjunctive force tying together the brother and sister, despite the emotional cut-off that occurs in their adulthood. In their childhood, Lincoln's Heaven symbolically reconciles messages of self-assertion and selflessness. But with Jake dead and the farm stolen, any relationship that promises self-gratification for either sibling is experienced as temporary and leads only to betrayal and loss. Their identity-creation partially follows gender roles, for Macon attempts to fulfill the assertive male role while Pilate attempts to be the nurturing female principle. Although a majority of critics see Pilate as the hero of the novel, she too seeks but ultimately fails to recreate the relationships of her family of origin.

Unlike both Macon and her father, Pilate is utterly indifferent to possessions, and the self-affirmation that "things" may imply. That Pilate floats as if unattached to the community is symbolically implied by Pilate's house lying on the perimeter of the socialized African-American community. As if in parody of Macon's conversion of land into deeds, Pilate owns only a dead man's bones, a geography book, and a rock collection, remembrances of places she visited, but where she could not stay. Like her father, Pilate rejects conventions and social verities, but Morrison is ambiguous in characterizing Pilate's deliberate choice of repudiation: "Her mind traveled crooked streets and aimless goat paths, arriving sometimes at profundity, other times at the revelations of a three-year-old." Pilate's last words are also ambiguous, expressing love, but also regret for her alienation: "I wish I'd a knowed more people. I would of loved 'em all. If I'd a knowed more, I would a loved more." In their extremes, Pilate and Macon unknowingly seek to recreate Lincoln's Heaven for their own families, but fail because they each deny in their characters the partial truths implied by their sibling. Macon's view of family life is frozen and enclosed around his self-aggrandizement, just as Pilate's is defined by self-denial and renunciation. Each extreme implies its opposite, but is incomplete without synthesis.

Pilate can reproduce her original family no more successfully than can Macon. Her family exposes her imbalanced character just as Macon's family reflects his. Her inability to understand the past's weight on her own spirit, an inability that jeopardizes her own family's welfare, is symbolically expressed by Pilate's failure to understand her dead father's cryptic messages. Just as she cannot understand that she carries the dead weight of her father's bones, she fails to understand fully how the loss of Lincoln's Heaven—the dead weight of her own past—has helped shape her treatment of Reba and Hagar. Like her mother, Reba cares nothing for property or possessions. Reba magnifies the destructive aspect inherent in Pilate's self-denial by allowing herself to be exploited by nameless lovers; in the text, moreover, she seems a nullity, "vacuous," lacking characterization or development. But it is Pilate's granddaughter Hagar, losing her own identity to Milkman's sexist whims, who suffers the fatal consequences of Pilate's original loss. "What," Guitar wonders, "had Pilate done to her?" As if in answer to Guitar's unspoken query, Morrison writes, "all they knew to do was love her." Their devotion, however, is another form of "anaconda love."

Although most criticism blames Milkman for Hagar's madness and death, Pilate and Reba are also partly responsible, for they are emotionally enmeshed in Hagar's life. In complementary relation to Pilate and Reba's exaggerated austerity, Hagar's life trajectory is yet another "spiral," but her self-renunciation is the converse of theirs. Her spiritual emptiness—"She had no self left"—is ironically balanced by her vast sense of entitlement: she believes that Milkman must love her, simply because she loves him. Her feeling of entitlement is a result of Pilate and Reba's enmeshment, their eagerness to give her everything. While they deplete themselves for her sake, she becomes the consummate consumer, receiving anything she asks for. Her mother and grandmother dress in rags, but Hagar is the epitome of fashion and elegance. She is, as Morrison says, "a spoiled child." Misunderstanding Hagar's statement that "Some of my days were hungry ones," Reba replies, "We get you anything you want, baby. Anything. You been knowing that." Even at 36, Hagar remains their "baby girl." Hagar dies insane, lost in her delusion that she can control another person's love with a suit of clothes. Just as the schizophrenic may emerge after generations of increasingly disturbed family interaction, so Hagar may be described as the (patho)logical consequence of Pilate's lost governor.

II
"Pressed Small": Ruth's Quest for Power

With this paradigmatic model of Macon's family of origin established, we can return to Macon's own family. The chaos of his present family life is in part a consequence of his attempt to reconsitute his family of origin. Macon chooses a wife who, he believes, will be adjunctive to this design, but because he insufficiently understands his own unexamined aim, Ruth is destined to create even greater chaos for him. Thus, Macon and Ruth's marriage may be conceptualized as a set of powerful psychic forces set in motion by the childhood families of each.

For Macon, Ruth signifies the symbolism of her Biblical namesake. She outwardly conforms to the stereotypical image of a devout housewife, and she adheres to the "separate spheres" doctrine deriving from gender definition, occupying herself with the duties of the household while he maneuvers in the larger world outside the family. Although she describes herself as "pressed small" by Macon, beneath her placid exterior Ruth struggles to wrest power from him. Her strength lies, paradoxically, in her weakness, her "smallness."

Ruth learned her strategy for gaining power through a weakness in her childhood's family, a family legacy of her enmeshment with her father, Dr. Foster. As "the most important Negro in the city," Dr. Foster is consumed—

like Macon—with acquiring property and wealth, and he treats Ruth as a servant, "useful" for housework and for his caretaking after his wife's death. Dr. Foster positions her as his child just as Macon will as his wife: a "thing" possessed. Ruth rewards his possessiveness by freely choosing her alienation for her father's sake: "I had no friends. . . . but I didn't think I'd ever need a friend because I had him. I was small, but he was big."

Ruth intuitively understands, however, that she can use her "smallness" as a mask to disguise her own efforts for control, regulating the family system that her father has established for his own benefit. Ruth is "devious" and "manipulative" in exercising control, especially when he becomes ill:

> She had the same calmness and efficiency with which she care for the doctor, putting her hand on death's chest and holding him back, denying him, keeping her father alive even past the point where he wanted to be alive, past pain on into disgust and horror at having to smell himself in his next breath.

Ruth discovers that her deference and servility can be her weapons. She enacts the role of the good daughter, "calm and efficient" in her duty to her father, though her effort to keep death at bay is contrary to her father's desperate wish to die. By ministering to him, she attempts to deny him the relief of death, even though she knows "that her father wanted to die." She ostensibly perpetuates her victimhood by prostrating herself before him, but through her service to him she also perpetuates the means of her power.

Ruth employs her strategy of control through manipulative weakness in her marriage. By marrying Macon, her social inferior, Ruth continues her role of self-abasement for her father's sake (since he encouraged her marriage), but simultaneously she asserts superiority within her marriage. Morrison neither exculpates Macon nor depicts Ruth as simply a masochist seeking suffering. Rather than becoming a helpless neurotic, Ruth uses Macon's battering to fortify her position as the center of power in the home.

Morrison describes Ruth as "leading her husband down paths from which there was no exit save violence." Ruth's daughter Corinthians understands her mother's method, "how her mother had learned to bring her husband to a point, not of power (a nine-year-old girl could slap Ruth and get away with it), but of helplessness. She would begin by describing some incident in which she was a sort of honest buffoon." By depicting herself as a "buffoon," she ruins Macon's "property" and denies him his dream of Lincoln's Heaven. She receives his abuse, but also renders him impotent before his children and consolidates their sympathy for her. Outside the household, Macon wields power as landlord, but within his family, physical power is the only alternative he believes he possesses. If one views the process of this family's functioning, Macon's violence represents his futile, reprehensible effort to offset the emotional power Ruth has garnered, ironically, through her own submission.

In the one incident of domestic abuse that Morrison dramatizes, the family dynamic of Ruth's self-abasement countered with Macon's violence is clearly elucidated. At dinner, Ruth happily tells of how she was humiliated at the Djvorak wedding, since she did not know (as a Methodist) that she should not take Catholic communion: "all were able to admire her honesty and laugh at her ignorance." At her telling of this trivial event, Macon loses control and hits her. What is the process of this conflict? By humiliating herself, Ruth unknowingly jeopardizes Macon's precarious design to reconstitute Lincoln's Heaven in his home; as a "silly woman" not worthy of his "ownership," she betrays him in his effort to "re-create the land that was to have been his."

Further, when she calls herself "Dr. Foster's daughter" at the wedding and "daddy's daughter" at the dinner table, she deprives him of his delusory "ownership" of her and erodes his self-respect and masculinity. In the face of this experienced "injustice" in his own home, he retaliates—a pattern, learned from Jake, that he has repeated since childhood. But by receiving his blow, Ruth wins her psychological victory over Macon in their war for Milkman's soul when he leaps to his mother's defense: "You touch her again, and I'll kill you," Milkman threatens. Momentarily, at least, Milkman forms a coalition with Ruth against Macon, but his defense of her could not, he knows, change the family dynamic: "It would change nothing between his parents. It would change nothing inside them . . . . The game would go on." His vain effort to "rescue" his mother, he intuitively understands, is doomed to fail because his parents' relationship has co-evolved through the decades.

This analysis of family process obviously does not excuse Macon for his battering, nor does it blame Ruth. An unreflective man, Macon is no longer a wounded child, and Morrison makes it clear that he is responsible for his reprehensible treatment of his wife and children. But understanding his battering within the context of the Dead's family functioning not only makes him a more complex character, but also gives a clearer vision of Ruth than as simple victim. Within his family, Macon continuously enacts the role of the insensitive, grasping brute because his vision of Lincoln's Heaven has failed. Ruth reciprocates by "calmly and efficiently" debasing herself because this is her only claim to control and power, especially over Milkman. As if in a dance, Macon rages in the home, then retreats to his real estate business to reinforce his masculinity and pride. He acts out Ruth's self-fulfilling prophecy of the brute, so that Ruth can continue her role as suffering, self-debasing victim. Each conspires to reinforce the psychological patterns of the other, for the process itself has become habitual and serves to rationalize their collective pain.

III
"You Can't Do the Past Over": Milkman's Enmeshment and His Release

If this family contained only these two polarities, these two conflicting part-ners, the system would ultimately collapse. The Dead family achieves home-ostasis (i.e., emotional stability) through the supression of the son, Milkman. Milkman is the focal point of the novel's thematics of enmeshment. Milkman provides Ruth with marital surrogacy (a male to serve), and Macon with a shadowy reflection of his own workings with Jake. Milkman, then, serves as the family's connective agent. Through him, because Macon's rage and Ruth's unsatisfied love are continually regenerated, they maintain a workable (though unhappy) balance. Milkman has been controlled by both father and mother. He has been triangulated into their power struggle, and it is his life's task to extricate himself.

Milkman's conception and infancy foreshadow his triangulation with his parents. Ruth schemes with Pilate to become pregnant with Milkman not because her baby would be "a person to her, a separate real person," but would be a "passion" intended "to hold them together"—that is, an attempt to control Macon. Predictably, her pregnancy provokes Macon's abuse in his attempt to abort Milkman. Ruth imagines Milkman's birth, her "one aggres-sive act brought to royal completion," as her victory over her husband. Her care of Milkman fortifies her triumph, since prolonged breastfeeding of Milkman, resulting in his nickname and Macon's public humiliation, rein-forces her self-image as the suffering servant who at least controls her home.

Far from acknowledging his son as "a separate real person," Macon too uses Milkman as a weapon for dominance and control of Ruth. Macon, like Ruth, infantilizes his son; as Milkman tells him, "You treat me like I was a baby." Although Macon sends his daughter to an exclusive school, he does not allow Milkman to attend college, coercing him instead to work as a real estate agent, a job providing evidence of Macon's victory over Ruth: "His son belonged to him now and not to Ruth." Macon also forces Milkman to adopt his values, even ordering Milkman to burglarize Pilate's house to steal her treasure: "Get it. For both of us. Please get it, son. Get the gold." Most disturbingly, Macon sets Milkman the example of his own domestic violence. When Milkman strikes Macon in defense of his mother, paradoxically, Milkman's blow precipitates in Macon "a grudging feeling of pride in his son." In fact, Macon hints that he covertly encouraged, then permitted his own beating: "I want you to think about the man you think you whipping. And think about the fact that next time I might not let you. Old as I am, I might not let you." "Letting" Milkman strike him may serve a purpose of which Macon is unaware at that point: to justify for himself that he can reveal his suspicion of Ruth's incest, and thereby fortify his own competing coalition with his son.

Milkman senses that his life is "pointless, aimless," and his drifting has roused the ire of some critics. Trudier Harris, for example, writes, "A spoiled brat, Milkman becomes a trial to our sympathies" Milkman, however, may be suffering from a depression at least partly a consequence of his parents' enmeshment with him, their desire to posses and control him completely. Their desire crystallizes around Milkman's choice of a vocation. He discovers that he is "excellent" in business dealings—a trait he absorbs from his father. The narrator describes his business talent with a positive tone, and implies that this could be a career path for Milkman, but for his own ambivalence. Why is he so divided about what to do with his life? At least partly, he is entrapped in his parents' battle over what he should become. Ruth wants him to go to college and become a doctor (like her father), for "she had as little respect for her husband's work as Macon had for college graduates." Thus, he is placed by his parents in an untenable situation: if he pleases one, he rejects the other. It is no wonder that, unable to make choices for himself, he feels "everybody wants something from me."

Enmeshed with both parents, Milkman tells himself that "you can't do the past over." This truism is precisely what Milkman must accept emotionally. Though he cannot change his family's history, even as events occurring a century earlier have helped chart a course for his life, he must develop a separation from his parents' emotional lives that will release him from his enmeshment. He can no longer exist as "a garbage pail for the actions and hatred of other people." Milkman's task is to allow "a self inside himself [to] emerge, a clean-lined definite self," an identity differentiated from the image imposed upon him by his parents for their own emotional purposes. Before this differentiation can occur, however, he must understand his parents as they are—ordinary and damaged as children themselves.

Prior to his acceptance of his parents' imperfections, he despises them both. He "would not pretend that it was love for his mother," for he had never "thought of his mother as a person, a separate individual, with a life apart from allowing or interfering with his own." For Milkman, Ruth is "an obscene child playing dirty games with whatever male was near—be it her father or her son." His relationship with his father is equally negative: "he differed from him as much as he dared." To see his parents in a different light is similar to a religious conversion, a spiritual transfiguration that leads to other fundamental changes in the way he relates to all people.

As critics have noted, Milkman's conversion occurs on multiple levels. He senses his connection with his ancestry, he learns domestic harmony with Sweet, he commits himself to the community at Danville, and he feels guilt at his treatment of Hagar. He learns to love Pilate. Antecedent to all these profound changes, however, is his differentiation from his parents' lives, an emotional sundering that occurs on his trip South. Milkman knows that he must "go solo" in more ways than one, for his enmeshment with Ruth and Macon have prevented him from empathizing with other people. Preoccupied with his parents' problems, he must learn to establish his own emotional boundaries so that he can tolerate his parents' suffering without becoming entangled in their unconscious expectations of him and their childhood losses.

But this separation is double-edged. He must also release them from his sense of grandiose entitlement, from his demands that they conform to his unrealistic and unreasonable requirements as perfect parents. Milkman is trapped in a "fairy tale mess"; unknowingly he has wished that his parents were a king and queen, with untainted pasts. On his trip, he can imagine his father as a child "[who] loved his father; had an intimate relationship with him; that his father loved him, trusted him, and found him worthy." The son of a wealthy man, Milkman has been given much, but he also resents the sympathy and understanding they have legitimately expected from him—not in return for their munificent gifts, but as a human obligation. He himself recognizes his refusal to sympathize with his parents as his own selfishness: "[H]e thought he deserved only to be loved—from a distance, though—and given what he wanted." Like the mother and father of Hansel and Gretel, to whom Morrison alludes, Ruth and Macon have damaged their children, but Milkman must learn to understand their pasts and forgive their parental transgressions.

His escape from enmeshment begins when he consciously releases both parents from his infantile desire for their perfection. As their son, he must be capable of listening to both parents without demonizing either one, taking sides, or absorbing their grief as entirely his own—all features of his earlier enmeshment with them. Because he could not be independent emotionally to understand their own childhood enmeshments, he could not respond to them without either corrupting his love for them or becoming enlisted in their struggle for control. His literal separation from them (during his trip South) permits an emotional detachment, one extending to them the freedom to have their own problems and to tell him about themselves. Milkman asks himself, "Why shouldn't his parents tell him their personal problems? If not him, then who?" His rhetorical question reveals his willingness to assume responsibility for his parents, but not to identify emotionally with them, to recognize their grief, but not to claim it as his own. At this moment, Morrison writes, a new identity begins to emerge, and he is reborn: "[H]is self—the coccoon that was 'personality'—gave way."

Milkman's liberating realization of his human obligation to his parents is symbolized by the disappearance of his hypochondriac limp, a "deformity [that] was mostly in his mind." At fourteen, Milkman notices that one of his legs was shorter than the other; he feels "shooting pains" and "believed it was polio." When he finally realizes his genuine connection to his parents, however, he experiences an "exhilaration":

> he found himself exhilarated by simply walking the earth. Walking it like he belonged on it; like his legs were stalks, tree trunks, a part of his body that extended down down down into the rock and soil, and were comfortable there—on the earth and on the place where he walked. And he did not limp.

Symbolically, Milkman can "walk alone," autonomous yet connected to Ruth and Macon by a generous sympathy that he had not felt before. He literally discovers his parental "roots"—symbolized in the image of the tree that describes his own new solidity. It is this change towards his parents that is the catalyst for the spiritual transformation he is about to undergo.

If Milkman's escape from parental enmeshment is understood as the narrative's central concern, his "flight" at the novel's conclusion comes into clearer focus. Failing to reframe the event within the context of Milkman's enmeshment, the critical tendency is to read this symbolic event too literally. Thus, critics interpret it both from a positive and negative perspective. His gesture has been seen as "suicidal," as a defeat of "the dragons of despair, nihilism, and sterility," as proof of his change into a "caring, responsible, communal adult," and as a cowardly escape from "the political possibilities inherent in human interaction with history." But if we read this scene within the frame of Milkman's affirming his family relations while simultaneously separating himself from the enmeshed structure that had heretofore been his entire emotional life, Milkman's liberation is, as Morrison asserts, a "marvelous epiphany."

It is therefore crucial to conceive of the events leading up to his flight within the framework of Milkman's family. He calls out to Guitar as his "brother," and he affirms (through his tribute to Pilate) his connection to his parents. His flight is both forward in family (in affirming his relationship with Guitar and Pilate) and away from enmeshment. As such, flying symbolizes the positive dimensions of the family, certainly an anomalous scene in this novel of damaged and suffering children. His decision to "surrender to the air" is a resolution to open himself to the emotions of others, his family's especially but not exclusively, without claiming ownership of these emotions, or control of the people experiencing those emotions.

Morrison thereby dramatizes her conviction that the individual self, as well as the family, is an agent of change; that the individual does not simply undergo the family's masked negotiations and transactions passively, but also to a certain extent shapes and chooses these processes, initiates and develops them. Milkman's life implies that the self's value inheres in its ability to change itself and thus become at least partially self-creating. Because Macon, Pilate, and Ruth could not face the suffering of their childhoods directly, they were incomplete as adults and looked for their emotional completion in their children. During his trip South, Milkman looks back. In doing so, he learns the wisdom to understand and forgive his parents, and in this way he frees himself from his enmeshment. For Morrison, it is possible to escape "anaconda love."

Chronology

1931   Toni Morrison born Chloe Anthony Wofford on February 18 in Lorain, Ohio, the second child of George Wofford and Ramah Willis Wofford.

1953   Graduates with B.A. in English from Howard University; changes name to Toni during years at Howard.

1955   Receives M.A. in English from Cornell University for thesis on the theme of suicide in William Faulkner and Virginia Woolf.

1955–57   Instructor in English at Texas Southern University.

1957–64   Instructor in English at Howard University.

1958   Marries Harold Morrison, a Jamaican architect.

1964   Divorces Morrison and returns with her two sons to Lorain.

1965   Becomes editor for a textbook subsidiary of Random House in Syracuse, New York.

1970   Morrison's first novel, *The Bluest Eye* published; takes editorial position at Random House in New York, eventually becoming a senior editor.

1971–71   Associate Professor of English at the State University of New York at Purchase.

1974   *Sula* published.

1975   *Sula* nominated for National Book Award.

1976–77   Visiting Lecturer at Yale University.

1977   *Song of Solomon* published, receives the National Book Critics Circle Award and the American Academy and Institute of Arts and Letters Award.

1981   *Tar Baby* published.

1984–89   Schweitzer Professor of the Humanities at the State University of New York at Albany.

1986   Receives the New York State Governor's Art Award.

1986–88   Visiting Lecturer at Bard College.

1987   *Beloved* published and is nominated for the National Book Award and the National Book Critics Award.

1988   *Beloved* awarded Pulitzer Prize in fiction and the Robert F. Kennedy Award.

1989   Toni Morrison becomes Robert F. Goheen Professor of the Humanities at Princeton University.

1992   Publishes *Jazz* and *Playing in the Dark: Whiteness and the Literary Imagination*.

1993   Receives Nobel Prize in literature.

1997   *Paradise* published.

Contributors

HAROLD BLOOM is Sterling Professor of Humanities at Yale University and Professor of English at the New York University Graduate School. His works include *The Anxiety of Influence* (1973), *Agon: Toward a Theory of Revisionism* (1982), *The American Religion* (1992), *The Western Canon* (1994), and *Shakespeare: The Invention of the Human* (1998). Professor Bloom is a 1985 MacArthur Foundation Award recipient and served as the Charles Eliot Norton Professor of Poetry at Harvard University in 1987–88. He is the editor of more than 30 anthologies, and general editor of several series of literary criticism published by Chelsea House.

WILFRED D. SAMUELS is Associate Professor of English and Ethnic Studies at the University of Utah. His articles and essays have appeared in *Black American Literature Forum, Callaloo, Umoja: Scholarly Journal of Black Studies,* and *Explicator.* He is author of *Five Afro-Caribbean Voices in American Culture, 1917–1929,* and co-editor of *"Our Spiritual Strivings": Recent Developments in Afro-American Literature and Criticism.*

VALERIE SMITH is Professor of English at the University of California, Los Angeles. She is author of *Self-Discovery and Authority in Afro-American Narrative* and editor of *African American Writing.*

STEPHANIE A. DEMETRAKOPOULOS is Professor of English at Western Michigan University. She is author of *Listening to Our Bodies: The Rebirth of Feminine Wisdom* and articles on a variety of subjects in the fields of literature, women's history and consciousness, and Jungian psychology.

KARLA F. C. HOLLOWAY is Associate Professor of English at North Carolina State University. She is author of *The Character of the Word: The Texts of Zora Neale Hurston*, as well as journal articles on Black women and politics, and oral language structures. She is associate editor of *Obsidian II: Black Literature in Review*, and on the editorial board of *Linguistics and Education: An International Research Journal*.

HARRY REED is author of *Platform for Change: The Foundations of the Northern Free Black Community, 1775–1865* and *Studies in the African Diaspora: A Memorial to James R. Hooker*.

RALPH STORY is a specialist in Afro-American literature who teaches at the University of Michigan, Ann Arbor. His poetry and articles have appeared in *Proud Black Images; Confrontation: A Journal of Third World Literature; Speak Easy, Speak Free; CLA Journal;* and *The Journal of Popular Literature*.

MICHAEL AWKWARD is Associate Professor of English at the University of Michigan, Ann Arbor, where he also teaches in the Center for Afro-American and African Studies. He is author of *Inspiring Influences: Tradition, Revision, and Afro-American Women's Novels* and editor of *New Essays on "Their Eyes Were Watching God"*.

DOREATHA DRUMMOND MBALIA is author of *Heritage: African American Readings for Writing* and *John Edgar Wideman: Reclaiming the African Personality*.

MARIANNE HIRSCH is Assistant Professor of French and Comparative Literature at Dartmouth University. She is editor, with Evelyn Fox Keller, of *Conflicts in Feminism*, and author of *The Mother/Daughter Plot: Narrative, Psychoanalysis, Feminism*, and *The Voyage In: Fictions of Female Development*.

LINDEN PEACH is author of *Angela Carter, English as a Creative Art, The Prose Writing of Dylan Thomas*, and *British Influence on the Birth of American Literature*.

BERTRAM D. ASHE is a doctoral candidate at the College of William and Mary.

JAN FURMAN is editor of *Slavery in the Clover Bottoms: John McCline's Narrative of his Life During Slavery and the Civil War.*

GARY STORHOFF is Associate Professor at the University of Connecticut at Stamford. He has published many articles and essays in journals devoted to American and African-American literature, and articles on family systems theory in the works of William Faulkner and Louise Erdrich.

Bibliography

Benston, Kimberly W. "Re-weaving the 'Ulysses Scene': Enchantment, Post-Oedipal Identity, and the Buried Text of Blackness in Toni Morrison's *Song of Solomon*," *Comparative American Identities: Race, Sex, and Nationality in the Modern Text*. Ed. Hortense J. Spillers. New York: Routledge, 1991.

Blake, Susan L. "Folklore and Community in *Song of Solomon*," *MELUS* 7 (1980): 77–82.

Branch, Eleanor. "Through the Maze of the Oedipal: Milkman's Search for Self in *Song of Solomon*," *Literature and Psychology* 41 (1995): 52–84.

Christian, Barbara. "Community and Nature: The Novels of Toni Morrison," *Journal of Ethnic Studies* 7 (February 1980): 65–78.

Clark, Norris. "Flying Back: Toni Morrison's *The Bluest Eye*, *Sula*, and *Song of Solomon*," *Minority Voices* 4 (Fall 1980): 51–63.

Coleman, James W. "Beyond the Reach of Love and Caring: Black Life in Toni Morrison's *Song of Solomon*," *Obsidian II* (Winter 1986): 151–61.

Cooper, B. E. "Milkman's Search for Family in Toni Morrison's *Song of Solomon*," *CLA Journal* (December 1989): 145–47.

Cowart, David. "Faulkner and Joyce in Morrison's *Song of Solomon*," *American Literature* 62 (March 1990): 87–100.

De Arman, Charles. "Milkman as the Archetypal Hero: 'Thursday's Child has Far to Go'," *Obsidian* 6 (Winter 1980): 56–59.

Fabre, Genevieve. "Geneological Archeology of the Quest for Legacy in Toni Morrison's *Song of Solomon*," *Critical Essays on Toni Morrison*, ed., Nellie Y. McKay. Boston: G. K. Hall, 1988. 105–114.

Harris, Leslie A. "Myth as Structure in Toni Morrison's *Song of Solomon*," *MELUS* 7:3 (Fall 1980): 71.

Hovet, Grace Ann, and Barbara Lounsberry. "Flying as Symbol and Legend in Toni Morrison's *The Bluest Eye*, *Sula*, and *Song of Solomon*," *CLA Journal* 27:2 (December 1983): 119–140.

Joyce, Joyce Ann. "Structural and Thematic Unity in Toni Morrison's *Song of Solomon*," *CEA Critic* 49 (Winter/Summer 1986-1987): 185–98.

Lee, Dorothy H. "*Song of Solomon*: To Ride the Air," *Black American Literature Forum* 16:2 (Summer 1982): 64–70.

MacKethan, Lucinda H. "Names to Bear Witness: The Theme and Tradition of Naming in Toni Morrison's *Song of Solomon*," *CEA Critic* 49 (Winter/Summer 1986–1987): 199–207.

Marshall, Brenda. "The Gospel According to Pilate," *American Literature* 57 (October 1985): 486–549.

Minakawa, Harue. "The Motif of Sweetness in Toni Morrison's *Song of Solomon*," *Kyushu American Literature* 26 (October 1985): 47–56.

O'Shaughnessy, Kathleen. " 'Life life life life': The Community Chorus in *Song of Solomon*," *Critical Essays on Toni Morrison*, ed. Nellie Y. McKay. Boston: G. K. Hall, 1988. 125–33.

Pinsker, Sanford. "Magic, Realism, Historical Truth, and the Quest for a Liberating Identity: Reflections on Alex Haley's *Roots* and Toni Morrison's *Song of Solomon*," *Studies in Black American Literature Vol. I: Black American Prose Theory*, eds. Joe Weixlmann and Chester J. Fontenot. Greenwood, FL: Penkevill Press, 1984. 183–97.

Rabinowitz, Paula. "Naming, Magic and Documentary: The Subversion of the Narrative in *Song of Solomon*, *Ceremony*, and *China Men*," *Feminist Re-Visions: What Has Been and Might Be*, ed. Vivian Patraka. Ann Arbor: Women's Studies Program, University of Michigan, 1983. 26–42.

Rosenberg, Ruth. " 'And the Children May Know Their Names': Toni Morrison's *Song of Solomon*," *Literary Onomastic Studies* 8 (1981): 195–219.

Royster, Philip M. "Milkman's Flying: The Scapegoat Transcended in Toni Morrison's *Song of Solomon*," *CLA Journal* 24 (June 1981): 419–40.

Scruggs, Charles. "The Nature of Desire in Toni Morrison's *Song of Solomon*," *Arizona Quarterly* 38 (Winter 1982): 311–35.

Smith, Valerie. "The Quest for and Discovery of Identity in Toni Morrison's *Song of Solomon*," *Southern Review* 21 (Summer 1985): 721–32.

Spallino, Chiara. "*Song of Solomon*: an Adventure in Structure," *Callaloo* 8 (Fall 1985): 510–24.

Weever, Jacqueline de. "Toni Morrison's Use of Fairy Tale, Folk Tale and Myth in *Song of Solomon*," *Southern Folklore Quarterly* 44 (1980): 131–44.

Wegs, Joyce M. "Toni Morrison's *Song of Solomon*: A Blues Song," *Essays in Literature* 9:2 (Fall 1982): 211–23.

Willis, Susan. "Eruptions of Funk: Historicizing Toni Morrison," *Toni Morrison: Critical Perspectives Past and Present*. Henry Louis Gates, Jr. and K. A. Appiah, eds. New York: Amistad, 1993. 308–29.

Acknowledgments

"Liminality and the Search for Self in *Song of Solomon*" by Wilfred D. Samuels from *Minority Voices* 5 (Spring-Fall 1981): 59–68. Reprinted in *Toni Morrison* by Wilfred D. Samuels and Clenora Hudson-Weems. © 1990 G. K. Hall & Co.

"*Song of Solomon:* Continuities of Community" (1985) by Valerie Smith from *Toni Morrison: Critical Perspectives Past and Present*, eds. Henry Louis Gates, Jr. and K. A. Appiah. © 1993 Henry Louis Gates, Jr. and K. A. Appiah.

"The Interdependence of Men's and Women's Individuation" by Stephanie A. Demetrakopoulos from *New Dimensions of Spirituality: A Biracial and Bicultural Reading of the Novels of Toni Morrison*. © 1987 Karla F. C. Holloway and Stephanie A. Demetrakopoulos.

"The Lyrics of Salvation" by Karla F. C. Holloway from *New Dimensions of Spirituality: A Biracial and Bicultural Reading of the Novels of Toni Morrison*. © 1987 Karla F. C. Holloway and Stephanie A. Demetrakopoulos.

"Toni Morrison, *Song of Solomon* and Black Cultural Nationalism" by Harry Reed from *The Centennial Review* 32:1 (Winter 1988): 50–64. © 1988 Centennial Review.

"An Excursion into the Black World: The 'Seven Days' in Toni Morrison's *Song of Solomon*" by Ralph Story from *Black American Literature Forum* 23:1 (Spring 1989): 149–158. © 1989 African American Review.

"'Unruly and Let Loose': Myth, Ideology, and Gender in *Song of Solomon*" by Michael Awkward from *Callaloo* 13:3 (Summer 1990): 482–98. © 1990 Charles H. Rowell.

"Inscribing an Origin in *Song of Solomon*" by Jan Stryz from *Studies in American Fiction* 19:1 (Spring 1991): 31–40. © 1991 Northeastern University.

"*Song of Solomon*: The Struggle for Race and Class Consciousness" by Doreatha Drummond Mbalia from *Toni Morrison's Developing Class Consciousness* by Doreatha Drummond Mbalia. © 1991 Associated University Presses, Inc.

"Knowing Their Names: Toni Morrison's *Song of Solomon*" by Marianne Hirsch from *New Essays on Song of Solomon*, ed. Valerie Smith. © 1995 Cambridge University Press.

"Competing Discourses in *Song of Solomon*" by Linden Peach from *Modernist Novelists: Toni Morrison* by Linden Peach. © 1995 Linden Peach.

"'Why don't he like my hair?': Constructing African-American Standards of Beauty in Toni Morrison's *Song of Solomon* and Zora Neale Hurston's *Their Eyes Were Watching God*" by Bertram D. Ashe from *African American Review* 29:4 (Winter 1995): 579–91. © 1995 Bertram D. Ashe.

"Male Consciousness in *Song of Solomon*" by Jan Furman from *Toni Morrison's Fiction* by Jan Furman. © 1996 University of South Carolina Press.

"'Anaconda Love': Parental Enmeshment in Toni Morrison's *Song of Solomon*" by Gary Storhoff from *Style* 31:2 (Summer 1997): 290–310. © 1997 *Style*.

Index